Patton's Hand of God

# PATTON'S
# HAND OF GOD

## J.E. SAMMONS
### RITA SAMMONS HARRELL
### NARRATED BY M. ANTON T.

# PATTON'S HAND OF GOD

© 2024 Rita Sammons Harrell

All rights reserved.

No part of this book may be reproduced or transmitted in any form without written permission from the publisher or author, except as permitted by U.S. copyright law.

The written portions of this book reflect the authors' recollections of a lifetime of experiences, supplemented by material provided in its original format to approximate the experience of a soldier in General George S. Patton's 2nd Armored Division, nicknamed "Hell on Wheels" and more specifically an engineering unit nicknamed "We Pave the Way" during World War II. The sources for this material include personal recollections and historical documents.

The images used in this book are from James Edward Sammons' personal collection and are believed to be in the public domain. Every effort has been made to ascertain the copyright status of these images, and due diligence has been exercised to ensure their lawful use. These images are provided for historical and educational purposes only, with explicit consent from the owner.

The Author, Narrator, and Publisher do not endorse any antiquated or offensive language or views on race or religion used in the book; some expressions have been retained as a record of the historical past. Readers are advised that historical content may include language or depictions that are now considered offensive or inappropriate.

While the publisher and author have used their best efforts in preparing this book, the purpose of this book is to educate and provide insight into historical events. The authors and publisher shall have neither liability nor responsibility to any person or entity with respect to any loss or damage caused or allied to have been caused directly or indirectly by the information contained in this book.

Printed in the United States of America

First Edition

ISBN 979-8-9905285-2-9 paperback
ISBN 979-8-9905285-0-5 hard cover
ISBN 979-8-9905285-1-2 ebook
Library of Congress Control Number: 2024908081

**Cover and Interior Design by:**
Chris Treccani

Created with the Millions to Legacy® Method

# DEDICATION

"This world is not my home, I'm just passing thru,
I hope to be around at 92."
**J. E. Sammons, September 12th, 2003**

Yes, Dad—you made it a little past 92,
and this is my heartfelt dedication, especially just for you.

Dad had a clear vision of his true mission in life from early childhood. Dad's clarity and precise recollections of the realities so honestly worded reflected his soul to the world in his story *GRAMPA'S WAR*.

This book could only be dedicated as a tribute to the strength of the brave men and their families of the 17th Battalion 2nd ARMORED DIVISION known as "the Patton Boys." A section of dad's book, *GRAMPA'S WAR*, is written precisely describing, who these men were. In the section, WHO ARE THESE MEN …FROM BENNING TO BERLIN, it is there, where I have listed one of my favorite passages. Dad also wrote about his "SIDEKICKS," comrades he brought together, so that all could relive their stories, and more importantly, support each other through the years.

> ### WHO WERE THESE MEN...FROM BENNING TO BERLIN?
>
> "General Patton knew what lay ahead of them, when on that day of his famous speech on a hillside at Ft. Bragg, N.C., he told these soldiers, "War is hell... and we are going over there and kick 'em in the ass, 'till their noses bleed!" Then, near the end of his speech, he raised a load roar, when he said, "When your grandson is on your knee 30 years from now and asks what you did in the Great War, you won't have to say you shoveled sh  in Louisiana!"
>
> **J. E. Sammons**

At Dad's annual reunions he would have a special name for each soldier. Always a funny connotation from the War. How many times would I hear Dad saying that familiar phrase… "Thanks buddy, you were a lifesaver."

*PATTON'S HAND OF GOD* brings home the gut-wrenching, raw reality of war and reveals the many depths and unselfishness of my father's experiences so that future generations will understand the sacrifice, love, and devotion that make a soldier a true hero—not to mention a terrific Dad! My father had such great love for his country and comrades.

This dedication is also for my Mom, Beatrice Chaon Sammons. She kept Dad alive in the foxholes with her inspirational letters and worked with him for 52 years to keep the reunion club going. Mom wrote letters to the soldiers' wives and inspired them, too. This couple—my parents—made sure every soldier in Company E was doing well and paid tribute to those who passed.

J.E. and the 17th Battalion, Company E, 2nd Armored Division were some of "Patton's Boys," soldiers selected by Patton as demolition warriors—"Hell on Wheels"—paving the way to our success in defeating the Germans. J.E. and his sidekicks in Company E paved the way through desert, mountains, sand, and snow. Listening to their stories, one realizes how great "Patton's Boys" really were.

I'd like to pay tribute to all of Dad's buddies who "had his back" throughout the war. There aren't articles or books about every one of these brave, special bridge-engineers of Company E, but each one of their specialized duties was critical. Combined, they were "Hell on Wheels" and an important part of the Allied victory in WWII. All of the following men were *"excellent soldiers, and great friends"* of J.E.

## It's an Honor Roll of Thanks to:

**George "Buttermilk" Whisenant**—always the first to get up and dance at reunions

**Thomas "TA" Walker**—poker buddy; always had a deck of cards

**Graham "Kid" Walker**—he called Dad "Sam"

**Edward "Eddie" Strickland**—always UP

**Robert Pryor**—A close friend who attended Ft. Knox Radio School with Dad

**Frank "Ziggy" Seeqmuller**—in charge of bridge sites

**William "Willie" Scruggs**—a poker buddy

**George "Georgie" Miller**—a lifesaver for Dad in battle

**George Mash**—a great mechanic who kept the tank tracks rolling

**Harry "Kupp" Kuppersmith**—worked in the supply department and shared his food packages with Dad

**Bill Karr**— a hit at the reunion parties

**Charlie Gnau**—a great help with the reunions

**Ray Ellis**—the right soldier when the going gets tuff; a gunner on Dad's half-track Johnny Diederickson—loved his beer and chicken in the war room at reunions

**Dwight "Coop" Cooper**—leader of Dad's half-track; fought with Dad in foxholes Herbert "BS" Barnes—funny bee _____ story

**"Mac" Atkins Pershing**—happy memories with families and reunions Charlie Althouse—Dad's close buddy in Germany; spoke German Russell Allen—a great engineer and a great friend of Dad's

**Mel Lascola**—a great supporter of reunions and family fun

**Alfred Provenzano**—Al and his wife Marian would dance through the night at the reunions

Both Mel Lascola and Al Provenzano were interviewed for an article that appeared on the front page of the *Baltimore Sun* during the 1977 reunion in Baltimore. At the very end of the interview, I found this interesting quote by Al on General Patton: "Patton was right" "he maintained that if Roosevelt had not stopped him, the General would have gone in and "cleaned out the Russians" "and we wouldn't have this problem with communism today."

History does repeat itself as we have seen recently in the news, with Russia's invasion of Ukraine. With today's instant visual content, it has many similar comparable battles to those that Patton and J.E. experienced, and now, we can see in full detail, the same results… loss of civilian lives.

# TABLE OF CONTENTS

| | |
|---|---|
| Foreword | xiii |
| Preface | xv |
| Introduction | xvii |

**GRAMPA'S WAR** — xix

| | | |
|---|---|---|
| Introduction to GRAMPA'S WAR | | xxi |
| Memoirs of Virginia - Childhood Stories | | 3 |
| Memoirs of War - Ready for War | | 25 |
| GRAMPA'S WAR: Benning to Berlin with Hell on Wheels | | 26 |
| Chapter I | The Journey Begins | 31 |
| Chapter II | New York – Casablanca – French Morocco | 43 |
| Chapter III | "D" Day – Omaha Beach – Normandy | 51 |
| Chapter IV | Omaha Beach – Belgium – Maastricht | 55 |
| Chapter V | Battle of the Bulge – Aachen – Berlin – Harry S. Truman – Presidential Citation | 59 |
| Chapter VI | Coming Home to America The Journey Ends | 69 |
| Chapter VII | Annual Reunions | 75 |

**Part 1: My Hand** — 127

| | |
|---|---|
| The Drugstore Cowboys | 133 |
| "Now I lay me down to sleep…I pray the Lord…" | 135 |
| GRAMPA's Farm on the Nansemond River | 137 |
| Movie Stars | 139 |
| Teenager Ava Gardner | 141 |
| J.E.'s Famous "Cousin Peggy" | 143 |

**Part 2—Patton's Hand** — 145

| | |
|---|---|
| From Benning to Berlin: Introduction to Hell | 147 |

| | |
|---|---|
| Who were these men of Battalion 17, Company E, 2nd Armored Division? | 149 |
| Next Stop…North Africa | 185 |
| Suddenly, One Of Our Own… Gone | 189 |
| Uncle Welly POW story | 193 |
| And the Big One… J.E. was there… The "Battle of the Bulge" | 197 |
| "WE PAVE THE WAY" …making Patton's tanks move at lightning speed! | 199 |

## Platoon Pictures — 201

| | |
|---|---|
| Engineering Platoon | 204 |
| Letters Not Forgotten | 207 |
| J.E. in Northern Africa, French Morocco, Tunisia, and Sicily" | 215 |
| From Sicily, ordered back to the UK… | 217 |
| Tidworth, England, 1944 | 220 |
| Finally D-Day + 1 | 225 |
| "The Map" | 229 |
| Final Victory Crossing The Rhine | 233 |
| "The Note" | 241 |
| The American Red Cross | 243 |
| Reunion Poem | 249 |
| Stories Written about D-Day | 251 |

## Part 3: "God's Hand" — 255

| | |
|---|---|
| President Harry S. Truman | 261 |
| President Eisenhower and Mrs. Eisenhower | 263 |
| President Ronald Reagan | 265 |
| President Bill Clinton | 267 |
| J.E.'s Correspondences | 269 |
| Crossing the Bar | 285 |
| Fifty-Two Years of Reunions | 303 |
| 1997 reunion, Three men at the table – the ladies | 305 |
| The 1992 REUNION ROSTER | 319 |
| 1992 Reunion Roster --- From: Russell G. and (Lillian) Allen To: Jo and (Pete) Zuko | 319 |
| J.E.'s Salute to "Hell On Wheels" …. And let Freedom Reign! | 327 |

## Epilogue — 329

| | |
|---|---|
| To my Dear Dad … | 331 |
| Acknowledgements | 333 |
| About the Author Rita Sammons Harrell | 335 |
| Appendix: Special Contributors | 337 |
| Special Mention: Michael O'Brien | 339 |
| Special Mention: How *Hospitality* Kept a Unit Alive!!! | 344 |
| And More Special "J.E. photos" … | 349 |

| | |
|---|---|
| Letter To The Editor | 355 |
| For The Record | 361 |
| APA Picture File List | 375 |
| Final Narration and Follow Up | 407 |

# FOREWORD

## M. Anton T.

My former history professor, Dr. Gordon Prange—who served as General Douglas MacArthur's chief historian, and whose 1981 published book was adapted into the film *Tora! Tora! Tora!*— always reminded us that the past is constantly shaping our future.

When I first saw General George S. Patton, it was by way of an old wood-framed color portrait of a glaring Army officer, chin jutting out, with shiny stars on the front of his helmet. The "general's portrait" was hung at eye level beside a second story bedroom window in the cottage that was to be my new home in America. The picture was one of many gifts donated by local parishioners in Bethesda, Maryland, to welcome a refugee family fleeing the 1959 Cuban revolution. There was also an ivory-handled six shooter in a black leather holster hanging on the tall wooden post of the bunkbed.

The little white cottage, nestled on Old Georgetown Road, had a gravel driveway that circled two towering oak trees. The oaks shaded the gardener's maintenance shed and an open garage for my father's 1959 Dodge. Every day at 6AM, the gardener would start his 10 foot- span lawnmowers, slowly sputtering towards the open range, and at the end of the day, leaving the countless acres of endless rolling hills, like a manicured PGA golf green. This open range of green fields (now part of the 300 plus acres of the fenced-in and closely monitored N.I.H. campus) surrounded the cottage and the 12- foot red-brick walls that guarded the cloistered Sisters of the Visitation's red brick covered estate. Both the cottage and the convent quarters are still present to this day.

Every week the gardener begged the cloistered sisters to take away my golf clubs, as the wedges were ruining his manicured lawn.

"No, please," the Mother Superior told the gardener smiling, "the boy has good aim, a steady hand… "The golf balls… all seem, to always land in front of the Virgin Mary's grotto. Surely, that's a sign from the Divine…and the young man's aim must've been guided, somehow, perhaps… by the hand of God!"

Nearly sixty years later, as the Covid-19 pandemic locked our nation into forced isolation in 2020, I reached out on social media to connect with many old friends, especially childhood classmates in Bethesda.

I found myself being pulled back in time… to that wonderful era, and parish—St. Jane De Chantal—which provided my family hope for a future at a time when we had none. I thought, here I had plenty of stories to write about, having grown up in an area that had allowed me in the 60's and 70's to cross paths with the rich and powerful in the Beltway Society—Senators, Congressional Representatives, Pro Athletes, even U.S. Presidents. Also finding out that there were those St. Jane De Chantal grade school classmates that had achieved some level of success… or so called, fame. One such classmate, Bob Redfield, 2 years ahead of me, had been named the Director of the Centers for Disease Control, trying to tackle the Covid-19 crisis, during that fateful year. But while Bob, the nation, and the rest of the world sought a Covid-19 vaccine, I was looking for a ray of hope to lead us into the future. I wanted to find a universal character, the representation of a "true American local hero"—someone who people from all generations—past, current, and future—would be able to relate to.

On Facebook, I connected with Rita Sammons, a former grade school classmate—now Rita Sammons Harrell. And after connecting on Facebook, we spoke on the phone.

"I have a great story," she told me. She sounded as if she was unwrapping a present that had been long ago shelved…put away, almost forgotten.

"My father, J.E., was part of Patton's 'Hell on Wheels' in WWII. He started a book he called GRAMPA'S WAR, with tons of pictures, but he never finished it. I was wondering if you could—"

Excitedly, I interrupted her. "You've got a historical treasure," I told her, "Something the world needs to know about…and needs to see, his pictures…his letters…his experiences with none other than General Patton!"

*PATTON'S HAND OF GOD* is a passage back in time, letting you experience a Depression-era childhood and four and a half years of WWII hell, through the incredible memory of Rita's father.

James E. Sammons was one of Patton's hand-picked soldiers, men who "paved the way" for the 2nd Armored Division's charge across Europe to defeat the Nazi regime. Hitler nicknamed Patton's boys, "Roosevelt's Butchers." After surviving the war, J.E. returned home and lived a bountiful life, a local American hero who inspired his WWII buddies—as well as Presidents Truman, Eisenhower, Reagan, and Clinton!

J.E. and his stories, that you'll enjoy in *GRAMPA'S WAR* need to be remembered, honored, and most of all, become a legacy for his family, and for every military family.

Let's dive into history — with General Patton, "Hell on Wheels," and J.E. and see how his Co. E buddies made sure Patton's tanks, ran at record breaking speeds, making sure that Hitler's Nazi regime was forever stopped. General Patton may have been credited with many Allied victories in WWII, but I assure you that J.E., and his "*We Pave The Way*" buddies, had plenty to do with it…and quite possibly as well --- the hand of God!

So, despite the fact I've traveled the world, met celebrities, politicians, artists, and even an occasional royal family member, I didn't realize that my quest of finding and presenting to the world what a "true American hero" was, had always been waiting for me, at my forever backyard, Bethesda.

Thank You, Rita Sammons Harrell, and J.E., for luring me back to Bethesda!

# PREFACE

My Dad meant everything to me. Before he passed, he handed me a book he'd compiled, *GRAMPA'S WAR*.

It wasn't until years after his passing that I really took a close look at it. Now, I'm sharing these preserved memories and pictures from a Corporal in Company E of the 17th Armored Combat Engineer Battalion, 2nd Armored Division. My father and his brothers in arms paved the way to success in WWII. J.E. Sammons had a devoted love for his country and family and faith in the hand of God.

In *PATTON'S HAND OF GOD*, you'll take an incredible, enlightening journey, following the footsteps of my father, James E. "J.E." Sammons, a true American hero.

# INTRODUCTION

This book has three parts. But it is only fitting that we start with *GRAMPA'S WAR*, the basis, the reason, and the honor of having *PATTON'S HAND OF GOD,* bring it back to life! These are the original type-written accounts, that were forever etched in J.E.'s mind, after surviving a world war. J.E.'s "Table of Contents" will provide an unparalleled journey, a true- historical experience of the pains of war, but a written legacy remembering and honoring those fellow "Patton's Boys" that never saw New York's welcome home, as well as those reunion lifetime friendships.

**Part 1, "My Hand,"** is filled with historical and motivational moments from J.E.'s youth. J.E.'s childhood in the 1920s and 30s in small-town Virginia were full of adventures. He grew up on the Virginia Peninsula in the shipbuilding town of Newport News. In the 1920's, Newport News was home to future stars of jazz and Hollywood. During the Great Depression, J.E.'s family moved to his grandfather's farm on the Nansemond River, across the James River from Newport News. Later, he returned to Newport News to work in the shipyard. This background developed the character of a man with a great love for family and freedom and helped shape the soldier he became.

**Part 2, "Patton's Hand,"** awakens the patriot in all of us, following J.E.'s service in the U.S. Army from his pre-war enlistment through seven grueling WWII battles. Raw facts and inspiring humor captivate throughout. After a brief stint in radio school in Fort Knox, Kentucky, J.E. joined Company E of the 17th Armored Combat Engineer Battalion of the 2nd Armored Division. Under the leadership of one of WWII's most renowned commanders, General George S. Patton. J.E. and his comrades trained at Fort Benning in Georgia and conducted maneuvers all across the Southeast. Training included rifle marksmanship and live-fire exercises. "Patton's Boys," as they came to be called, were inspired by Patton and felt a camaraderie with their general.

The specialized task of the 17th Engineers was to clear land mines, build or demolish bunkers, trenches, bridges, and roads. Their work enabled the 2nd Armored Division's tanks to advance—hence their motto: "We Pave the Way." When the war began, the 2nd Armored Division, nicknamed "Hell on Wheels," and fought its way from North Africa to Sicily to

Normandy, across northern France, the Ardennes, and the Rhineland straight through to Berlin, Germany.

The work of the 17th Armored Combat Engineer Battalion was key to the 2nd Armored Division's success in each of its seven WWII campaigns. They embarked from New York harbor in the middle of the night and sailed for 13 days to reach Casablanca, dodging German U-boats the whole way, then joined Operation Torch and the invasion of North Africa. After fighting in Sicily, they landed at Omaha Beach in Normandy, where J.E. spent the night in a foxhole reciting Psalm 23. They fought in the Ardennes Offensive, in the Battle of the Bulge, and built a bridge across the Rhine River into Germany in under seven hours.

There was sadness and loss throughout J.E.'s four and a half years of war, but also humorous and inspiring situations. "Just another bloody battle," he would say. He endured hunger from low rations, lost his commander, and labored under gunfire and bombs to build bridges.

After victory in Europe, President Truman came to Berlin to award J.E. and the other extraordinary men of the 2nd Armored Division a special Presidential Citation. As General Patton said, "Wars may be fought with weapons, but they are won by men."

History does repeat itself, and today Ukraine is facing an evil invasion by Russia and fighting for its freedom. Let freedom reign in Ukraine!

**Part 3, "God's Hand,"** covers J.E.'s homecoming, safely sailing back into New York Harbor. "What a beautiful sight!" J.E. said, when the Statue of Liberty came into view. There wasn't a dry eye on the ship that night. In 1946, J.E. and one of his war buddies started Company E reunions that continued for 52 years. Even after the war, these soldiers still had each other's backs. I remember seeing these grown men with tears in their eyes and tissues in their hands as they relived moments from the war, each one adding details the others hadn't known. Witnessing their bravery and love for one another as I grew up, I came to understand why J.E. had to keep them together through the reunions. There was no therapy for these WWII vets—just themselves, cigarettes, and beer. Part 3 is filled with J.E.'s passion for his comrades in arms, and his writings are a legacy to all of our military families, their children and grandchildren.

We start with J.E.'s book, *GRAMPA'S WAR*, in this book, we have combined these experiences, adding to J.E.'s earlier life, and finishing it up with the successful reunions that he annually had.

J.E. wrote, spoke about, and provided interviews about his intimate experiences during WWII, but actually tried to sort of, downplay its "hell," with colorful stories about his comrades during, and after the war with his reunions. Following J.E.'s lead, we have interwoven *GRAMPA'S WAR* into a family legacy, *PATTON'S HAND OF GOD*, which describes how a simple man, growing up during the Great Depression, could survive such a hell with Patton, and embrace freedom with those that helped J.E. attain it.

All these stories would be forever preserved, in *GRAMPA'S WAR*, as my father wanted, and I just merely finished it for him with *PATTON'S HAND OF GOD*, publishing both legacies into one, so that our entire family, and the rest of the world, can appreciate James Edward Sammons….an American Hero, and my Dad!

**— Rita Sammons Harrell**

# GRAMPA'S WAR

*GRAMPA'S WAR* is a book with the original manuscript from Corporal James E. Sammons, as a radio morse code communicator, cycle rider, halftrack driver and jeep driver of commanders. The eyes and ears of J.E. clearly had great perception and recollections that inspired his hand to write his 7 battles in Benning to Berlin which then became *GRAMPA'S WAR*. His spirit and love of his country kept his humor through the most difficult wartimes, and he also shares his helplessness in a foxhole with bombs blasting all around him. I hold the original little bible he held in his hand reciting Psalm 23 over and over. And now my hand is handing to generations to come these unique stories of 7 Battles with of an extraordinary soldier serving in World War II, my dad.

— **Rita Sammons Harrell**

"I remember a time during the war when we were pushing the Germans through France, Belgium, and Holland to the German border at Aachen, the gateway to the 2nd Armored Division to the Weser, Rhine, Elbe, and Berlin. Hitler gave orders to hold the line at all costs at the German border—as no enemy soldier was to set foot on the soil of the Fatherland. We fought for those three weeks in the November rain and cold to breach the line at Aachen, alongside of the 30th Infantry Division as the 14th, 78th, and 92nd Field Artillery of our division fired 75 mm."

— **J. E. Sammons**

**Figure 3** Insignia of the 2nd Armored Division

# INTRODUCTION TO GRAMPA'S WAR

## M. Anton T.

Events in history proceed like falling dominoes—one occurrence inevitably triggers the next. Some things—like an egg cracked out of its shell into a frying pan—can never be undone. I had a professor who liked to say that we live "from womb to tomb"—in other words, our time is limited to the span between the womb and the tomb. Understanding what J.E. Sammons did between womb and tomb requires an explanation of the Great Depression and the environs around Newport News, Virginia, where he grew up.

J.E.'s mother's cousin, Marguerite "Peggy" Upton, soared to fame in the 1920s. She is known to history as Peggy Hopkins Joyce—and known to J.E.'s family simply as "Cousin Peggy." After joining Ziegfield's Follies in 1917, she went on to stardom as an actress in the 1920s, keeping company with such Hollywood legends as Charlie Chaplin and W.C. Fields. She was undeniably one of the most controversial women of the Roaring Twenties, a precursor of the modern liberated woman. Her six marriages to wealthy men earned her a misplaced reputation as a gold digger. Author Rita Sammons Harrell plans to publish a book on Cousin Peggy that sets the record straight.

The Great Depression—widely considered to be the worst economic slump in modern history—began in 1929 and continued until 1939. At the end of the Roaring Twenties, the stock market crashed in October of 1929. Millions of Americans—and investors worldwide—saw their stock holdings evaporate nearly overnight. Events cascaded in an unstoppable domino effect.

The panic of the stock market crash caused people to lose faith in the banks. Countless people tried to withdraw their funds at the same time. Banks typically did not have enough cash on hand, so they had to sell assets to cover the withdrawals. In many cases, these "runs" on the banks caused the banks to fail. As banks failed, more Americans—even those who never had money in the stock market—lost their savings.

Making matters worse, the Hoover administration thought the government should not intervene in the economic situation. Consumer spending and investments declined, causing businesses to slow down, putting millions of people out of work. By 1933, when unemployment was at its worst, 15 million Americans were jobless.

Bread lines and soup kitchens became commonplace. Homelessness skyrocketed. Many people drifted from place to place, looking for work or simply for their next meal. As millions went hungry, many farmers lacked the cash to pay harvest labor, leaving crops to languish in the fields. Drought conditions in the Great Plains region triggered massive dust storms, some of which flung topsoil as far away as the Atlantic Ocean. In the 1930s, more than 2.5 million people left the "Dust Bowl" in search of better conditions.

In 1932, President, Herbert Hoover, was swept out of the White House with the election of Franklin D. Roosevelt in a landslide. In his inaugural address, FDR said, "The only thing we have to fear is fear itself." FDR sought to reassure beleaguered Americans, speaking to them directly over the radio in his fireside chats. He also took immediate action to relieve the dire economic conditions, enacting a series of reforms known as the New Deal. This included the Tennessee Valley Authority (TVA) and the Works Progress Administration (WPA), which provided employment for millions and built important regional infrastructure. It also included the Social Security Act, which provided unemployment insurance and support for the elderly and disabled.

Growing up in the throes of the Great Depression, J.E. Sammons and his family were affected, too. His hometown—the port city of Newport News, Virginia—was hard-hit, but the Sammons family, like many other Americans, left the city for J.E.'s grandfather's farm. Future Hollywood star Ava Gardner moved to Newport News with her parents and six siblings from the North Carolina tobacco fields; for a short time, she was J.E.'s high school classmate. Future jazz greats Pearl Bailey and Ella Fitzgerald lived on the other side of Newport News in the African American "Blood Fields" neighborhood.

The domino effect reached far beyond the borders of the United States—the woeful economic conditions of the 1930s extended worldwide. In Germany, desperate times helped fuel the rise of Adolf Hitler's Nazi Party, and Hitler's nationalistic aggression led to war in Europe in 1939.

Although the United States was not immediately involved in the conflict, President Roosevelt saw the need to support Britain and France in resisting German expansion. As defense production geared up, the American economy finally began to shake off the Great Depression.

In December 1941, as J.E. Sammons wrapped up his military training, he thought he would soon be headed home to Newport News on furlough. The Japanese sneak attack on the American naval base in Pearl Harbor, Hawaii on December 7th shattered that plan and changed the course of his life.

The Great Depression was over, but the United States was headed into the bloodiest war the world had ever seen. J.E. Sammons, as part of General George Patton's "Hell on Wheels," would be in the thick of it.

# SPECIAL SECTION

Prelude to:

# GRAMPA'S WAR

Original Typewritten WWII and Photographic Memoirs

J. E. Sammons

# MEMOIRS OF VIRGINIA

## Childhood Stories

## LIFE AS A BOY IN VIRGINIA

The following is my memory of some of the events as a boy in Newport News in the 1920's & 30's. I can assure you there were many-many more.

Newport News is a seaport city on a peninsula with the water of Hampton Roads on one side and James River on the other. Divided by 30 or more C&O railroad yard tracks, bringing coal and other supplies from the West to and from overseas. There are 3 bridges over these tracks that divide uptown from the East end. The 25th St.,28th st.,& 34th St. bridges. Washington Ave.was uptown big time & Jefferson Ave.was small time. Warwick Ave.was a dirt street under the bridges to the boat harbor. My uncle Clinton Brock was the Engineer & builder of the 25th & 34th St.bridges. The other large industry was the Shipyard located in the North end. Population was 35 to 40 thousand of which 15,000 worked in the shipyard & 5 to 6 thousand at the C&O railroad.

James Edward Sammons born 6:00 P.M.Friday Sept.12,1919 at 2814 Jefferson Ave.,Newport News,Virginia. Third child of William Henry & Daisy Lee (Wilroy) Sammons. One older brother William Wilroy and one older sister Vera Delane.

The first I remember at 2814 was sitting in a buggy on the sidewalk and a neighbor named Ivan Davidson,a red hair wonderful Russian Jewish man that retired after playing a horn in the John Phillip Sousa Band. I remember his long bushy moustache & pinching my cheek & singing a tune in Russian.

My next remembrance was after we moved around the corner to a larger home at 618 28th St.when I was about 3. This seemed great after the smaller row home,even though we only had a small gas stove for cooking & electric lights hanging from a cord on the ceiling. No central heat only a flat sheet metal coal stove in the dining room. Mom would heat the water in a pot on the gas stove & our Saturday night bath in the wash tub. In winter Dad would wrap the water pipes under the house to prevent a freeze. The back yard came with a large overhead trellis grape vine with delicious white grapes. Dad would set a crock of grapes to ferment for wine in the winter. The law allowed one gallon per family. From wood crates that furniture came in,we would haul scrap boards in our wagon with the nails still in,over the 28th St.bridge from the J.H. Bell Furniture Co.that they gave us from the trash pile. After removing the nails and used Dad's hammer & saw (when he was at work),we built a two story house in the back of the yard behind the coal shed. It had a special trap door hidden in the roof like we saw at the Tom Mix cowboy silent movies. ONe day while playing cowboys & indians I jumped from the coal shed onto our house & forgot about the trap door and landed at the bottom with torn & bleeding hands & a sore butt. One day while playing cowboys & indians my brother Wilroy jumped over a fence & ripped out the seat of his pants. From then on his name was "RIP" Sammons. I remember our first dog "Snooks",My Mom's sister Aunt Lydia in Norfolk sold their home as her husband Uncle Leonard purchased the Hotel Preston in dowtown and no dogs were allowed in their suite.

## MY DOG "SNOOKS"

He was Spitz & Terrior and was loyal to our family of five. Do not invade his territory - the front door & porch, unless you were one of the family of five. He tore the pants several times of our mailman, so Mom would bring him inside the home before the mailman's arrival time each day or one of us would meet the mailman on the front sidewalk and receive the mail. Snooks was not a lap dog. Snooks went with Mom everyday to the grocery store and guarded her all the way. One Spring I came from school and Snooks was dead at the front door. I wrapped him in a blanket and buried him 4 ft. deep in the back yard next to my garden. Snooks was 14.

Figure 4 - My dog Snooks

The day after Snooks arrived he decided he did not like his new friends or home and decided to sneak out and go home. After 3 or 4 days of search he was found near the boat harbor as I guess he decided not to try and swim the 5 miles across Hampton Roads to Norfolk. We brought him home and he soon adjusted to his new family. Later he followed Mom everywhere she went.

We lived in a Jewish & Greek neighborhood and had many nice families in our block. Next door lived the Arnoff's that owned a little grocery store on Jefferson Ave. I remember grandmother Arnoff died and seeing her in the living room in a plain wooden coffin and they said it had holes drilled in the bottom for the insects. Across the street lived the Scholls that owned a small drug store at 25th & Jefferson and had 3 beautiful daughters (to me) that worked in the drug store. Next door to them lived our barber Jake Brenner who gave me my first haircut and I cried. Two homes to our North lived Mr.& Mrs.Kaplan that had a son the age of my brother and they were good friends. One night he invited Wilroy over to see and listen to their new radio. For some reason I tagged along and in a small room on a table was a large black box with two large numbered dials with a horn speaker on top. The only thing I remember hearing was static. They said late at night they could receive KDKA Pittsburgh and WLW Cincinnati. That was my first contact with radio. This would been about 1924.

Across the street lived one of my best school friends,Bryan Weaver. As a Sgt. in the 29th Infantry he was killed D day at Omaha Beach. Mrs. Lazzious a nice jewish lady that lived about 4 houses away would bring Mom matzo and wine every jewish holiday. My playmate Tullie Rea also lived across the street. Christmas 1922 Santa brought me a little rocking chair and to this day I still have it.

Just a few blocks away was Warwick Ave.,the black (African American) area. We were told not to go in this area. I remember the many times we walked across 28th St.bridge on the way uptown or to church and looking down on a dirt street Warwick Ave.and the unpainted wooden shack houses that harbored moonshine whiskey and loose women in this red light district. Pearl Bailey & Ella Fitzgerald lived in this area.

After WWI the city built a Victory Arch at 25th & West Ave. I remember a soldier parade when the last soldiers returned from France. I remember Sunday's in the summertime after Sunday School & Church, Dad would bring out the wooden tub with the hand crank & spindle on the back porch. Mom would fill the tube with ice cream ingredients, Dad would pack ice and salt all around and we kids would take turns cranking & cranking until Dad said it was frozen - then we had ice cream and Mom's homemade cookies for Sunday dessert. We kneeled at the bed every night to say our prayers - "Now I lay me down to sleep I pray the Lord my sole to keep". etc.

Dad was promoted to Asst.Supt.Union Life Insurance Co., then we moved to a new brick row home at 623 29th St. There we had 3 bedrooms and one bath plus dining, kitchen and a large pot belly coal stove to heat the entire house. We even had a copper coil gas hot water heater in the kitchen. One bath at a time in the tub then 2 hr.re-heat. We had a small back yard and a one car garage for the 1924 Chevy Dad bought later. I remember Dad reading the headline - Lindberg Flies the Atlantic to Paris. I remember one night our next door neighbor, Mr. Arnott and his son my playmate invited Dad and I over to listen on their new radio the Jack Dempsey - Max Schemelling fight. Mr. Arnott was office Mgr. for the C&O railroad. His wife was bookkeeper for Shapiro's Dept. Store.

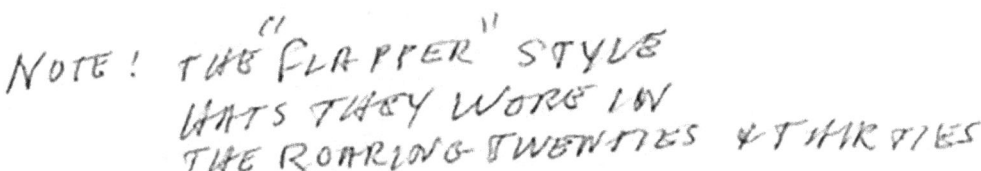

Figure 5 Mom and Dad, 1930

They had one older daughter, Marietta and one son, Buddy that was my age and we played baseball, football, cowboys, marbles and all the other things that little boys do. Dad bought an Atwater-Kent console radio and it was Amos & Andy and Bing Crosby Pepsodent program every night after dinner. Next door lived Mr. & Mrs. Rhodes. They were older and retired then moved away - but not before they gave me their golden cat named "Goldie". Goldie the cat with the L shaped tail. Someone had closed a door on his tail and it healed in an L shape. We became good friends.

I remember my first birthday party I was invited too, just two doors away for Helen Roth and we played spin the bottle in the yard and I got to kiss (on the cheek) the birthday girl. That was my first love at about six.

Dad bought a used 1924 Chevy the one with the high top and square windows, 4cyl. for 125.00. We kept it in the garage until Sunday then to church and Sunday afternoon ride. When it was running good we would make it to Hampton, Buchroe Beach and sometimes to Williamsburg. In 1928 they had the Grand Opening of the James River Bridge, at that time the longest in the world - 5 miles. Everyone was invited to drive over and back free the first Sunday. We gassed the Chevy (Amaco American) 15¢ per gal. got in line and waited for hours to cross. Finally we got the thrill and over we went a couple miles to a turnaround at the Log Cabin Restaurant and headed back to the bridge. By this time the leaking radiator was boiling hot. We pulled off the road and from under the front seat (no trunk) Dad got out a jug of water, two eggs and a can of black pepper and after it cooled poured in the mixture and we made it safely home.

Everyday we had the milkman (Mr. Anderson), the ice man (10¢ piece) for the ice box. Every Friday the fish man who came in his horse drawn flat bed wagon covered with ice and fish. Mom always bought fish, cleaned them and we had fish every Friday for dinner. The milk man, Mr. Anderson lived three houses away and had two lots for his house and cow shed with two milk cows. His cows would MOO when needed milking and we kids would tell him his kids were calling. On Halloween we would put his front porch rocking chair on top of the street light pole and 2 inch fire crackers in mailboxes. We played baseball & football on every vacant lot. I knew all the neighborhood cars and license numbers as a hobby - Whippet, Moon, Star, HUpmobile, Ford, Chevy, Essex, Hudson, Buick, LaSalle, Packard and Graham-Paige. Our landlord Mrs. Doty (a widow) came each month in her LaSalle Coup'e to collect. Chrysler made 3 models - Chrysler "52" 4 cyl. 2 dr. Coup'e - Chrysler "66" 6 cyl 4 dr. Sedan & Chrysler "77" 8 cyl Super sedan. Aunt Josephine my Mothers sister bought a new Chrysler "52" with wooden oak spoke wheels and Fisk tires for 450.00.

Each morning before leaving for the office, Dad would leave a one dollar bill on the dining table for Mom to buy the days food supply. On Saturday he left 5.00 for the weekend and Sunday dinner. Each morning "Snooks" was waiting on the front porch for Mom to go to market. He would run ahead and then wait at each store along the way as he knew it would first be the A&P then D. Pender grocery and Kramers Meat Market. On return home he would walk along with Mom. "Snooks" did not like the mailman or anyone going onto the front porch except the family. One day he tore the mailman's pant leg. He was a mix of Spitz & Terrier and would challenge any big dog. Onetime a big Airdale picked him up by the stomach and shook him upside down until I pulled them apart.

Figure 6 Family Picture – Aunt Josephine, Aunt Paige, Mom and Dad

There was a man named Hooper that lived at Mrs. Cooper's boarding house on Marshall Ave., who was called Walking Hooper. On weekends he would walk the C&O railroad tracks to near Richmond and back.

When I was in grade school at Walter Reed I had two girlfriends I was in love with, Harriet Brown & Ruby Amory. I did quite a juggling act in carrying their books while walking home with them, without either one seeing me with the other. I would wait at school until one or the other was a block or two ahead and I would go with the other. I had a feeling they both knew how to play the game.

Uncle Clinton Brock, the Engineer, Lawyer and builder of the overtown bridges and Camp Stewart during World War I, Built a large home in the high rent district and owned several other empty lots that we used for baseball & football. Uncle Clinton (married to my Mom's sister) told me that each time I made the Honor Roll at school he would give me a dollar bill. I made a few bucks that way.

My Sunday school teacher was Mr. Shawl, a Master Locksmith who was handicapped and walked with a cain had a little shop in the back of Duncan's Repair Garage on 28th at Jefferson. One morning he got a call from Mr. Shapiro that his money safe was jammed and he could not open for business Shapiro's Dept. Store on Jefferson Ave. Mr. Shawl came and being the expert he opened the safe in about two minutes and told Mr. Shapiro the charge was 100.00. Mr. Shapiro yelled and said no pay that much, so Mr. Shawl closed the safe, spun the lock and told Mr. Shapiro to open it himself and started for the front door. Mr. Shapiro yelled comeback – I pay.

We had a sand lot baseball team and played after school, Saturday's and all summer. Wilroy, my brother was our star pitcher and I played short-stop. Our big playing field were the empty lots between Halprin's Grocery at 31st & Jefferson and Helmers Feed Store at 32nd & Jefferson.

When Dad bought the '24 Chevy it needed tires. I remember going to the Esso Station at 30th & Jefferson and Dad bought four new Atlas Cord tires that lasted about 3000 miles & cost 4.00 each. (Big Event).

When I was old enough I got a job at the A&P on Jefferson Ave. delivering groceries in my Radio Flyer wagon from 7:00 A.M. to Midnight Saturday for 75¢ and all the over ripe bananas that would not keep until Monday. When I was a little older I was promoted to clerk and worked Thursday after school to 7:00 P.M. Friday after school to 9:00 P.M. and Saturday 7:00 A.M. til Midnight for 5.00. When the store was not busy I was sent to the back room to weigh sugar, beans, rice and prunes into one & two pound brown paper bags with water sealing tape.

Leon Boyd the barber, had a 2 chair barber shop behind Tony Koskinos drug store & ice cream parlor at 28th & Jefferson. Leon gave me the job of shining shoes, janitor and errand boy. My pay would be what I could earn shining shoes. I built a shoe shine stand from scrap wood from J.H. Bell Furniture Co. throw away furniture crates. Dad gave me some of his black paint and I shined shoes after school and all day Saturday for 5¢ a pair. On a good saturday I could earn 75¢. For this privilege I swept & mopped the floor and ran all the errands. Leon was a friend of the Mgr. at the local State ABC Liquor Store and each Saturday he would give me a note to take to the Mgr. In a brown paper bag (I looked) I would bring back a bottle of Rock & Rye Whiskey. At close, 9:00 P.M. Leon would pull the shades tell me to go home, lock the door and he and fellow barber & friends have their Saturday Night. Haircut was 15¢ – shave & haircut 25¢.

In the summertime we had 5 or 6 Church Baseball Teams that I watched play after school and sometimes bat boy. After dinner most of the players would meet in front of Tony Koskinos (Greek) Drug Store and I would listen as they played each game over again plus the Yankees & Washington Senators. We were called Drug Store Cowboys.

Figure 7 Sammons Family Picture

That was our evening of excitement.

Each summer during our school years Mom would get out the old big tan leather suit case, then we knew we were going to Grampa's farm on the Nansemond River for 3 weeks of vacation. It was street car to the C&O depot then the passenger liner (The Virginia) to Norfolk then on the Edgerton Bus Line across the Portsmouth ferry, then past Driver to Wilroy Station. Then the mule buggy ride back to the homestead and river. This is a 30 mile all day trip. We fished, crabbed, fed the chickens, gathered the eggs, fed the pigs & cows, rode the mules, ate watermelon, apples, peaches and got stung by the yellowjackets.

On our summer vacations at Grampa's farm, behind the corn barn in the cow pasture Grampa had parked his 1923 Buick Touring Sedan that had died. So we kids would play driving to town behind the wooden steering wheel and leather seats. The worn canvas top leaked when it rained and the isinglass snap-on panel side windows were cracked and broken.

Also at the homestead we went swimming in the creek in the cow pasture and dove off the cattle bridge, while keeping an eye on the rattle snakes coiled up sunning on the bank. We swam in our underwear.

Gramma Wilroy told me the story of the "Biggie Bird". A family from Italy bought a farm next to one of Grampa's 3 farms and Grampa taught him how we farm in America and each Thanksgiving we celebrate with one of the wild turkeys that are plentiful on the farm. Grampa didn't see the Italian farmer for several days after Thanksgiving, so he went over to see if he was O.K. He told Grampa that for Thanksgiving he shot and killed a biggie bird turkey and they were all sick from the "Biggie Bird". He had killed and they had eaten a buzzard instead of a turkey for thanksgiving dinner.

In those days Grampa was known as a "Steamboat Farmer", as he grew and shipped by boat, potatoes, spinach, squash, sweet corn, green beans, and watermelons from the wharf he built on the Nansemond river. In addition, he grew peanuts, cotton, corn and hay for the animals. He shipped loads to Baltimore, and New York markets. One time he shipped a boat load of green beans in one bushel baskets and by the time the boat reached New York Harbor the market was overloaded and the price had dropped to almost zero, so he wired the ship captain to dump the beans in the New York Harbor and return the empty baskets.

When Dad, Wilroy & I were truck farmers operating the farm during the depression we hauled sweet corn, potatoes & watermelons in our truck to the Norfolk Saturday Produce Market. In order to get a good spot location at the market Saturday morning, we would go early Friday night and sleep in the truck and on top of the load and usually sold out by noon. We also cut hauled & bailed marsh grass from the 500 acres of marsh land. Our bailer was mule drawn and my job was to pull the wires thru and tie each bale as it pressed thru the bailer. Dad & I would haul a 2 ton load to the Norfolk Shipping Docks to meet the banana boats from South America. They preferred our grass to hay because it was tough yet soft and they could use it several times Regular hay would crush at the bottom.

Figure 8 Granpa Wilroy's Farm Home

One day I entered the banana ripening room and saw at least 1000 green bunches hanging on hooks to ripen. The manager said I could have any on the floor. On the way home I ate at least 10 half green bananas. At home I wasn't hungry and I told my Mom what I had done - she said most likely I would be in the hospital before dawn with green gripes, whatever that is? I'm still here.

Around the turn of the Century a young man came to the U.S.A. from Italy and settled in Wilkes-Barre,Pa. He roasted and sold peanuts on the street in paper bags for 5¢ each to earn a living. Business was good. He saved his nickels and opened a shop in the peanut capitol of the world - Suffolk,Virginia. He bought,roasted and sold peanuts with good success and soon called it Planters Peanuts.

During the great depression of the thirties our family moved to my Grandfather's farm a few miles from Suffolk,Va.on the Nansemond River. I was but a young boy. Two farms down the river lived a man and his wife on a beautiful river farm with servants,a beautiful home and a large pier with a boat dock. We kids used Grampa's 12 ft.row boat for fishing and swimming. I remember one time we decided to row down the river to see this home,yard and boat and dock and take a close look at the beautiful yacht. We tied up at the dock and was greeted by a man asking why we were there. He was the gardener and handyman. We just wanted to see up close this beautiful 75 ft.solid mahogany trimmed in white yacht. The name on each side of the yacht said "ROMA". On some weekends the "ROMA" would go up the Nansemond river to Suffolk and return. We would run out to the river bank when we saw the "ROMA" coming around the bend. We would wave and yell and the pilot would either wave or toot the whistle and if Amedeo Obici was on the deck he would wave. This was quite a thrill to we kids,as very few luxury yachts travelled this small river.

Each day we walked from our river farm out to the highway (2 miles), to wait for the Model T Ford school bus and each morning about that same time a big black sedan would go by slowing to about 5 mph.as the chauffeur was approaching the Southern Railroad Crossing at Wilroy Station on his way to Suffolk and Planters Peanuts. We kids of course were all eyes. There in the back seat of the long black sedan was a small man wearing a wide brim black felt hat,either reading a newspaper or business papers,thanks to a little spotlight attached to the corner of the back seat. That man was Amedeo Obici the founder of Planters Peanuts.

On Grampa's farm we grew about 100 acres of peanuts each year and I remember the truck loads of peanuts and delivering and selling them to Planters Peanuts in Suffolk for about 2¢ a pound. Uncle Bernard Simmons travelled the 48 States for more than 40 years buying & selling peanuts by the carload.

On our return home from school each day the Model T Ford school bus would let us off at Wilroy Station and we would visit with Mr. Heath at his Southern Railway watchman's shack located 6 ft.from the railroad tracks and the highway. The shack included a bench Tom,Edgar and I sat on,a rocking chair with the rockers sawed off with a potato sack stuffed with straw on the seat,a small pot belly stove and a large spittoon as Mr.Heath always had a wad of tobacco in his cheek. Half of the tobacco spit hit the spittoon and half hit the wall or floor. He told us the latest news from his newspaper and news of the world as we had no radio at the farm.

At 3 o'clock he changed shifts with Mr. Tom Holland who also had a chew of tobacco in his cheek. Mr. Heath would leave with his lunch bucket and head home in his little Whippet auto. After a few stories from Mr. Holland, Tom, Edgar & I would pick up the mail and make the two mile walk back to the farm and our daily chores. That was our news of the day.

Each year we would go as a family in the 'ole Chevy to visit Aunt Annie (Dad's Sister) her husband Uncle Willie Faison and family at Emporia. One time my cousin, Marvin had a nest of white mice and I talked Mom into letting me bring one home to play with. It's fun what you can do with a little white mouse, a piece of cheese a peanut and cookie. I trained it to go up my sleeve across my shoulders and come out the other arm. Plus several other minor tricks.

Every year Mom would invite Dad's sister, Aunt Annie, Uncle Willie, son Ray & wife Cora and the other children to our home for an all day get-together & large dinner of Fried Chicken, Country Ham, Butter Beans, all the trimmings and pineapple pie. They arrived in Ray's nearly new Model A Ford. Sitting around after the big meal we would ask Ray how he liked his Ford (we had a Chevy) and he would say - "She Perks". After that with Dad, Wilroy & I it became a standing joke saying if asked how our '24 Chevy was running it was - "She Perks".

On 4th of July Mom would invite her 5 sisters and families for a full dinner and celebration. I remember one person in particular, Uncle Bernard who was married to Mom's sister Ruth. He was at least 6½ ft. tall with his expensive linen palm beach suit with gold chain attached to his gold watch in vest pockets, large diamond ring and hard flat brim straw hat. He was called "High Pockets". Uncle Bernard Simmons was also my Dad's cousin and traveling salemen for Planters Peanuts in Suffolk. He traveled by train across the country buying & selling peanuts by the carload. One of his employee benefits was a large granite tombstone. He had carved into this stone a replica of his traveling suitcase and below his name it said - "My Last Trip". He is buried at Cedar Hill Cemetery in Suffolk at Grampa Wilroy's large lot.

Each summer our church sponsored an all day picnic at Buckroe Beach. Mom prepared a large basket of fried chicken, ham, potato salad, homemade rolls and all Mom's cookies you could eat. What a thrill!, when we walked down to Jefferson Ave. to board the 3 car special street cars waiting and a 3 mile ride to Buckroe Beach. Dad gave us each 1.00 to spend. Wilroy & I headed for the roller coaster (10¢) then the fish pond (10¢) then the merry-go-round (5¢) & a free ride if you caught the brass ring. Wilroy was good at that. Then it was into the penny arcade to crank the cinescope for (1¢) to see the bathing beauties, then the beach, swimming and sunburn. We were now ready for the fried chicken, cookies and street car home. We looked forward to this special day every year.

One summer I distributed 500 movie flyers to homes each week for the Palace Theatre - for 2 free tickets to the movies.

In the mid-twenties we received our first radio station - WGH (World's Greatest Harbor). It was located on the 2nd floor above a retail store between 28th & 29th St. on Washington Ave. It was only a 5000 Watt station heard mostly in the city. We kids would climb the long dark wooden stairs to see a man in a glass enclosed room with a large microphone hanging from the ceiling and a sign that said - "Quiet On Air".

Figure 9 Family Photo

In the summertime Wilroy & I would go clamming in Hampton Roads off Buxton Ave., when the tide was low and sandbars about 200 yds. out. We had an old garden rake & Wilroy would dig the clams. I would clean them and put in a tow sack. We would dig as many as we could carry (about 4 doz.) and sell to neighbors for 25¢ a dozen. We also fished the Warwick Machine Pier and Pier A. We caught mostly catfish & eels that we sold to a Mrs. Roth on 28th St. for 15¢ each.

Wilroy delivered the Saturday Evening Post and I delivered Liberty Magazine for 5¢ each and we had about 30 customers and our profit was 2¢ each. I also had a Times Herald daily paper route of about 40 customers. The daily was 5¢ and Sunday was 10¢. My commission was 2¢ daily & 4¢ Sunday. One of my customers was our Asst. High School Principal, Dr. Stanley R. Lamar and he always gave me a 5¢ tip.

On the night of the Bruno Hauptmann execution I waited at the Daily Press until about 10 P.M. until word came down by wire and the extra from the Daily Press. I worked the street car tracks on Washington Ave. from 25th to 35th until midnight yelling "EXTRA" and sold about 30 copies and earned 60¢.

Dad bought a lot on Powhatan Parkway near Buxton Ave., 2 blocks from the water and on our Sunday ride would go by as Dad was planning the home of his dreams. When the depression hit, Dad sold the lot so we could eat. No one was buying insurance instead of bread. In the early thirties Dad got a job as a maintenance man repairing & painting the fleet of Liberty Ships from WWI that were tied up at Yorktown and were used again in WWII.

Across the street from #1 firehouse at 28th & Huntington Ave. was the J. Hugh Caffey Funeral Home. They had the body of a black man about 6½ ft. tall that no claimed. In time he became petrofied and they stood him up in the corner of the back room. One Halloween 3 fireman from the fire house decided to sneak him out on the street for a scare. In the process he fell on one of the fireman and broke his leg. That ended their Halloween. They later buried him in Potters Field.

Next to the corner at 25th & Jefferson Ave. was a 10 ft. front Greek Coney Island Hot Dog Stand with the grill of hot dogs in the window. When Wilroy earned a dime mowing a lawn we would hurry to the Hot Dog Stand and buy 3 Coney Hot Dogs for 10¢. He would eat 2 & I would get one. 65 years later the 2 sons & grandson of this Greek man served Wilroy and I Coney Island Hot Dogs at their Greek Restaurant they owned and operated since 1950 in St. Petersburg, Florida.

At 18th & Jefferson Ave. was the African-American Dixie Theatre and one time Lionel Hampton & his band were playing there and Tullie Rea and I were curious to see the crowd & pictures out front. So we went (our parents did not know) and at the ticket window it said Admission 25¢ colored Only. We didn't have the 25¢ either.

Two row houses from us lived our happy policeman - Billie Saunders. He walked "The Beat" each day & I remember him waving his 3 ft. bullie stick going to work. He had a son - Billie Jr. that was an Engineer at the shipyard engineer school & practiced his Banjo everyday after work and drove everyone nuts. He bought a new 1929 Chevy and Friday his payday would pay me 10¢ to wash his car for the weekend.

When living at 623 29th St.Wilroy & his buddies decided they wanted an auto to sport around in so, Wilroy,Bill Faison & Wilmer Austin (later killed at the Battle for Midway),went to see their other high school buddy, Ike Spooner who's Dad owned Spooner's Junk Yard. For ten dollars they bought a 1920 Motel T Ford with the high top carriage type body with the big round window in the rear. No way would they be seen in that, so they found another body from the junk yard,a 1925 Ford 4 dr. soft top. They stripped the body down to a convertible with no top and removed the 1920 body & tried to install the 1925. This took many days after school and weekends, plus a few choice words. Finally we rode around town in this convertible until one day the engine blew. It was back to Spooners Junk Yard.

About 1930 was built a new beautiful theatre at 33rd & Washington Ave.,named the Paramount. In front of the stage the Mighty Hammond Organ would rise thru the floor from the basement with Gladys Lyle playing beautiful music for about ten minutes before each show. About 50 years later when they tore down the Paramount, they saved the beautiful Hammond Organ. Later it was installed at the Alexandria Theatre & Bea and I went to see & hear it once more. We did not know the person playing but what a memory thrill. (They are tearing down buildings I watched them build).

The Imperial Theatre at 30th & Washington Ave. had a Polo Paddle Ball contest one Saturday morning on the stage. I bought a bolo paddle for 10¢ & practiced all week. There were about 20 in the contest including three girls. Of all things!! a girl won 1st prize (5.00) & I won 2nd prize (Mickey Mouse Watch).

When Dad came home from work on Saturday he gave us kids 25¢ for the Buck Jones, Hoot Gibson or Tom Mix silent movies. We would stop at Woolworth's 5&10 for a pound of peanut butter kisses for 10¢ & 10¢ for the movie. On the way home we would stop at Tony Koskinos Ice Cream Parlor for a 5¢ Eskimo Pie. That was our weekend treat.

We had one rent-a-car in town and it was named U Drive It. One dollar a day plus 5¢ per mile. The mileage meter was in the right front wheel.

Virginai had a BLUE LAW - no store open on Sunday except prescription drug stores. No baseball,football or any sports. The jewish people got around the law by closing on Saturday - hence we had hot vienna bread on Sunday from Brenner's Bakery to go with the Sunday leftovers. One Sunday Dad gave Wilroy a dime for a hot loaf. I went with him and on the way home we ate most of the hot loaf. After a loud reprimand Wilroy was given another dime and this time we had bread.

Dr. Creasy came to town and opened a prescription drug store across the corner from Tony Koskinos with soda fountain,ice cream & patent medicine. Dr. Creasy was a kind man and trusted everyone to his dispair. A couple years later he had a cash shortage and hired me as a soda jerk and collection agent, to try and collect unpaid accounts on a 50/50 basis. I did collect a few dollars and wore out a lot of shoe leather.

When the depression hit Wilroy was old enough to work after school and Saturday to help with food money. After graduation from Newport News High School he worked full time as an apprentice printer for Mr. Eager Wood of the Wayside Press and earned 15.00 a week for a 6 day work week. When Wilroy completed his apprenticeship and became a master printer, John Berryman owner of Peninsula Printing Co. near 24th St. on Washington Ave. hired Wilroy to supervise the shop and a pay raise of 20.00 a week.

At the East end of Wickam Ave. to the water of Hampton Roads was the Old Dominion Golf Course. Tullie Rea and I would check into the Caddie Shack and get a number. Sometimes we would caddy 18 holes for 75¢ or 9 holes for 35¢. If our number was not called we would hunt lost golf balls and sell them for 25¢ or best offer. On the way home we would be so hungry we would stop at a Coney Island Hot Dog Stand on 25th St. between Marshall & Wickam Ave. There we ate up our earnings for the day. In the late thirties they made the golf course into a subdivision of nice homes called Stewart Gardens. At the South end on Hampton Roads on the water was built the Dodge Boat Corp. the builder of speed boats.

This golf course in WWI was called Camp Stewart and an embarking point for soldiers overseas. Uncle Clinton Brock was the builder for Camp Stewart in WWI.

Winters were much colder in Newport News in those days, as we usually had several 6 to 10 inches of snow and no snow plows. The only vehicles moving were the street cars. One of my playmates had a sleigh and we would take turns sliding down 28th St. bridge on the ice and snow. Four homes North lived our high school basketball coach Julious Conn. I played football in high school under coach Mike Byrne.

At Williamsburg, Virginia they had the 150 year Sesqui-Centennial celebration of the Commonwealth of Virginia, a six day celebration (never on Sunday) in conjunction with the completed Historic Restoration of Colonial Williamsburg by the Rockefeller Foundation. Wilroy and several of his high school classmates were selected as ushers & guides for the event. On Saturday, the final day of celebration we gassed up the Chevy and made it to William & Mary College football field (wooden bleachers only) and sat for a long time in the hot sun to listen to speeches by Governor Byrd of Virginia, Governor of New York, Frankin D. Roosevelt, and the President of the United States, Herbert Hoover. Wilroy was one of the ushers to help Franklin D. Roosevelt to his seat on the speakers platform located at one end of the field.

I had two pairs of pants known as nickers, one pair for school and play and one pair for Sunday School & Church and our Sunday ride. When I wore holes in the knees Mom would sew on a patch from the scrap material in her sewing basket. These patches were called "Hoover Badges".

I remember on Sunday ride in the Chevy to Yorktown to see and enter the General Cornwallis Cave. I brought home a piece of rock from inside the cave, that I still have in my 1938 Cremo Cigar Box.

I remember one summer the great evangelist Billy Sunday came to town and put up a large tent on the Casino Grounds with saw dust floor and wooden seats with great success. A few years later the great evangelist Mordici Hamm came to town and built a large tent in the same location that was blown down by a summer thunderstorm. He re-built and the second day another storm toppled the tent. He packed up and left town saying, "The Devil is in this Town".

When I was a freshman at Newport News High School, I had a classmate named Ava Gardner. Her Dad located a job at the shipyard and moved the family from North Carolina. She was a beautiful girl and the favorite with the football & basketball stars, of which I was neither. After Graduation it was on to New York and Hollywood as an Actress and later Married Frank Sinatra.

In the early thirties the shipyard & C&O railroad were laying off many people and there was not any work in town. We could not make expenses so Mom's brother, Uncle Bud and sister Josephine asked us to join them at Grampa's farm home on the Nansemond River as Grampa & Granma were deceased and they had plenty of room and to stay with them until the depression was over. - - So we moved to Grampa's farm.

Uncle Bud operated the farm with the help of two black families that lived in the two tenant houses on the farm. Aunt Josephine did the cooking and the chickens. A little later Mom's sister Della, husband Tom Kittrell and the two boys my age (Thomas & Edgar) moved in with us as Mr. Kittrell had closed his grocery store near Suffolk. We now had 3 sister cooks. Mr. Kittrell soon opened the closed grocery store on the highway at Wilroy Station. Thomas, Edgar & I walked two miles each way out to the highway and a 3 mile ride in a model T Ford school bus to DeJarnette High School at Driver, Va. We carried a brown bag lunch of a cold leftover biscuit with homemade jam and a hard winesap apple from the orchard. We were too embarrassed to eat with the other students in the lunch room that had bologna or ham on fresh bread with store fruit. So we ate out on the playing field alone. Later Mr. Kittrell closed the unprofitable grocery store at Wilroy Station and located a job in Portsmouth. The Kittrell's including Uncle Bud moved to Portsmouth and Tom located a job at Rodman's Barbeque. That left our family and Aunt Josephine to manage the farm. We hired two new black families for the tenant houses to help Dad, Wilroy & I to run the farm. Wilroy worked full time at Peninsula Printing and brought home the food. Dad fed the cows, hogs & mules. Aunt Joe did the chickens & eggs, Mom did the cooking and I worked in the field with the tenant hands and milked 2 cows twice a day. Moving to the farm from the city was quite a shock - no electric (kerosene Lamps), no running water (well in the yard) and a 3 hole privy down the hill with a Sears & Roebuck catalog. Big wood stove in the kitchen with attached hot water tank for washing dishes and baths. On the farm it was early to bed and early rise. I would go to bed tired about eight-thirty before the last Southern train from Danville to Norfolk at 9:00 P.M. My bedroom window overlooked the Nansemond river and bridge the Southern Railway train would cross before blowing the whistle for Wilroy Station. I would listen and always knew if it was going to stop - 3 longs & 1 short meant- STOP - and 2 longs & 2 shorts meant - going on thru to Norfolk. About 50 years later Wilroy and I visited Smithsonian in Washington and were thrilled to see one of these Special Locomotives on display. This was a Special Fast Start, High Speed one of a kind short distance locomotive built in England with special 6 ft. diameter wheels (1-3-2) painted bright green with gold trim.

My sister, Delane went to Newport News, lived with Aunt Paige, found a job and later married Tommy Cutchins, Captain of #1 fire station on Huntington Ave. I graduated from DeJarnette High School in 1938 and went to Newport News to live with Delane & Tommy and to find a job as business was getting better. With the help of Tommy Cutchins I located a job as a carpenter's helper with the Virginia Engineering Co. building tobacco warehouses at Morrison.

These were completed in 1939. I then located a job at the Newport News Shipbuilding & Drydock Co. in the Engineering Dept. blocking boilers and the engine room with insulation on the passenger liner U.S.S. Brazil. ( Little was I to know that 3 years later I would travel to North Africa to fight a war on the U.S.S. Brazil).

My brother Wilroy, opened his own printing Co."The Commercial Printer" at 28th & Huntington Ave. in 1941.

Life was good, so I bought a 1932 Chevy Sport Coup'e at Hutchins Chevrolet 24th & Huntington Ave. - 125.00 with 10.00 down & 5.00 a week. I was earning 65¢ per hr. and paid by the shipyard every Friday in Silver Dollars & change.

In the meantime, the farm was sold and Dad, Mom & Aunt Joe moved to Newport News at 849 26th St. I continued to work at the shipyard until I was drafted in October 1940 and reported for one year selective service in the Army on January 10,1941.

**NOW** - you know part of the story of a happy boy - poor in wealth, rich in LOVE & the LORD living the 1920's & 30's, survived the Great Depression, World War II, wed a beautiful girl and became a Dad.

## ABRAM EDGAR WILROY, SR.
## 1841 – 1924

Abe Wilroy's forefathers came to America from England on the 2nd ship load of Capt. John Smith and landed at Jamestown, Virginia in 1608. Abe Wilroy was born in Virginia and drafted in the Civil War in 1862. He joined Co."I"61st Virginia Regiment Mahones Brigade 24th Virginia Infantry General Anderson's Army. Fought and was captured during the battle at Fredericksburg in March 1865. As a prisoner of war he rode a wagon train for 2 weeks to Fort MOnroe, Virginia that was called (The Rip-Rap). On the prisoner wagon train he met a fellow soldier named Joseph Holloway from Norfolk, Virginia and they became good friends.

After a few months, little food and few guards at this Fort on the Chesapeake Bay they found a ten foot board, cut it in half and after dark when the guards were in for the night they swam the 4 miles across Chesapeake Bay on the boards (bleeding stomachs) to the home of Joseph Holloway. At home he met Joseph's father & mother, 2 sisters and 1 brother. There he met Joseph's sister Josephine Holloway. They fell in love and when the war was over they married at the Holloway home in Norfolk.

Abe Wilroy bought his first home on the Nansemond River and a big mortgage next to his older brother John and his farm on the river. He became a very successful farmer shipping potatoes, melons, green beans and other produce and other produce from the wharf he built on the river to the Baltimore & New York markets.

Abe & Josephine had 2 boys and 6 girls that they educated through Finishing School (college today). He purchased 2 additional farms in the area. The Southern Railroad running from Norfolk to Danville built a station and produce platform going through this village named – Wilroy Station and it made 2 passenger stops each day.

I remember one summer on the farm Grampa sitting in his rocking chair on the porch & his corn-cob pipe. I remember his funeral and his being laid-out in the big parlor room with his long white beard and full head of white hair. He is buried at Cedar Hill Cemetery Suffolk, Virginia.

P.S.  I have one living cousin, Hilda Wilroy Duke daughter of Abram Wilroy, Jr. She is 105 years of age.

Ed Sammons – Grandson

Feb 10, 1865

This letter written home during the battle of
Fredericksburg by my Grandmothers brother -
Joseph Holloway and copied to be readable by
my first cousin Hilda Wilroy Duke and later
given to me.
Joseph Holloway and my Grandfather - Abram
Edgar Wilroy served together in Co. I 61st
Virginia Regiment, Mahones Brigade, 24th Virginia
Infantry, General Anderson's Army.
They were both captured during the battle at
Fredericksburg and rode a wagon prisoner train
for 2 weeks to reach Fort Monroe, Virginia -
known as the - RIP - RAP and prison for confederate
soldiers. Joseph & Abram searched and found two
pieces of wood board one foot by five feet long.
Late one night they escaped from Ft. Monroe which
is on the water and paddled on the boards across
Hampton Roads to try to reach Joseph's home in Norfolk.
After four miles of surfing and bleeding stomachs
they made it to Josephs home. There Abram met Josephs
sister Josephine, fell in love, married and the eight kids
are history, which I have yet to tell.

```
            PEGGY HOPKINS JOYCE
           ACTRESS - MOVIE STAR
           BROADWAY - HOLLYWOOD
                1885 - 1936
```

This is a family happening my Mother told me :

My grandmother Josephine (Holloway) Wilroy married to my grandfather Abe Wilroy had an older brother Joseph who fought and was a prisoner in the Civil War with my grandfather, Abe Wilroy (that's another story to write) and her younger sister Rebecca (HOlloway) Hopkins. Rebecca and her husband lived in Norfolk, Virginia and for summer vacation would come in their horse & buggy with their baby daughter Peggy, to visit my grandmother Josephine and her family at the farm on the Nansemond River. My Mother and her sisters as young girls played with and baby-sit Peggy Hopkins.

Peggy Hopkins graduated in Norfolk from Finishing School (College) and became a beautiful young lady.

She was discovered by Broadway in New York and acted in many shows on Broadway. Next she was offered the silent movies in Hollywood and did several movies with the great actor Jack Oakie and other Hollywood stars. Later she met and married a lumber millionaire tycoon from the Northwest named Joyce. They both loved horses and had them on their California Ranch.

A few years later they took a voyage to Europe and then to a horse resort in England. One day they were on a sleigh ride together and the horse became frightened and ran. It overturned and both ended in a hospital where they both died several days later. They had no children.

I remember the family discussion about her death, but do not know who attended her funeral.

Ed Sammons

**Editorial correction:** Peggy did not lose her life in the sleigh ride with her husband at that time and lived until 1957.

# MEMOIRS OF WAR

## Ready for War

# Original Table of Contents – J. E.
## GRAMPA'S WAR: Benning to Berlin with Hell on Wheels

### TABLE OF CONTENTS

```
FORWARD
INTRODUCTION    THE MEN OF THE 2nd ARMORED DIVISION
                MILITARY HISTORY - JAMES E. SAMMONS
                MILITARY HISTORY - CO."E" 17th ARMD. ENGR. BN.
CHAPTER I       THE JOURNEY BEGINS - VIRGINIA - BENNING - TEXAS - CAROLINA
CHAPTER II      NEW YORK - CASABLANCA - FRENCH MOROCCO
CHAPTER III     "D" DAY - OMAHA BEACH - NORMANDY
CHAPTER IV      OMAHA BEACH - BELGIUM - MAASTRICHT
CHAPTER V       BATTLE OF THE BULGE - AACHEN - BERLIN
                PRESIDENT HARRY S. TRUMAN - PRESIDENTIAL CITATION
CHAPTER VI      COMING HOME TO AMERICA - THE JOURNEY ENDS
CHAPTER VII     ANNUAL REUNIONS - 1946 - 1997
                THE BRIDGE COMPANY, JIM BURT CONGRESSIONAL MEDAL OF HONOR
                STORY OF THE FAMOUS GIRDLE
                GENERAL PATTON'S BOYS
                FILIPINO STOWAWAY SOLDIER
                WHAT GOES AROUND COMES AROUND
                THE COLONEL AND THE CORPORAL
                REUNION LETTER MEMORIES
```

## FORWARD

These writings are dedicated to my wife Bea. Without her daily letters of encouragement, faith and support during the war, it would have been very difficult to look forward to the next sunrise. I am forever grateful.

I began writing my memories and making tapes in 1978. I was aware that my children and grandchildren would appreciate knowing about the side of war that they would not read about in newspapers and history books. This is a father and now grandfather's "take" on a war I survived that had some lighter sides which were not always known.

These events are a portion of the many battle campaigns during World War II as a soldier of Co."E" 17th Armd. Engr. Bn., U.S. 2nd Armored Division, 1941-1945. Ft. Benning, Ga. to Berlin Germany by way of North Africa, Sicily, D day Omaha Beach, Normandy, France, Belgium, Netherlands, Battle of the Bulge and Germany.

We, the fighting men of the famous 2nd Armored Division WW II have come a long way. This is twilight time and oh, what great memories we have shared at our annual reunions. After more than 50 years it is much easier to talk about the war. These stories are about my 4½ years of war. I leave the ugly and bloody events, which were many to the movies and to historians.

My forefathers landed at Jamestown, Virginia in 1608 and fought the Indians. My grandfather fought and was a prisoner of war with General Anderson's 24th Virginia Infantry in the Civil War. My father, a Marine of the 1st U.S. Marine division, fought the Filipino Insurrection War, the Boxer Rebellion in China and the Spanish American War. To these brave soldiers I say, I've tried to carry on this tradition, fighting to keep our freedom.

## THE MEN OF THE U.S. 2nd ARMORED DIVISION
## 1941 – 1945

<u>WHO WERE THESE MEN - BENNING TO BERLIN ?</u>
Gen. Patton knew, they were farm boys, city slickers, drug store cowboys, high school and college graduates who volunteered or were drafted to help preserve our freedom. These men were welded into a solid fighting unit by General Patton.

<u>WHO WERE THESE MEN - BENNING TO BERLIN ?</u>
They were young Americans from all parts of our great Nation with names like, Atkins, Brown, Barnes, Gnau, Masch, Mecler, Miller, Powell, Strickland, Stewart, Walker, White & Young. Just to name a few.

<u>WHO WERE THESE MEN - BENNING TO BERLIN ?</u>
Ask the people in North Africa, Sicily, Normandy, Belgium & Holland. They felt their strength, friendship and freedom.

<u>WHO WERE THESE MEN - BENNING TO BERLIN ?</u>
Talk to Hitler's elite SS Storm Troopers, they felt their armor and determination. They called these men - " **ROOSEVELT'S BUTCHERS** ".

<u>WHO WERE THESE MEN - BENNING TO BERLIN ?</u>
These were the soldiers that were reviewed and honored on the German autobahn at Berlin, Germany in July 1945 and awarded the Presidential Citation in person by Harry S. Truman, President of the United States.
In attendance were countless dignitaries of war including, Sir Winston Churchhill, Field Marshall Sir Bernard Law Montgomery, Sir Alan Brooke, Sec.of War Henry L. Stimson, Gen. Dwight Eisenhower, Gen. George C. Marshall, Gen. Omar Bradley and of course Gen. George S. Patton, Jr. their first Commander.

<u>WHO WERE THESE MEN - BENNING TO BERLIN ?</u>
Gen. Patton knew, the day of his later famous speech on a hillside at Ft. Bragg, N.C., when he told these soldiers, " War is hell and we are going over there and kick 'em in the ass till their noses bleed". Then near the end of his speech he said, " When your grandson is on your knee 30 years from now and asks what you did in the great war, you won't have to tell him you shoveled sh-- in Louisiana ".

<u>WHO WERE THESE MEN - BENNING TO BERLIN ?</u>
They have travelled, celebrated and remembered their war buddies for more than 50 years. Each year at a different location they meet in memory of those men that helped defend and preserve our freedom in this great land. They know who they were and who they are.

<u>WHO WERE THESE MEN - BENNING TO BERLIN ?</u>
Just ask their wives, children, grandchildren, relatives & friends.

<u>WHO WERE THESE MEN - BENNING TO BERLIN ?</u>
I know, because I was fortunate enough to be one of these men and so were some of you.

God Bless - thank you for being here.(Part of final speech 10/97).

<u>WORLD WAR II</u>
<u>MILITARY HISTORY</u>
TECH 5  JAMES EDWARD SAMMONS SERIAL # 33040248
CO. "E" 17th ARMD. COMBAT ENGR. BN.
U.S. 2nd ARMORED DIVISION
JAN.10,1941 - MAY 26,1945 HONORABLE DISCHARGE

<u>BATTLE CAMPAIGNS :</u>

    NORTH AFRICA - FRENCH MOROCCO - TUNISIA
    SICILY - GELA - PALERMO
    D DAY 2 - OMAHA BEACH - NORMANDY - SAINT LO
    CENTRAL & NORTHERN FRANCE
    CENTRAL EUROPE - BELGIUM - NETHERLANDS
    ARDENNES - BATTLE OF THE BULGE
    RHINELAND - AACHEN - SIEGFRIED LINE - RHINE RIVER BRIDGE - MAGDEBURG


<u>BATTLE AWARDS :</u>

    SILVER STAR
    BRONZE STAR
    INVASION ARROWHEADS - 2 - GELA SICILY - OMAHA BEACH NORMANDY
    DISTINGUISHED UNIT CITATION - BRIDGE OVER RHINE
    NORMANDY JUBILEE FREEDOM MEDAL - D DAY LIBERTY
    FRENCH CROIX de GUERRE - LIBERTY & FREEDOM
    NETHERLANDS RESISTANCE CROSS - BATTLE AT MAASTRICHT
    BELGIUM FOURAGUERE - BATTLE OF THE BULGE
    PRESIDENTIAL CITATION - IN PERSON BY PRES. HARRY S. TRUMAN
    GENERAL PATTON SPECIAL AWARD
    EUROPEAN AFRICAN MIDDLE EASTERN CAMPAIGN MEDAL
    AMERICAN DEFENSE SERVICE MEDAL
    GOOD CONDUCT MEDAL
    NATIONAL DEFENSE MEDAL
    WORLD WAR II VICTORY MEDAL


<u>DIVISION STATISTICS :</u>

    12000 MEN    1702 MILES IN COMBAT
    7089 KILLED - WOUNDED - CAPTURED
    4911 SURVIVED

# CHAPTER I

## The Journey Begins

Virginia – Benning – Texas – Carolina

GREATEST GENERATION
MEMORIES OF A SOLDIER
WW II 1941 - 1945

My writings are dedicated to my wife Bea. Without her daily letters of encouragement, faith and support during the war, it would have been very difficult to look forward to the next sunrise. I'm forever grateful.

I began recording my war memories on tape in the seventies. This part of my life I must tell the children so they know Dad & Grampa.

We, the fighting men of the famous 2nd Armored Division (Hell on Wheels ) have come a long way. This is twilight time and what great memories we have shares of 52 years of annual reunions. After more than 60 years, it is much easier to talk about the war. These are some of the events during my 4½ years of war. I leave the ugly * bloody events, which were many to the movies and to the historians.

My forefathers landed at Jamestown, Virginia in 1608 in the second boat load of Captain John Smith and fought the Indians. My grandfather fought and was a prisoner of war with General Anderson's 24th Virginia Infantry in the Civil War. My Father, a Marine in the 1st Marine Division fought in the Filipine Insurrection War, the Boxer Rebellion in china and The Spanish American War.

To these brave soldiers I say - I've tried to carry on this tradition fighting for our freedom.

Ed Sammons
17th armd. Combat Engr. Bn.
2nd Armored Division  ( Hell on Wheels )

## VIRGINIA TO BENNING TEXAS AND CAROLINA

The journey began when President Roosevelt picked my number from the fish bowl in October 1940 at the Nation's Capitol, along with other future members of the 17th Armd. Engr. Bn., U.S. 2nd Armored Division. From Ft. Meade, Md. we were sent on a two day train ride to some place called Ft. Benning, Ga. After arriving at Ft. Benning the train backed into an area called Harmony-Church and we stepped out in sand over our shoes to an 'ole time regular Army Master Sgt. - "Yelling, On the double". We found out later his name was Sgt. Vause and after our basic training he moved on to the next recruits for their basic training.

The next day after we arrived at Ft. Benning, we were called together in a large auditorium and told some of the facts of life and some of the facts of life at Ft. Benning, Ga., by Captain Hurley, who was later our Colonel and Battalion Commander and was killed by a mine during the invasion of Sicily. He told us that Ft. Benning was a different Army Camp from any other Army Camp, because across the river was a place called Phenix City, Ala. It was a city of corruption and our casualties were at least one a day from stabbings and gun fights. He finally ended his speech with - "Fellows remember, it doesn't take any brains to cross the bridge to Phenix."

We began three months of basic infantry training including full field pack twenty-five mile forced marches at night, followed by six months intensive engineer training including many types of portable, trestle, pontoon and fixed river bridges plus bazooka guns, land mines and other explosives.

After completion of basic infantry training the Battalion decided to start a monthly publication of events. They held a contest to name the publication. I entered the contest and named it "Armored Castle", won the two dollar cash prize and had my picture on the front cover of the first issue. 2 bucks bought a lot of cokes & peanuts at the PX.

We built all types of bridges from Tenn. to Louisiana and Texas to North and South Carolina on maneuvers with Gen. Patton. The General put us through an intensive and rigid training program. George S. Patton, Jr., came to our Division as a Colonel in charge of our tank regiments. His Green Hornet uniform he designed and wore was a big laugh to us and the War Department, as they did not approve it for our Armored Divisions.

I remember Ft. Bragg, N.C. when we were there on maneuvers in an outpost area. One day the entire Division was assembled together as there was to be a speech by General Patton and that was the day he made his later famous speech about "War is Hell", crying and yelling. I will never forget his closing words when he said, "We are going over there and kick 'em in the ass until their noses bleed - there is one thing you men will be able to say when you get back home and you may thank God for it. Thirty years from now when you are sitting around your fireside with your grandson on your knee and he ask you - what did you do in the great World War II, you won't have to say well, I shoveled sh-- in Louisiana."

One of the most unusual soldiers in our Company was a full-blooded Indian, a volunteer from a reservation near Telleson, Arizona. We called him Big Chief. He was very tall, strong and very quiet. Did his job but payday was something else. He liked his fire-water and each payday he took off toward Columbus, Ga. He usually got as far as a tavern called the LAST CHANCE. It was the first place to get a drink on the way to Columbus and the last place to get a drink on your way back to camp. Big Chief usually stayed there until his money and fire-water were gone. He came back to the barracks one night a little beat-up and we were told there were several M.P.'s laying on the railroad tracks behind the LAST CHANCE, that had tried to arrest him.

I remember Big Chief in particular one day when I was on guard duty. After we had returned to the guard house from RETREAT and the changing of the guard, the new shift went to eat, except Sgt. Jack LaVassar and myself. All of a sudden a G.I. from "A" Company came running into the guard house and asked us to come and help, as there was trouble in the "A" Company Mess Hall. We asked what was happening. He said Big Chief was there on the warpath. Big Chief went into the front entrance with a bottle of fire-water in hand and a war cry, just as "A" Company sat down to eat. When they heard and saw Big Chief coming in, they all ran for the side door exit. He turned over a few tables of food on his way through and out the back door. We told the cook from "A" Company to go back, as we in no way would go near the "A" Company kitchen and try to stop Big Chief, as he was in our Company and we knew his talents when he had a bottle of fire-water and was on the warpath. After a few paydays, the Officers and men knew Big Chief too and they seemed to turn their heads on payday. Nobody knew where Big Chief was or gone and nobody really cared until he started trouble. He would drink until he could drink no more, then usually go off behind the barracks down into the wooded area and sleep it off. The next day he was back to normal.

In regard to Francisco J. Beltran, the Indian in our Company, one of the last times I remember Big Chief was after we broke out of the St. Lo battle in France and began to move toward Paris. As you know we moved quite rapidly and captured many German soldiers and equipment. One day we came upon a large hill or small mountain known as the Falaise Gap. On this hilltop were a number of elite SS German soldiers. We surrounded them and on to the top of the hill we captured those that had not escaped. We found a large arsenal of German hand grenades (potato mashers). A little later we were told that Big Chief had found a bottle of fire-water and was throwing potato mashers against the trees and somebody was going to get killed. It took six of us to calm him down, take away the hand grenades and he finally passed out. The next day he was ready for battle again. That was our buddy, Big Chief!

I remember my first paycheck, we were paid 21 dollars a day, once a month. My cash amounted to $12.00 and change, on the envelope it said, the balance was for laundry.

We had a loan shark in our Company by the name of Pvt. Mel LaScola, who would loan you $5.00 for $10.00 payday. He had a small portable table and each payday he would set up shop at the end of the payroll line to collect. Business was good.

In the latrine was a sign that read - Please stand close the next dogface may be barefooted.

At Ft. Benning when we were teaching fellow soldiers how to drive a 2½ ton truck and the larger semi-trailer trucks, we had a fellow by the name of Robert Moseley, who did not have too much education and to shift the gears you must double-clutch. He had trouble with the gears and I kept telling him you must double-clutch in order to synchronize the gears when you shift. He finally looked down at the floor of the truck and said, "I don't see two clutches". He was known from then on as "Double Clutch Moseley". About 32 years later at one of our annual reunions at Winston Salem, North Carolina, I met Robert Moseley again and the first thing he said to me was - "I'm Double Clutch Moseley".

I remember South Carolina maneuvers and a Company Commander by the name of John H. Ray, he was a lover, of Dutch Masters cigars and Coca Cola. In our half-track we must always keep the supply adequate. One afternoon he ran out of cigars and told me to go and get a jeep from Sgt. Taylor at the motor pool and don't come back without a box of Dutch Masters cigars. It was late in the afternoon and I drove at least 50 miles and I finally ended up in Albermarle, N.C. I found the cigars and headed back to the maneuver area where we were located, in the meantime, the Company received orders to move. I drove all night but was unable to locate our Company. I finally caught up with them the next day and a LOUD REPRIMAND!

I remember South Carolina maneuvers of 1941. We spent 3 days building and taking down trestle bridges across the Pee Dee river near Cherow, South Carolina. The day we were to load up and move to another location, two of the fellows bought a gallon jug of white lightning from the local natives and located it near the bridge site. The maneuver plan was to be loaded and move out after dark to practice travel in blackout conditions. By the time to move out most of the fellows that drank were already blacked out. Our Company Commander, Captain Carter went from cab to cab trying to find someone sober enough to ride with. MIRACLES DO HAPPEN! We travelled about 30 miles that night through woods, fields and back roads in blackout and the next morning everyone and all the vehicles were accounted for without a scratch. ONLY HEADACHES !

In between this time I spent 3 months studying the Morse Code at Radio Communications Command School at Ft. Knox, Kentucky and graduated in August 1941, fully qualified at sending and receiving the Morse Code and maintaining short wave radios. One of my best friends while attending radio school at Ft. Knox, was a fellow from Chicago by the name of Bob Pryor. On our only days off, Sunday, we toured many interesting places in Kentucky. He was a member of the 92nd Field Artillery of our division and after graduation we each returned to our own battalion. We did not meet again until 35 years later at the 1976 2nd Armored Division Reunion in Philadelphia. He is Chairman of the 2nd Armored Division and we keep in touch.

Our one year of draftee training was completed in time for us to be discharged and home for Christmas 1941. Sunday afternoon December 7th, while listening to the radio - came word of Pearl Harbor. Next day our discharge papers were trashed - we were in for the duration.

Leo (Hawkshaw) Mecler and Paul Cannady were the only two cooks I knew that could feed 180 soldiers on 2 large cans of Spam, a box of corn starch and 2 large cans of green beans.

In the Spring of '42, we, the 2nd Armored Division left Ft.Benning, Ga. for the last time and travelled to South Carolina for additional maneuvers. We built several types of bridges across the Pee Dee river in South Carolina in addition to intensive maneuvers.

In late September we arrived at the Ft.Bragg reservation outpost and bivouacked among the underbrush and sand dunes. There we re-assembled, caught our breath, had a shower, washed our clothes, changed from summer to winter uniform and the food was a little better than "C" rations.

We then underwent a vigorous combat training program and final tune-up for war. We listened to the famous General Patton speech and were told we were ready for battle. Then came the weeding out process. The goldbricks, misfits and undesirable were transferred out of the Division. We found out later that these men ended up hauling supplies to the front battle lines in Italy.

We did not know where we were going until we arrived at Ft.Dix, New Jersey. We loaded our tanks, half-tracks, trucks and other equipment and our Division of soldiers on a 135 car train headed North. At this time a few German spies had been caught in New York and along the East Coast. To make sure our Division arrived safely at Ft.Dix to prepare for overseas, the order was - each flat car of the train was to have a guard ride on board with a loaded weapon for security. I volunteered to ride the flat car of my half-track as a guard - for the adventure of a Hobo Soldier, from Ft.Bragg to Ft.Dix. It was a 3 day journey on a flat car going about 10 to 15 miles per hour. We were given a brown paper bag that contained a spam sandwich and apple for lunch. Along the way civilians greeted us with waves and American flags. Later that day before dark, we stopped in Virginia near a railroad station for a pit stop and another brown bag with a sandwich and piece of fruit. After a long, cool and dark night we arrived the next morning at the train yards near Washington, D.C., for toilet and breakfast which was coffee and donuts. After another long day and night through Maryland, Pennsylvania and New Jersey we finally arrived at Ft.Dix, New Jersey to move into cold wooden barracks and prepare for the long boat ride from New York - to where we did not know. This was the beginning and the end of my Hobo Soldier adventure.

At Ft.Dix, New Jersey before sailing for North Africa most of the fellows that lived near the area and could make it home, took the train or bus home most every night. After a few of 2 hours sleep per night or less, Jerry Maher fell asleep on the train late one night returning from Long Island to Ft.Dix and woke-up early the next morning in Baltimore. The next night when we were going to the Mess Hall to eat, we saw Jerry Maher out in the bitter cold walking with a rifle and full field pack.

LATRINE DUTY – FT. BENNING, GA. 1942

BASIC INFANTRY SOLDIER TRAINING WITH GENERAL PATTON – JAN. 1941
(NOTE PRE-WAR EQUIPMENT)

Figure 14 - Patton addressing the soldiers at Ft. Benning, Georgia – picture taken by J. E.

CHOW TIME AT THE MESS HALL - MARCH 1941 FT. BENNING, GA.

BRIDGE BUILT ON LOUISIANA MANEUVERS - 1941

FT. KNOX, KY. RADIO COMMAND SCHOOL - 1941
(NOTE CIVILIAN CLOTHES)

## HOBO SOLDIER

In the Spring of '42 - we, the 2nd Armored Division left Ft. Benning Ga. for the last time and travelled to South Carolina for additional maneuvers. We built several types of bridges across the Pee Dee river in South Carolina in addition to intensive maneuvers.

In late September we arrived at the Ft. Bragg reservation outpost and camped among the pine trees and sand dunes. There we re-assembled, caught our breath, had a shower, washed our clothes, changed from summer to winter uniform and the food was a little better than "C" rations.

We then underwent a vigorous combat training program and final tune-up for war. We listened to the famous Gen. Patton speech and were told we were ready for battle. Then came the weeding out process, the goldbricks, misfits and undesirable were transferred out of the Division. We found out later that these men ended up hauling supplies to the front battle lines in Italy.

We did not know where we were going until we arrived at Ft. Dix, New Jersey. We loaded our tanks, halftracks, guns and other equipment and 12000 soldiers on a 135 car train headed North. At this time a few German Spies had been caught in New York and along the East Coast. To make sure our division arrived safely at Ft. Dix to prepare for overseas, the order was each flat car of the train was to have a guard ride on board with a loaded weapon for security. I volunteered to ride the flat car of my half-track as a guard - for the adventure of a hobo soldier from Ft. Bragg to Ft. Dix. It was a 3 day ride on a flat car going about 10 to 15 miles per hour. We were given a brown paper bag that contained a spam sandwich and apple for lunch. Along the way civilians greeted us with hand waves and American flags.

Later that day before dark we stopped somewhere in Virginia near a railroad station for a pit stop and another brown bag with a sandwich. After a long cool and dark night we arrived the next morning at the train yards near Washington, D.C. for toilet and breakfast that was a cup of coffee and two donuts. After another long day and night through Maryland, Pa., and New Jersey we arrived at Ft. Dix, New Jersey and moved into cold wooden barracks and prepared for the long boat ride from New York - to where we did not know.

This was the beginning and end of my Hobo Soldier adventure.

Ed Sammons

Figure 18 J. E. and Friends

### GERMAN U-BOAT TORPEDO

While at Ft.Dix in November '42 they loaded our tanks & half-tracks on ships at the Brooklyn Army Base and in the middle of the night we loaded on board with full field pack & duffle bags. We sailed out of New York harbor before daylight and joined a convoy of ships off the coast of Virginia that included a commando assault team of our Division that had been training on the Virginia beaches. We now had a convoy of 24 ships to cross the Atlantic. The ships travelled 4 abreast and 6 deep and changed course every 6 minutes as it took a German U-Boat 7 minutes to aim & fire a torpedo. After 13 days we landed at Casablanca, French Morocco to help clear out the Germans and silence the French.

After many air raids by the German Heinkel Heavy Bombers we managed to move 12 miles north of Rabat into a heavily wooded cork forest. U.S. War Dept.(SSI) told us that Hitler was preparing to send 2 Panzer Divisions from France thru Spain across the Rock to attack British Gen. Montgomery and our forces from the rear & Rommel would defeat the allies in North Africa. The 2nd Armored Division was ready.

We began to run out of food thanks to the German U-Boat torpedo sinking of our food supply in the Atlantic. Our Battalion Commander Col. Hurley told each Company Commander to assign a task force to supply food for the men of each Company from the market in Rabat. I was assigned to head a task force to help feed Co."E". I chose a driver from our Engineer Section, a former buyer on the New York produce market and a soldier from Maine that spoke French fluently. We purchased eggs by the 30 doz. case, bread, chicken, oranges, wine, pastry and other items we could eat. One day while shopping in Rabat we located a bakery. Their specialty for the day was chocolate eclairs. We bought their entire stock (over 200). We were quite the hit back at the cork forest. On two occasions on our market trips to Rabat we passed a small village where the Arabs were having an auction buying & selling young working girls 10 to 15 years in age. The larger and stronger girls would bring the higer prices.

We had lunch before returning to camp in the cork forest at Andre's French Cafe. Andre with his handlebar mustache & white apron had only two items on the menu - eggs & hard french bread. We washed it down with champagne Andre had hidden from the Germans. We traded cigarettes and french francs. After a few times going to market we met a lovely lady and her 19 year of age college daughter, Hilga. Hilga spoke - English French, Arabic and Spanish. They invited us to their home to celebrate their National Holiday (our thanksgiving). We arrived at their home in our army truck after several wrong turns to a big beautiful white home on a hilltop overlooking the Atlantic Ocean. We met her husband and family and they served us fruit, seafood, aged vermouth and their national dish - COUS-COUS. The next day while dining at Andre's cafe in Rabat and telling him about our visit, Andre informed us that we dined yesterday with the High Commissioner (Governor) of French Morocco his wife and family.

Soon we began to receive food thru the Port Of Oran & moved into Algiers. Ed Sammons

# CHAPTER II

New York – Casablanca – French Morocco

## NEW YORK – CASABLANCA – FRENCH MOROCCO

With full field pack and duffle bag, we loaded at night and left New York harbor before daylight and then joined a convoy of ships off Norfolk, Va. We now had a convoy of 24 ships. The ships travelled four abreast, six deep and changed course every six minutes, as it took a German U Boat seven minutes to aim and fire a torpedo. After 13 days we landed at Casablanca in December 1942, to help clear the Germans out and silence the French in French Morocco.

When the ground fighting was over and we began unloading our equipment, we had daily air raids by the German heavy bombers at night and strafing by German fighter planes during the day, trying to destroy us, our equipment and any other ships that tried to dock. I remember one day at the docks we had a raid and we were told in event of an air raid there was a concrete wall down the center of the pier and to stand against the wall. During an air raid one of the fellows got too excited and ran the wrong way and overboard into the water. I remember my buddy, Kid Walker, throwing him a rope and we pulled him out of the water and onto the pier. On another time at the docks, I was not there, but told this later - during a strafing raid, one of the fellows from another Company was against the wall when a piece of shrapnel hit his canteen, punctured it and water ran down his leg and he began to yell for help as he was bleeding to death. We always carried our canteen of water on our belt as we did not drink the local water.

We had an Italian soldier by the name of Eleo Iacovitti, drafted from Niagara Falls, N.Y., who was born in Italy, came to the U.S., became a citizen and joined our Company. He was a nice guy, spoke very broken English and was always joking. At Casablanca due to the congested area we dug foxholes and slit trenches deep enough and long enough to hold three men parallel. One night during an air raid three fellows jumped into the same hole for cover and while waiting for the raid to end, trying to be funny as usual, Eleo goosed the fellow below him and asked him if he had filled his pants yet. Well, it turned out that the soldier below him was Lt. Frank Arnone and he was Eleo's platoon leader. I don't recall Eleo trying that one again.

The highlight of an evening in North Africa was for a group of the fellows to gather around our Command Half-track for any news or music from BBC or Axis Sally. We could usually pick-up Axis Sally and her American songs and telling us lies about the war and home and that all our wives and girlfriends were cheating on us. So a great night, in the African Desert while guarding Gen. Montgomery against attack from the rear, was standing by our half-track listening to the radio in between the snakes, coyotes, mosquitoes and jumping kangaroo rats.

During the fighting in the North African desert, one story brought back to us when we sent up replacements was, a Major in Recon., that dressed as an Arab, borrowed a donkey and rode into a town in Tunisia, among the Germans, recorded in his head the location of their tanks and gun positions, then rode back to prepare for tomorrows successful attack.

While living in the cork forest North of Rabat in French Morocco, food supplies became very low, thanks to the U boats in the Atlantic.

Our Battalion Commander, Col. Hurley, told each Company Commander to assign a task force to supply food for the men of each Company, from the local market in Rabat 12 miles away. I was selected to head a task force to help feed Co."E". I chose a truck and driver from our Engr. section, Robert Shaffer, a soldier who had been a buyer on the New York produce market, Harry Kuppersmith and a soldier from Northern Maine, that spoke French fluently, Edmond Fongemie. We purchased eggs by the 30 doz. case, chickens, good wine, bread, oranges and other items we could eat. We had lunch before returning to camp in the cork forest, at Andre's French Cafe. Andre, with his handlebar mustache and white apron had only two items on the menu, eggs and hard french bread - we washed it down with champagne he had hidden from the Germans. We traded cigarettes and French Francs. After several weeks going to the market we met a lovely lady and her daughter, who spoke English, while shopping at the market each time. Later the lady invited me and my crew of three to their home to celebrate their National Day - Our Thanksgiving. We arrived at their home in our 2½ ton Army truck after several wrong turns, to a big beautiful white home on a cliff overlooking the Mediterranean Sea. We met her husband and family and they served us fruit and aged vermouth with their National Dish called - Cous-Cous. The next day while dining at Andre's cafe in Rabat, and telling him about our visit, Andre informed us that we dined yesterday with the High Commissioner of French Morocco, his wife and family.

One day while shopping in Rabat, we located a bakery. Their specialty for the day was chocolate eclairs. We bought their entire stock (200). We were quite the hit back at the cork forest for dinner dessert.

On two occasions on our market trips to Rabat of three times a week, we passed a small village where the Arabs were having an auction, buying and selling young girls from about 10 to 18 in age. The larger and stronger looking girls would bring the highest prices.

After leaving the cork forest we moved to Algiers. We were not at all welcome by the French Foreign Legion as we looked like the Armored Division they resented. Before the bloodshed we moved to an area near small Arab villages and into sand, rock and brush area we called "The Brush Pile", near Oran. At night for entertainment Battalion Hdqtrs., set up a movie screen after dark with a black & white movie from the thirties. While at the movies the Arabs would raid the tents and steal our equipment and clothes. One night Captain McCauley from Hdqtrs. decided he would stay and guard the tents while we were at the movie. He shot and killed an Arab stealing clothes from a tent. The next morning the Arabs came and hauled his body away on a cart, and said - "An eye for an eye and we will get one of you".

A few days later we were granted passes to go to Oran. Each truck was marked and was to meet us at a certain location for the return trip. That night I missed the 17th truck and was forced to return on the last truck available which was a 67th truck. The 67th area was located about three miles from the 17th area. The driver let me off at a crossroad before he turned for the 67th. I was now on my own, following the moon and stars to find our location several miles away. I came upon an Arab village and could hear them chanting - "An eye for an eye and one of you". I took a long detour around the village crawling on hands and knees over sand and rocks, praying they would not see or hear me in the moonlight.

I finally made it past the village and they were still chanting and I began to run as fast as I could over rocks and hills. I finally found our location, arriving at my half-track in the wee hours bruised, bloody, exhausted and a prayer to the Lord.

We saw many German prisoners marching by us on their way to Oran and the ship to America after the fighting ended in Tunisia. They were sailing to our homeland and we were going to fight our way to their homeland. What an odd feeling to say the least.

In July 1943 the invasion of Sicily was executed by "Operation Husky" and part of our battalion joined General Patton and his race across Sicily. Our battalion Commander, Col. Hurley was killed in Sicily when his jeep ran over a land mine near the beach.

Moving on from North Africa, Sicily and the Mediterranean to England to prepare for "D" day I recall the British ship we were privileged to travel on, it had come from Egypt and had been out of home port in England for more than 18 months. We were on board with a number of British Commando's going back to England from the fighting in Italy and they were in the next compartment from us. The bread we were eating was quite heavy and soggy and we found out later it was being made from the flour that had been in the hole of this ship for more than 18 months and had become wet and moldy. After eating this bread for 3 or 4 days, being G.I.'s we became curious as to whether the British Commando's were eating this bread and the other horrible food, such as dried lima beans for breakfast. So in looking in on them we found at meal time they would take their slices of this bread and beat it on the table then hold it up to the light of the port hole and look at it. Being G.I.'s we asked what they were doing. They told us they were knocking the weevils out before they ate it, of course we had been eating this bread for several days. After that we went back to our "C" rations. We had emergency "K" rations, but Lt.(Long John) Coughlin said anyone caught eating them would be court-marshalled. You know the sh-- list he was on and at our 1946 and first reunion, a couple of the fellows really told him off.

We did not know how long of a boat ride this was going to be to England on this British ship. As we passed the rock of Gibralter after midnight there came an alert, a general alarm, prepare to abandon ship, as several German U Boats were coming down from the lower coast of France to attack our convoy. The ship quickly turned West - full speed ahead. The ship was vibrating for hours as we headed toward New York. There were a couple of fellows, like Mel LaScola that were taking bets we were going to New York. After 14 days we finally arrived at Liverpool, England. After that ride, I could understand why the Germans were winning the war. As we came down the gangplank at Liverpool there was a British band playing great homecoming music, apparently the British Commando's were heroes and I guess they thought we were too. They played quite well until one of our G.I.'s tossed a coin to the leader. They promptly stopped playing and marched away. We were loaded on British compartment trains to go to Tidworth Barracks. At that time aboard the train before it left for Tidworth, I received my one and only free cup of coffee and donut from the American Red Cross. I will never forget, because later during the Battle of the Bulge in the freezing cold and snow I did not have a dime for a donut and cup of coffee from the American Red Cross.

NORTH AFRICA - FRENCH MOROCCO - CASABLANCA

with  GENERAL GEORGE S. PATTON JR.

In October '42 the 2nd Armored division (Hell on Wheels) moved from Ft, Bragg to an overseas stageing area at Ft. Dix to prepare for the invasion of French Morocco in North Africa - all except one battalion of the 2nd Armored Beach Rangers that went to Virginia Beach to practice beach landing. They were part of the greatest amphibious operation in history up to date. The invasion fleet consisted of 850 vessels.

The division was divided into 3 combat commands - A - B - Reserve. Command A landed North of Casablanca at Port Lyautey while Command B invaded the Coast South of Casablanca at Safi. The target was to capture the French Garrison near Casablanca and all resistance in between. The 17th Engrs.& 41st Infantry defeated the French Regiment at Safi. After a 3 day battle the French Garrison and all forces surrendered. General Patton marched into Casablanca and signed a peace treaty.

I was in Command Reserve and we landed a few days later at Casablanca where we encountered daylite strafing by German fighter planes and night time heavy bombers while landing at Casablanca. After several days and many air raids and a few casualties we moved North near Rabat into a heavely wooded Cork Forest.

We began to run low on food thanks to the German U-Boats sinking our food supply in the Atlantic. Our Division Commander ordered each Company Commander to assign a task force to help supply food for his men. I was assigned team leader to help feed 200 men of Co."B". I chose an A-1 truck driver, a former buyer on the NY produce market and a soldier from Maine that spoke French fluently. We purchased eggs by the 30 doz. case bread, fruit, pastry and other food we could eat. Our american paper money with the blue seal was not acceptable by French Morocco, so we exchanged our blue seal dollars for printed gold seal dollars sent to us from Washington. The French and Arabs considered the gold seal as gold. Later we exchanged our american money for french franc's. The exchange rate was 3 to 1, so we made a few bucks. On 2 occasions on our market trips to Rabat we passed a small village where the Arabs were having an auction buying and selling young working girls 10 to 15 of age. the larger and stronger girls would bring the higher prices.

We had lunch before returning to the cork forest at Andre's French Cafe. Andre with his handle bar moustache & white apron had only two items on the menu, eggs & french bread. We washed it down with the champagne he had hidden from the Germans. After a few times going to market and through our friend, the owner of the egg market we met a lovely lady and her college daughter, Hilga. Hilga spoke English, French, Arabic and Spanish. They invited us to their home to celebrate their National Day (our thanksgiving). We arrived at their home in our army truck after several wrong turns to a big beautiful home on the Atlantic Ocean. They served us fruit, seafood, aged vermouth and their national dish Cous-Cous.

( CONTINUED )

The next day while dining at Andre's Cafe in Rabat and telling him about our visit, Andre informed us that we dined yesterday with the High Commissioner (Governor) of French Morocco his wife and family. Hilga became a good pen pal as we kept in touch by letter during the war.

The 1st Armored Division landed at Oran and moved into Tunisia to help British General Montgomery in his desert battle with General Rommel. The 1st Armored Division suffered more than 2000 casualties in their first battle.

The U.S. War Dept.(SSI) said that HItler was preparing to send 2 Panzer Divisions from France through Spain across the Rock to attack General Montgomery and our forces from the rear. We then moved from the Cork Forest to Algeria to protect General Montgomery and Allied Forces. In Algeria we received a cold reception from the French Foreign Legion as they resented our modern war equipment and american soldiers. After a Clash, as we were cramping their style, we moved 40 miles from Algeria into Spanish Morocco near Oran. Soon we began to receive food supplies from the Port of Oran. Among the African sand, rocks and scrub bushes we prepared for the invasion of Sicily in July 1943.

Ed Sammons
Co."E" 17th Armd. Combat Engr. Bn.
2nd Armored Division   (Hell on Wheels)

LIFE IN THE CORK FOREST WHILE TRAINING FOR THE INVASION OF SICILY

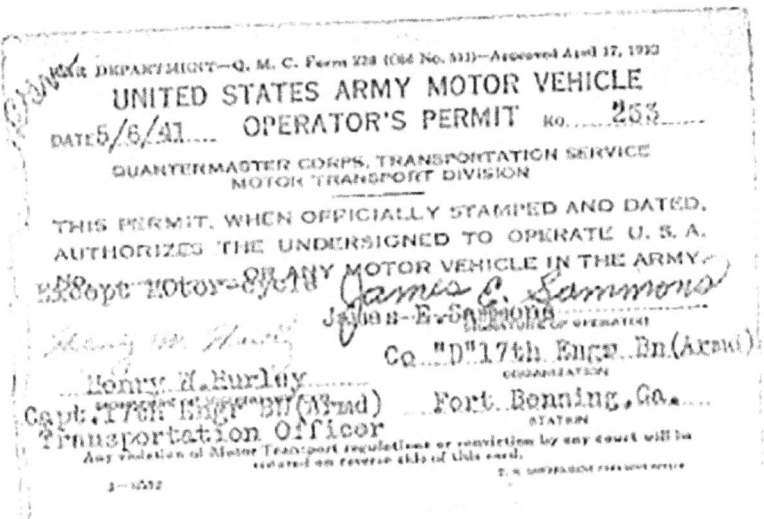

THIS IS A COPY OF MY ORIGINAL ARMY VEHICLE OPERATORS LICENSE
THAT TRAVELLED WITH ME IN MY WALLET FROM BENNING TO BERLIN

Figure 20 J. E. Motor Vehicle Operator's Permit

## GELA TO PALERMO
## WITH
## GENERAL PATTON

In July '43 the 2nd Armored Division invaded the island of Sicily. We landed at Gela and fought our way around the left side of the coast toward our target Palermo. Our first encounter with the Italian Army and their pre-war guns was no match for the 2nd Armored Division. However, our Battalion Commander, Col. Hurley was killed at Gela. We encountered the German Herman Goering Panzer Division on our way to Palermo. Gen. Montgomery with British forces landed at the same time to clear the right side of the island and fight the German 15th Panzer Division on their way to Palermo. Gen. Patton was heard to say - we will beat Montgomery to Palermo if it takes a truck load of dead G.I. dog tags. We beat Gen. Montgomery and the British to Palermo. There the fighting ended. After a few weeks we were loaded on an English Ship with a commando group of British Rangers returning to England as hero's for their invasion of Italy.

That boat ride to England dodging German U Boats was another rough and exciting war event.

Ed Sammons

# CHAPTER III

"D" Day – Omaha Beach – Normandy

## WHITE CLIFFS OF DOVER

In Dec.'43 at Liverpool England we boarded a compartment train and I received my first & only coffee & donut from the American Red Cross. We were taken to Tidworth Barracks on thr Salisbury Plain. Tidworth Barracks were built before WWI red brick 2 story buildings with 2 soldier bunk beds with straw mattress. 6 wash bowls & 6 toilets for 40 soldiers per room in 20 bunks.. With no showers. This later proved to be premium facilities after "D" day. We received new tanks, half-tracks, guns and other equipment for a "D" day invasion. We prepared our vehicles and did 20 mile full field pack marches at night and were ready for the invasion. I spent one week at a special gunnery school for machine guns shooting at airplane targets over the White Cliffs of Dover. At the Tidworth Theatre we enjoyed movie star James Cagney and his Yankee Doodle Dandy Stage Show from Hollywood. We were given in groups of 6 - six days R&R in London. Our group stayed at the Reed Hotel near Piccadilly Square. The 2 person and driver of little London cabs had a 1 gallon gas ration per day and Glenn Green and I toured London ruins, bridge and Chinatown for 2 hrs. for 2 shillings (50¢). We rode the plush and fast subways to every end of London suburbs looking for food (and Girls).

A few days after returning to Tidworth from London a german bomb went down the elevator shaft of the Reed Hotel. Lucky Again!

Ed Sammons

## D DAY AT OMAHA BEACH
## NORMANDY, FRANCE JUNE 1944

We arrived at Tidworth Barracks, Tidworth, England on Dec. 12, 1943, to prepare for the invasion at Normandy, France. In Nov. 1942, we landed in North Africa meeting little resistance by the French. We then moved into Tunisia to help the British in the Spring of 1943, then on to the invasion of Sicily in the Summer of 1943. We spent a cold, wet, and miserable Christmas of 1943 at Tidworth Barracks, which was built before WWI and had only a fireplace for heat and a four stall toilet with six cold water bowls for washing and shaving with sixty soldiers per barrack. This was cold but good - as it was all down hill from Tidworth to Berlin.

In Jan. 1944 we began to receive our third fleet of tanks, half-tracks, plus all the other equipment necessary to invade and fight a war, as an Armored Division. ( We lend-leased our first vehicles we brought with us from the States, to the French in North Africa and left our second fleet in Sicily. ) As the weather in England improved, we began heavy training and physical conditioning, including 25 mile forced marches at night in the hilly terrain.

We began to road test, maintain, and modify our equipment from experience in previous battle. We completely waterproofed our vehicles to be capable of enduring six feet of water at invasion. We were previewed, reviewed, and interviewed by Generals Ike, Bradley, Brooks, Field Marshall Montgomery, and Sir Winston Churchill, and were ready for the invasion and battle in April 1944. Now we stood ready, waiting and trying to guess the date.

Finally, the call came to move-out and down the coast near Portsmouth. There we entered a barbed wire enclosure with no outside contact. We were bedded down after the best of food, ( chops, steak, fresh veg. & fruits ) that we had eaten since leaving home. It gave you a certain feeling of - fattening before the kill - and our "Last Supper".

We were then taken in small groups into private guarded closed tents - told when and where we were going, given an emergency survival kit which included a chocolate bar, codeine tablets, and a large bandage for stuffing a body wound. Our American and English money was exchanged for French franc's. We were issued a map of the coast of Normandy, with a thin tissue paper overlay, ( to be eaten in event of capture ) showing our target location on D plus 2, which was a town about three miles inland by the name of Le Molay.

We were then issued two complete sets of under and outer clothing that was impregnated in event of gas warfare. After about two days you began to smell like a walking chemical plant with the itch.

The first wave to hit the beach at daylight June 6, 1944, ahead of our combat team was the 29th Infantry Division. The 101st paratroopers had landed D minus 1 and holding positions toward Carentan and sustaining heavy losses. They were to secure a beachhead two miles deep while the LSD's would return to load our tanks and half-tracks at the Portsmouth docks. The initial forces encountered fierce resistance climbing Omaha Beach, suffered heavy casualties, loss in time, and returned several times to Portsmouth with as many of the wounded as the ships could carry.

This delayed our loading all day and by the time we were loaded and reached Omaha Beach it was late in the day D plus 1. The tide was out and the infantry had not penetrated far enough inland for our landing and maneuvering into battle position.

We spent the night ( nightmare ) about 2000 yards off shore amid the bombardment by U.S. Battleships and bombing plus strafing by German planes. Bombs went over and landed all around us, lucky, no direct hit on our LST. About daylight our LST 321 hit Omaha Beach in about four feet of water, the big doors opened and I found myself driving the lead half-track into the water and up a narrow winding sideway path trying to reach the top. I saw several signs that said "Achtung Minen", before reaching the ridge on top of Omaha Beach.

At the top I drove around and past many dead German soldiers scattered about the top of the hill. By this time the heat gauge on the dash of my half-track was in the red zone. However, I had to continue to move inward in order for the vehicles behind me to clear the ridge. Then I could stop long enough to remove the dum-dum waterproofing from the engine and other parts with the elbow length thick asbestos gloves I was wearing.

Our crew on board for this landing were - Capt. James McAdams, Commander, Sgt. Dwight Cooper, Crew Chief, Cpl. Ray Ellis, Turret Gunner, Cpl. Carl Smith, Radio Operator, (Morse Code), Pfc. Fred Boland, Rear Gunner and myself. In addition to Command Half-track Driver, I was back-up Radio Operator and qualified as Expert Gunner.

Our first night over the top of Omaha Beach a German bomber hit one of our 10 ton ammunition trucks about 500 yards from our location. What a blast! At daylight we found only a belt buckle and twisted metal of the two soldiers and the truck.

The next few weeks we maneuvered in an area about three miles from the beachhead, enduring night bombings and daylight strafing by the Germans while surviving on C and K rations and water we brought along in five gallon cans. No water to wash your face and hands, only to drink. We did not realize until later how great the possibility that the Germans could have pushed us back into the English Channel, as we had no air cover due to the bad weather. The Germans would light flares and drop bread-basket bombs on us at night. We spent the nights in foxholes.

We fought our way through the hedgerows toward St. Lo, as we waited for good weather. One morning the sun came out and there was a great roar in the sky. We looked toward the channel and the sky was black with B-17 and other U.S. bombers coming to our rescue. I was later told that more than 5000 U.S. planes flew over us that July day 1944. They pulverized the St. Lo area in front of us, killing about 250 of our soldiers as a few bombs fell short of the target. When we moved through, it was just a pile of rubble as the tank bulldozers made a path through St. Lo for us to move on.

These events are what I saw and did in general, before, during and after the invasion of Omaha Beach. This was just the beginning - it was on toward Paris, Belgium, Holland, Battle of the Bulge, and Berlin. That's another long, cold, and bloody episode.

James E. Sammons 7/87

# CHAPTER IV

Omaha Beach – Belgium – Maastricht

## OMAHA BEACH - BELGIUM - MAASTRICHT

After the nightmare in the water off Omaha Beach, we were strafed every morning in the hedgerows at daylight and early evening just before dark by German Messerschmidt fighters and at night by the heavy bombers. They would drop flares and then the 500 lb. bread basket bombs. In order to survive you had to be in a foxhole and away from the hedgerows. I spent many nights in a foxhole reciting the 23rd Psalm. We had a soldier in our Company that claimed to be an Atheist. However, he was among the first in a foxhole each night. We lost several men every night and one night the German bombers hit our area very hard and when I came out of the foxhole in the morning, we found in foxholes near us several men dead from a direct hit, including one of our medical doctors, Capt. Kelly. I was part of the detail driving one of the jeeps. Sgt. Cooper placed a blanket over Capt. Kelly in the back of the jeep and we drove back behind the line where we gave his body to the Medics. The Medics told me that last night we lost more than fifty 2nd Armored men from the German bombing raids. We could not break-out of the hedgerows and advance toward St.Lo due to the German resistance and no air cover due to the bad weather.

After the breakthrough at St.Lo and out of the hedgerows we had the German 1st Panzer Division and the 352 Infantry Division on the run. They would stop at every obstacle and town along the way. Our next big fight was at the Falaise Gap, a small mountain area on our way toward Paris. The Germans put up a fight as they controlled the high ground. After a two day battle, the Germans retreated. At the top of the mountain we captured two luxury trailers used by the German High Command. Our next battle was for Elbeuf. About this time food supplies were beginning to catch-up, so one night our Chief Cook, my good friend Dick Hazen, (you must always be a good friend of the chief cook), said we had enough supplies that tomorrow early daylight before we move on, we would have powdered eggs and pancakes. Always being hungry, I volunteered to help prepare one of the few meals we would receive from the kitchen truck. We prepared and I cooked pancakes for 180 men at daybreak. I got my fill of both. We had about 10 pancakes left-over that were quickly eaten by Joel Bouchard, a Frenchman from Maine. Next meal was back to "C" rations. The next time I was lucky for food was a stop in Belgium due to bad weather. We had pancakes and coffee in the rain. After taking each town the French Underground wearing the Cross of Lorraine, would come out of hiding to greet us, then march the town Mayor and all the town folks who had collaborated with the Germans to the town square and promptly shot the men and shaved the heads of the women.

Each day we were running low on food and gasoline for our vehicles as we moved rapidly across France and liberating as we went. One day in the middle of France we stopped to wait for food and fuel to catch up, there was a terrific dog fight of American and German fighters overhead. The German planes won that battle and one of the American planes came down in flames. The pilot bailed out and landed close to our half-track, while the other planes retreated. He stayed with us over-night, we shared our "C" rations and he returned to England the next morning. When the pilot left he gave us his fleece lined jacket & boots saying, "Where you are going you will need them and where I'm going they have plenty".

## FIGHTER PILOT BOOTS

After landing in Normandy at Omaha Beach D-2 we attacked the 2nd German Panzer Division that had the 101st Airborne Division trapped near Carentan After 3 weeks of battle we finally broke thru Saint Lo and continued to chase the 2nd Panzer Division across France One afternoon on a hot July day there was a dog fight overhead by the German Messerschmidt planes and the U.S. 8th Army Air Force P 51 fighters During the fight the German planes downed two P 51's and the others retreated back to England One of the P 51 pilots ejected and landed by my half-track We became friends and he stayed with us until a way back to England When he left he gave me his fleece lined leather vest and fleeced lined leather boots and said - "Where you are going you will need them - where I'm going they have plenty of them" When we finally reached Belgium still fighting the 2nd Panzer Division then the battle of the bulge - the pilot was so right In our fight in 10 degree ice & snow the boots were the difference between frozen feet and not frozen feet

        Just one of the many life saving events

Ed Sammons

# PATTON'S HAND OF GOD

We headed toward Paris, but that glory was for the French 2nd Corp. So we headed toward Belgium, capturing and liberating many towns in France and our goal was to reach and free the Belsen-Olson concentration camp in Belgium, then reach the Rhine and Elbe rivers. Hitler's latest orders were to stop us at the Rhine. One day on our way in France we stopped as we were low on gas and food. We divided our gasoline so every vehicle had enough to continue as food and gas supplies were too far behind. Our Battalion Commander, Col.Correll, said we would perhaps be there a couple hours for rest and hope for food and gas. Ray Ellis, gunner on our half-track, George Miller, jeep driver and Paul Geneski, one of our medics decided to go back in a jeep a couple of miles to a little town we just passed through to get eggs and french bread and we would eat. On the road back they were stopped by a Frenchman who said there are German soldiers in the small wooded area ahead on the edge of this small town. So they decided to try to capture the German soldiers in the small patch of woods, and if they had German Lugars, it would be very profitable. The plan was for George to stay on one side and Ray would creep around to the other side and they would meet in the middle. Paul was to stay with the jeep and if he heard shots, was to come with his medic bag. When George and Ray met in the middle they saw five German soldiers sitting on a log. One was an Officer, one a Sgt., and three privates (two Lugars). They did not resist when challenged by George and Ray, even though they were German SS Storm Troopers. So Ray decided to show them how tough G.I.'s were, so he lined them up facing a tree pretending to shoot them. Then he shot over their heads to scare them. In the meantime, Paul, the medic, hearing the shots came running. They marched the five Germans out and onto the front of the jeep and drove them back until they found the French Underground to turn them over. They turned over the soldiers but not the two Lugars and a large leather briefcase carried by the Officer. The briefcase was full of new French Francs made in Germany for payroll. In the meantime, we received orders to move forward, without the missing three. We travelled about thirty miles or so by midnight where we stopped for rest and hopefully food and gasoline. A couple hours later from my sleeping bag I heard a noise. It was George and Ray. I will never know how they were able to find us, especially on a dark night. They brought no food, only a briefcase and two Lugars. The next day, after more pursuit of Germans we stopped and finally received "C" rations and gasoline. Ray examined the briefcase and found it contained more than $15,000 dollars in French Francs, all new 50 and 100 franc notes in serial order. George, Ray, and Paul divided the money and flipped for the Lugars. They hid the money in their duffle bags, except George, who put his in the glove compartment of his jeep. Later when we reached the Belsen-Olson concentration camp in Belgium, Sgt. Cooper of our crew opend the jeep glove compartment and part of George's money fell to the floor of the jeep. No one would tell where the French Francs came from. (We finally told Sgt. Cooper at our 50th Annual Reunion in 1995.)

One day in Holland we stopped for rest near a coal mine and the Dutch invited us to take a shower at the mine. I remember the shower and between the flying coal dust and dirty floor I did not feel very clean after the shower. A shower in a Dutch coal mine is some experience. That was my first shower since the cold ones at Tidworth.

# CHAPTER V

Battle of the Bulge – Aachen – Berlin – Harry S. Truman – Presidential Citation

BATTLE OF THE BULGE

```
                    HEADQUARTERS
                 FIRST UNITED STATES ARMY
                        APO 230

                                          5 January 1945
```

SUBJECT : Enemy Equipment Counted in CELLES (P-0675) Pocket.

TO      : Commanding General, 2nd Armored Division.

THRU    : Commanding General, VII Corps, APO 307.

    1. The Second British Army has reported that the final count of enemy equipment found in the CELLES pocket is as follows :

<u>Destroyed or Captured</u>

  81 tanks
   7 assault guns
405 vehicles, all types
  74 guns

    2. It is believed that the bulk of this equipment belonged to the 2nd Panzer Division and that the tanks probably represent almost every operational tank in that division, since the German Panzer Div now contains a total of from 100 to 120 (maximum) tanks. The 74 guns represent the normal complement of over six battalions and would account for the complete divisional artillery and AT battalions normally under a division.

    3. The action of your division therefore destroyed the 2nd Panzer Division as an armored division. This division has always been composed of first-class personnel from Austria, and therefore its overwhelming defeat by your division is regarded as an outstanding and distinguished feat of arms.

    4. Please accept my heartiest congratulations to you personally and convey them to the officers and men of the 2nd U.S. Armored Division.

                                  /s/ COURTNEY H. HODGES

                                  Lieutenant General, U.S.A.,
                                        Commanding.

Added in Marshal Montgomery's own hand :
    My very best congratulations to the 2nd Armored Division.

                                  /s/ B.L. MONTGOMERY,
                                    Field Marshal.

               1st Ind.

HEADQUARTERS VII CORPS, APO 307, United States Army, 6 January 1945.

To : Commanding General, 2nd Armored Division, APO 252, United States Army.
    It is a genuine pleasure to transmit this fine letter of commendation from the Commanding General, First Army, and Field Marshal Montgomery, to which I add my heartiest congratulations.

                                s/ J. LAWTON COLLINS.
                                t/ J. LAWTON COLLINS.
                                Major General, U.S. Army,
                                  Commanding.

The weather turned bitter cold with snow. The American Pilot that gave us the fleece lined jacket and boots back in France, was right, as we used them on outpost watch. They were the difference between frozen and not frozen feet. We fought our way toward the Rhine river. (See the Colonel and Corporal story).

After crossing the Rhine a G.I. would say - "Give me a dime", and you would say, for what, then give him a dime to hear him say, "Thanks you just contributed a dime to a Yank that crossed the Rhine, don't be an ass and begin to whine, get your dime like I got mine".

After the Rhine river battle and completing the bridge across the Rhine, we came upon a small abandoned village and a large warehouse. The warehouse was loaded with French Wine, Brandy, Cognac, German Grundig Radios (with the magic green eye) and boxes of yellow raincoats. In the homes we found eggs, bread and other food. Added to the booze from the warehouse, I can remember an all-night party and celebration, for we knew not what tomorrow would bring and I can still hear the windows being opened and dirty dishes and pans going out - because a G.I., after he eats in a German enemy house, he does not do the dishes - he just throws them out the window. That's what we did!

The race was on again capturing town after town and then across the Weser river. One morning our Company was ordered to capture the town of Hamlin, of Pied Piper Fame. In the town square was a three story hotel. We moved in with little resistance and gave the hotel residents thirty minutes to clear out. The German soldiers retreated to the edge of town. It looked like a Chinese fire drill for the next thirty minutes. We searched the hotel and found a German Army Major hiding in bed in his underwear pretending he was ill. We found his uniform neatly hidden in a closet. That night on outpost guard at the edge of town, the Germans counterattacked. We fought them off with no casualties at our half-track outpost. The German soldiers were not so lucky.

Fighting our way toward Magdeburg, we overran an airfield and as we approached, we saw the last German airplane take-off. Searching the hanger for Germans, we only found a warm coffee pot, some food and many Japanese pure silk parachutes. After that it was on to bridge the Elbe river near Magdeburg.

We were then halted and not allowed into Berlin, until later. That victory was for the Russians. The war was finally over for us. I was told I was going home with the first 2500 soldiers with the most points for combat service and also the American red Cross reported to me that my Dad was very ill and I should return home. To qualify all of the first 2500 soldiers had a minimum of 110 points. I had more than enough plus more than 1700 miles in combat and seven battle campaigns.

I would be amiss if I did not mention the hardships we endured during the war in North Africa, Sicily and "D" day to Berlin. Like not having enough and the proper food, sleeping in the same impregnated winter clothes for months, no bath or shower, our bathroom was stradling a slit trench, washing our face and hands in our helmet, drinking local sour wine for water and washing your impregnated clothes in gasoline.

Through France, Belgium and Holland the people were so happy to see us and their freedom, they shared with us what little food they had such as eggs and hard bread. We were grateful.

We had two fellows in our Company by the names of Howard Gouge and Ed Dudley, who were known as washing machine Gouge & Dudley. In North Africa in the cork forest they suspended a used oil drum with holes in the bottom from a tree and one would climb the tree and pour a bucket of water into the drum and on the G.I. below. That was our shower. Along the way through France, Belgium, Holland and Germany they salvaged machine parts and made a washing machine and washed our coveralls for a buck.

After the war Ed Dudley, as an Engineer invented several automatic and electronic devices for the fish canning industry on the West Coast. Howard Gouge became a fireman on the Litchfield Railroad Line going from the Kentucky coal mines to the North Carolina coast. After 10 years as Fireman, Howard became Chief Engineer on the line and retired after 34 years. Howard invented several automatic devices for the washing machine industry including an automatic back-washer.

About 47 years later, in 1992, came a knock on our front door. My wife answered and there stood a man wearing a Detroit Tiger baseball cap asking to see Ed Sammons. My wife asked if she could tell him who was calling. He said "NO, I'm an 'ole army buddy visiting friends in North Florida and I drove an extra 200 miles to see him and to find out if he still remembers me". After a few minutes at the door I still could not recognize him. We invited him to come in and he finally said, "I'm Washing Machine Gouge". We had a wonderful 2 hours talking about our war years together. We invited him to stay for dinner and he said No, as he had to meets his friends in North Florida tonight.

What a gratifying feeling to know and see a World War II buddy I hadn't seen in all these years and to think he drove those extra miles just to see and talk with me.

FOOTNOTE :

DURING THE SEVEN BATTLE CAMPAIGNS WE CHANGED PASSWORDS EVERY NIGHT AT MIDNIGHT. WE CONFUSED THE GERMANS WITH PASSWORDS LIKE - BLACKHAWK STONEWALL CHEROKEE AND GERONIMO.

BUILDING THE BRIDGE ACROSS THE RHINE MARCH 1945

L-R FRED BOLAND    JACK WAITE
RHINE RIVER BRIDGE

ED SAMMONS AT THE RHINE

RAY ELLIS IN COMMAND HALF-TRACK
AT THE RHINE

CAPT. JAMES E. McADAMS COMPANY COMMANDER
AT REST AFTER WE BUILT THE BRIDGE AND
THE INFANTRY AND TANKS ARE ACROSS

Figure 21 J. E. Bridge building across the Rhine

## HELL DAY ON THE RHINE

Mar.'45 on our race and route of the German Panzer Divisions from D day, France, Belgium, Holland, Battle of the Bulge to Berlin we overran air fields, Belsen-Olsen concentration camp small towns and battle at Hamelin to get to the town of Wesel on the Rhine. At the Rhine the orders were to remove land mines, raft the infantry assault forces across and build a bridge for our infantry & tanks. We found a good location the night before below a cow pasture. Before dawn we started. I located our half-track about 50 yrds. from the approach site with our crew. We dug fox-holes and maintained Morse Code radio silence as the Germans were listening. Our 142nd Signal Co. laid a telephone line from our half-track to Battalion Command, half mile away which was linked by wire to the 78th field artillery who were to direct fire across the river to cover us from small arms fire and 88's coming in. We were in constant contact by telephone from the fox-hole with Battalion Command. After daylight the Rhine was fogged in and the Piper Cub planes of the 78th were grounded and of little help to the 17th Engr. Bn.

Our Battalion Commander - Col. Correll came in his jeep to direct and check our progress. His driver parked the jeep behind a barn. Afew minutes later an 88 hit the barn and jeep killing Col. Correll's driver. In the midst of all the excitement, noise and dense fog the 88's were killing cows in the pasture and several of us. Later we learned the 88's were mounted on a track firing 4 rounds and moving up and down the Rhine. Richard Kane, one of our medics was helping the wounded by me when hit in his back by a large piece of shrapnel. Lucky Again!

Although the Germans hit the bridge twice blowing out a section each time and 7 comrades we managed to build the longest bridge (1152 Ft. in 7 hrs.) under heavy fire (a record) for our infantry and tanks to cross. Company "E" was decorated with the Presidential Citation in person by President Harry S, Truman when we reached Berlin. We lost 21 comrades that day.

Ed Sammons
Co."E" 17th Armd. Combat Engr. Bn.
2nd Armored Division

Figure 22 J. E. Bridge Building

HARRY S. TRUMAN
PRESIDENTIAL CITATION
JULY 1945 – BERLIN, GERMANY

HELL ON WHEELS – MEETS HELL ON WATER

During our race from Omaha Beach to Berlin, we finally reached the Rhine River in Germany in March 1945, by way of the battle of the Bulge. We built a 1152 ft. bridge under extreme fire in record time of 7 hours. The German 88's hit the bridge twice during construction blowing out a section each time. We lost 21 men that day. "E" Company of the 17th Armored Combat Engineers was awarded the Presidential Citation and decorated in person by the President of the United States, Harry S. Truman, on the Berlin Autobahn. This was the first Presidential Citation award by a President **in person on foreign soil.**

In attendance were countless dignitaries of war including – Sir Winston Churchhill, Field Marshall Sir Bernard Law Montgomery, Sir Alan Brooke, Secretary of War Henry Stimson, Gen. Dwight Eisenhower, Gen. George C. Marshall, Gen. Omar Bradley and of course our first Commander, Gen. George S. Patton, Jr., who said with tears in his eyes – " The only trouble with the American Soldier is that he doesn't know how good he really is ".

THIS IS THE ORIGINAL HERSHEY TROPICAL CHOCOLATE WRAPPER THAT SURVIVED D DAY 1944, OMAHA BEACH, BATTLE AT ST LO, WITH 1st ALLIED SOLDIERS TO LIBERATE BELGIUM, BATTLE AT MAASTRICHT, BATTLE OF THE BULGE AND ACROSS THE RHINE UNDER HEAVY FIRE TO BERLIN. THE CHOCOLATE BAR WAS IN MY SURVIVAL KIT FOR D DAY THAT INCLUDED CODEINE TABLETS, A BANDAGE FOR STUFFING A LARGE BODY WOUND AND A FINE PAPER OVERLAY LOCATION MAP TO BE EATEN IN EVENT OF CAPTURE.

Figure 23 Hershey's Chocolate Wrapper

# CHAPTER VI

Coming Home to America
The Journey Ends

## COMING HOME TO AMERICA

I will never forget riding in the back of a 2½ ton covered Army truck for miles and miles on the hard wooden seats, only to see where you had been and not where you are going. Then on a 40 & 8 cattle car ride for many more miles with very little food or sleep. We arrived near Paris and the French Army fed us stew from a big open pot in a field, before a trip to Cherbourg where we were to take a ship to N.Y.

After riding several more days in the 40 & 8's we arrived tired, dirty and hungry at Cherbourg, France. They fed us again and were put up for the night in an old French Army brick building with a straw mattress in an old wooden bunk. The next day we lugged our bags and marched a long way to the pier and stood for more than two hours looking at the ship we thought we were going home on. After this long time an Officer came along and said there was a change in plans and we were not going on that ship. That's the Army for you!

We were then taken back to Le Havre by an old French train to go on a ship that was taking German prisoners to the U.S., and we were to be their guards. On the way back to Le Havre we began to think Cherbourg, France was the closest we would get to the U.S. After several more days of rough riding and little food on the old train, we arrived at Le Havre. We then boarded a locomotive tender ship which was open in the center with railroad tracks. It was empty and the hole in the center was to be filled with German prisoners and we were to guard them to the U.S.

At Le Havre, we were told the war had ended in Europe and no more German prisoners would be sent to the U.S. So they put us aboard this empty locomotive ship by the name of U.S.S. Lakehurst.

Several hours later the ship sailed for New York. Once along the way, there was a sailor on board and he had a record player for our entertainment and apparently only two records, because they were the only two records he ever played. He would hook it up to the loud speaker system during the day and play the two songs over and over again. I remember standing on deck and listening to "Mairze Doats" and the other song was "Don't Fence Me In", as we looked out over thousands of miles of water in the Atlantic Ocean.

I will never forget coming home and steaming into New York Harbor one May morning in 1945. Just after the sun was up and we were all up on deck, as we did not want to miss the beautiful site. We saw the New York Skyline and as we came into the harbor there was the "Ole Girl"- the Stature of Liberty with the sun shining on her face. She was saying, Welcome Home! I recall standing next to me was a Captain from the 29th Infantry Division and he had been wounded and awarded many medals and decorations in action and he was coming home with our group. I don't think I have ever seen one person shed anymore tears than he did, of course my eyes were not dry by any means. Without a doubt, I'm sure that was one of the greatest moments for each and every soldier on board the U.S.S. Lakehurst that beautiful May morning in New York.

LANDING AT BROOKLYN ARMY BASE
MAY 1945
NOTE : HOSPITAL SHIP U.S.S. HOPE
IN BACKGROUND

RIDING THE 40 & 8's
ACROSS EUROPE ON THE WAY HOME

ABOARD THE U.S.S. LAKEHURST
COMING HOME TO AMERICA MAY 1945

Figure 26 Coming home to America – May 1945

We were taken by train to Camp Kilmer, New Jersey and assigned a bed for the night. Then we went to the Mess Hall to eat. As we went in the cooks asked us what we would like to eat and they would prepare it for us. I remember eating a large steak and asking for a head of lettuce with any kind of dressing. They brought the food and I ate the entire amount.

Each soldier was returned from Camp Kilmer to the original Army Base where he began. I returned to Ft. Meade, Maryland. The Army said, I had too many battle campaign points to go to the Pacific war. Three days later I was given an Honorable Discharge, 100 dollars in cash and a Greyhound bus ticket to my hometown from which I began. The final end of the journey.

The memory of the men of the 2nd Armored Division is permanently memorialized by a monument at Medal of Honor Grove, Valley Forge, Pa., along with General George Washington and many other fighting men in our history.

NOTE : CHAPTER III OF THIS BOOK IS ON PERMANENT DISPLAY AT THE NATIONAL "D" DAY MUSEUM, NEW ORLEANS, LA.
DR. STEVEN E. AMBROSE, DIRECTOR, AUTHOR & HISTORIAN

## FAREWELL TO WAR
## GOING HOME – END OF THE JOURNEY

After the battle at the Rhine we were halted at Magdeburg, Germany. Berlin was for Russian Glory. I was with the first group of 2500 soldiers with combat service to come home as promised by General Eisenhower. I will never forget riding in the back of a 2½ ton army truck for many miles on the hard wooden seats only to see where you had been and not where you are going. In France after a pot of stew in a field, we were put on 40 & 8 cattle cars with little food and sleep for many miles. Later we rode an old steam train to Cherbourg for a ship to America. After the usual Army mix-up we were taken from Cherbourg to LeHarve on the old train where we finally boarded the locomotive tender ship U.S.S. Lakehurst. Another 11 day ride across the Atlantic. Once along the way a crew sailor had a record player for our entertainment. He apparently had only two records. He hooked it to the loudspeakers during the day and played the two songs over & over. We listened to "Mairze Doats" and "Don't Fence Me In" as we looked out over thousand of miles of water of the Atlantic Ocean.

I will never forget the U.S.S. Lakehurst steaming into New York that May morning 1945. We were all on deck to see the "Ole Girl", Stature of Liberty with the sun shining on her face. She was saying "Welcome Home". I recall standing next to me was a Captain from the 29th Infantry who had been wounded and awarded many medals and coming home with our group. He had tears in his eyes and mine were not dry either. We were taken to Camp Kilmer and the cooks prepared premium steaks and all the other food we could eat.

I would be amiss if I did not mention the hardships we endured in 2½ years of war in North Africa, D Day Omaha Beach, France, Belgium, Holland to Berlin. Like not having enough and the proper food, sleeping in the same impregnated army clothes for months, no bath, no shower and our bathroom was stradling a slit trench. Washing in our helmet, drinking sour wine for water and washing our impregnated clothes in gasoline. In France, Belgium & Holland the people were so happy to see us and their freedom they shared with us what little food they had such as eggs & hard bread. For this we were grateful.

Each soldier was returned to the original army base where he began. I returned to Ft. Meade, Maryland. The army said I had too many battle campaign points to go to the Pacific. Three days later I was given a Honorable Discharge, 100 dollars in cash and a Greyhound bus ticket to my hometown where I began.

The memory of the soldiers of the 2nd Armored Division is permanently memorialized with a monument at "Medal of Honor Grove", Valley Forge,Pa. along with General George Washington and many other fighting men in our history.

Ed Sammons

Thank the LORD - TODAY - I'm 85 with my family at my side
I have travelled part of the World that is free
But have many things yet to do and see
I've been around the block a couple of times
Listened to many stories, tales and rymes
General Patton was right you see
when he told me about my grandson on my knee
I survived the African Desert, jumping kangaroo rats,
snakes, mosquitos, heat and all of that
In Sicily we beat Montgomery to Palermo
as we fought hard and fast
Patton got the glory - Montgomery came in last
In England we bridged the Thames
Jolly ole' British thought I was one of them
In France we brought freedom and sights to see
as we fought our way thru Normandy
1st Allied soldiers in Belgium we were greeted with joy
their freedom they have forever more
In Holland we were greeted with
wooden shoes and beautiful flowers
A loving welcome and our first shower
Hitler ordered - HOLD THE LINE - MAKE A STAND
no Allied Soldier is to set foot
on the soil of the Fatherland
I was a yank that bridged the Rhine
to help defeat Hitler just in time
Yesterday belongs to GOD - Tomorrow is in his hand
So I must do my best TODAY - To make it something Grand

Ed Sammons

9/12/04

# CHAPTER VII

## Annual Reunions

### 1946 – 1997

*The Bridge Company, Jim Burt Congressional Medal of Honor Story of the Famous Girdle*

*General Patton's Boys*

*Filipino Stowaway Soldier*

*What Goes Around Comes Around*

*The Colonel and The Corporal*

*Reunion Letter Memories*

*The Last Reunion "Goodbye"*

*Tributes --- by U.S. Presidents: Truman, Eisenhower, Reagan, & Clinton*

*Sidekicks*

Figure 27 Family Photo

## These Reunion Letters...

These Reunion Letters are the response back to each member of the 17th Battalion 2nd Armored Division, the soldiers their wives, children & many friends of the families. I did not include all the pre-order forms and information of each location as JE would send out to hold the date and create interest but added the responses of the aftermath of the highlights of each reunion as written by J.E. and contributions by my mom Bea.

The Reunion letters are from 1977 through 1997 being the "Last Hurray" in Myrtle Beach, SC. The very first reunion gathering was held in 1947 at the Hamilton Hotel in Washington DC. As I have attached a copy of the original pre-stamped card that J.E. sent out to the entire 17th Battalion. These Reunions were also formed by Dad's best friend and buddy – Charlie Gnau and other Trustees — Eddie Strickland, George Whisenant, Mac Atkins, Dwight Cooper, T.A. Walker, Herbie Barnes, and George Masch. The locations of the reunions were held mostly along the north and southeastern states, hosted by each soldier and their family. This formed the original group that started in 1946, with the purpose to keep their memories alive while having a good time enjoying the freedoms they secured during WWII.

J. E.'s reunion letters were not collected until after raising a large family and working hard with sometimes 2 jobs to keep us kids in our private school uniforms. These annual events were looked forward to each year. I remember the NY World's Fair and all the incredible amounts of food, fun, with all the families and friends. As kids we would pal around with each age group and play funny pranks on everyone. This was also organized and prepared by the Axillary group of women who you will read about in Dad's story of the Famous Girdle.

**— Rita Sammons Harrell**

THE BRIDGE COMPANY
Co. "E" 17th ARMD. ENGR. BN.
WE PAVE THE WAY

HELL ON WHEELS - MEETS - HELL ON WATER

Captain James M. Burt, Commander of "B" Co. 66th Armd. Tank Regiment, 2nd Armored Division, recipient of the **CONGRESSIONAL MEDAL OF HONOR** and his lovely wife, Edie were host for a pre-reunion "Shish-Ka-Bob" at their home in Wyomissing, Pa., celebrating the 41st annual reunion of Co. "E" 17th Armd. Engr. Bn. August 27-31, 1986, Reading, Pa.

Attending the party from the 66th were, Don Evans, Curtis Jones, Calvin Yoh and their wives representing the " Alter of Battles " of the 2nd Armored Division Monument at Valley Forge, Pa. Attending from "E" Co. were, Ed Sammons, Chairman, Herb Barnes, Trustee, George Masch, Trustee and their wives.

Jim Burt remembered the 1941 maneuvers in Louisiana and Texas, when one night their tanks, the Red Force were ordered to attack the Blue Force across the Red River and be near the river at daylight, as "E" Co. was to ferry the infantry and initial assault forces across, then build a bridge across the Red River for the main force to attack. When the tanks arrived at the bridge site, "E" Co. of the 17th had rafted the initial assault forces across and completed the entire bridge and were dining on "C" rations for breakfast. However, the tanks never crossed the bridge - the enemy force ( Blue ) sent a plane ( Piper Cub ) to bomb the bridge. The flour sack landed almost in the center of the bridge and the umpires declared the bridge destroyed. "E" Co., the Bridge Co., was baptized and became " Hell on Water " from Benning to Berlin.

Ed Sammons
10/86

Co."E" REUNION CLUB
17th ARMD. ENGR. BN.
2nd ARMORED DIVISION
1946 - 1997

**STORY OF A FAMOUS GIRDLE**

In 1979 at Co."E" 's Annual Reunion at Spencer, Nebraska - someone brought in a girdle to our then Country Store. No one bought it although the selling price had been reduced several times. Finally Russ Allen came along and offered the ladies 50¢ for it. The sale was made, and therein lies the story of a Nebraska farmer's wife foundation garment. In 1980 - Russ and Lillian packed the girdle in a beautiful box of gift wrap and blue ribbon and brought it to the Annual Reunion in Bethesda, Maryland, Hosted by Ed & Bea. The Allens told Ed that they had brought a mystery gift to be auctioned off. Since a couple other members had brought mystery gifts, Ed didn't have a clue as to the contents. We still had the Country Store at this time, so the auction was something new! The bidding was hot and heavy especially between Mac Atkins and John Diederickson and Mac made the last and final bid. It cost him $27.00 Imagine the surprise when the beautiful wrapped box was opened - behold THE GIRDLE FROM NEBRASKA! Russ Allen knew and recognized a real gem of a gimmick! That girdle has travelled many many miles since then -always beautifully wrapped and bringing in $547.00 to our Reunion Fund. It became such a fun thing, and soon we converted our Country Store Fund Raiser to our annual auction, with everyone bringing a gift or two. In 1997 by an ironic twist of fate at Myrtle Beach, South Carolina our final reunion, the girdle was back in the beginning hands of our man - Russ -- and so ends a saga.

GENERAL PATTON'S BOYS
40 PLUS YEARS OF WAR MEMORIES

This is the true story I told at our 44th Annual Army Reunion in Niagara Falls, New York, about our wonderful celebration in Spencer, Nebraska at our 34th Annual Reunion in 1979. ----
I could tell you about the battle of North Africa, U Boats, Arabs, Sicily, Omaha Beach, Battle of the Bulge and General Patton. However, you have read and heard these stories many times and some of us have experienced these battles. So I am delighted to tell you the unique story of what happened after thirty some years of reunions, to the men of Co."E" 17th Armd. Engr. Bn., 2nd Armored Division that fought together for more than four years, covering more than 1700 miles in combat from North Africa to Berlin.

It all started when we gathered for our first reunion at the Hotel Hamilton in Washington, D.C. in 1946. We held our 1964 reunion in New York while attending the World's Fair. We celebrated our 25th again in Washington, D.C. We were in Gettysburg for our 30th reunion and topped it off at Disney World for our 40th.

We were invited to have our annual reunion in Nebraska at the Ranch of one of our members of Co."E". It was near a town of 700 with one 15 room Motel. The townfolk turned their extra bedrooms into Motel rooms for more than 100 people. When we arrived for the four day reunion, the main street was lined with American Flags and Banners. They built a large float for all the soldiers to ride on and then had a big parade down Main Street. They had an all day picnic, barbecued a 300 lb. pig, stuffed with potatoes and sourkraut and barrels of beer was brought in along with a troupe of Square Dancers.

Saturday night at the Armory they held a dance with a live band, prizes and refreshments. I talked with one gentleman farmer of about 85 in years, and he said to me - " He was glad to know that the people from back East were HUMAN ". This was all in addition to our usual events such as the Ladies Country Store, Business Meetings and Sunday Banquet at the one and only Steak House in town. They brought gifts and farm produce to our Country Store and one item they brought, has gone to every reunion since, selling each year for more than 20 dollars. ( That's another story ").

I asked several of the townfolk, during our stay - Why they did all this for more than 100 people they had never met ? Their answer was - "Never before and never again will 100 people, 2nd Armored Division Veterans of WWII and their families gather in their little town of 700 for a four day celebration and reunion of some of the fighting men of General Patton and the Big War".

TO THE PEOPLE OF SPENCER, NEBRASKA - IT WAS CAUSE FOR CELEBRATION


Ed Sammons
9/89

## FILIPINO STOWAWAY SOLDIER

As Co-Founder and Chairman of our Company Army Reunions since WWII, we were holding our 41st annual reunion in 1986 at Reading, Pa. At this reunion I met for the first time in 41 years a combat soldier friend of our Battalion. We fought together from Ft. Benning to Berlin. In all the war years I only knew him as a friend, comrade and fellow G.I. He was jeep driver for his Company Commander and I was half-track driver and radio operator for my Company Commander. We would meet at Company Headquarters and talk while waiting for our Company Commanders as they planned our next move. Sometimes these meetings lasted a long time, as we discussed our situation today, we hoped to see each other tomorrow, win the war soon, return home and back to our lives.

I did not know Andre Cortez and his wife Linda were going to attend our 41st reunion at Reading, Pa., as I had not received their reservation. The second night of the reunion Bea and I went to the hotel dining room for dinner. There was a long line for seating at the dinner hour. We exchanged greetings with the couple standing behind us. We noticed he used a cane. Soon we were called to be seated at a table large enough for four. We asked the Hostess if she would seat them at our table as he was obviously disabled. Deep down in my subconscious I thought he just might be a member of our group. I certainly did not recognize this dignified, slightly built man in his dapper silk suit nor his lovely and charming wife.

They accepted our invitation to join us for dinner at our table and thanked us profusely. I inquired if they were in Reading for a visit, sightseeing etc. - the answer to which was - " I'm attending a reunion of my Army Group ". ( They rode a bus from New York, just to see his army buddies ). We looked at each other in amazement - we were 'ole buddies, found each other after all these years. Unbelievable ! I had to ask about the cane - had he been injured during the war ? He didn't seem to want to talk about it - but Linda told us that Andy had been standing on a street corner near home waiting for the bus ( never owned a car ) and a jogger came running around the corner, knocked Andy down and he wound up in the hospital with a broken hip that never healed properly due to his early years of malnutrition and was forced to use a cane.

Andy relaxed - lit one of his Philippine cigars, offered me one while we awaited our food services. He began to tell who he was, where he came from and our war years together. After a couple of cocktails and cigars, we listened to this incredible story - - - -

J. E.'s Filipinos Stowaway Story has all the elements of a dedicated solider and how he strived and starved in seeking his childhood dream of his "America" homebound journey. J. E. wrote this story with a heavy heart and with such great respect and admiration for Andre Cortez. All that this soldier encountered, before even entering WWII, and how his determination and sacrifice was never-ending.

Andre received the Silver Star, 2 Bronze Stars, 2 Invasion Arrowheads, Belgian Crois de Guerre and the Presidential Citation. Andy became the beacon of light that ignited all those in attendance at the 41st Reunion banquet and not a dry eye in the house. After 41 years, Andre & his wife entered the hotel dining room and walks in with a cane as this unbelievable story begins.

**—Rita Sammons Harrell**

Andy was born in Manila of Filipino catholic parents and the oldest of 13 children. They were very very poor and as the eldest he felt he had to help support the large family. His dream was the dream of his parents - to get to the U.S. and specifically to the Filipino area of Bedford-Stuyvesant in New York City. There were Filipinos there who had made their way from Manila. If he could get there - friends would help him. He watched and waited for the best opportunity. He spent time at the ship docks watching the U.S. merchant ships coming and going.

His chance finally came. He secretly stowed away in the hole of a ship bound for the U.S. After about two weeks at sea and only scraps of food he salvaged from the garbage at night and no water he became so desperate he decided to take a chance and come out of hiding. He was soon discovered by a crew member and dragged up to the main deck for all the crew to see. They at once decided to throw this underfed kid overboard to the sharks. The crew chief suggested they best deliver him to the Captain and get his O.K., before they threw him overboard. Andy was taken to the Captain's quarters. The Captain looked at this scrawny, dirty boy of 14 and had other ideas. He dismissed the crew, said he would care for the boy until the ship landed in America. He kept the boy in his quarters with food, drink and a bunk.

On arrival at San Francisco, the Captain called his sister and asked her to meet him at the dock as he had something for her. His sister arrived in a beautiful chauffeur-driven automobile. The Captain gave his sister the vagrant. They drove to a fashionable home and estate overlooking the bay. He was given a small room, food, his clothes and 50¢ a day. In exchange he was to be the house boy, yard boy and general handyman.

He worked very hard and being all his personal needs were met by his employer, he saved every cent he was paid and in a little less than two years he had amassed enough money for his bus fare to New York City. His dream come true ! He indeed found Filipino friends there who took him in, cared for him and sent him to catholic schools. While attending school he was able to find part-time jobs so that he could send money to his family.

In 1938 Andy became a U.S. citizen, met and married a young lady from a well-to-do family in the Philippines. Her family had sent her to New York to attend Fordham University. After graduation and during the war she taught in the New York Public School System. In 1941 Andy was drafted into the army and joined me and other draftees in the 17th Armored Engineer Battalion, U.S. 2nd Armored Division at Ft. Benning, Georgia. About this same time a Colonel named George S. Patton, Jr. joined our Armored Division.

For his wartime combat service Andy was awarded the Silver Star, 2 Bronze Stars, 2 Invasion Arrowheads, Belgian Croix de Guerre and the Presidential Citation.

Returning to civilian life, Andy decided to join the Merchant Marine. His beloved Linda was teaching the children they never had. Not having children of their own, they invested their moderate amount of savings in bringing several nieces and nephews to the U.S. and paid for their college educations. They proudly told us of their family members who are teachers, lawyers, doctors and engineers. God works in mysterious ways to further his kingdom on earth.

Andy and Linda never had a penchant for the material things - such as a home or even a car. Andy retired from the Merchant Marine after 34 years and wife Linda retired as a District Supervisor for the New York Public School System. As he told us his story - he told us they still lived in the modest rented apartment in the Bedford-Stuyvesant area. Then a decision - they decided to return to the Philippines and build a home for their extended family. Each summer they returned there for a long visit.

Suddenly the four of us in the once crowded dining room were aware of the intense quiet around us. By now everyone had left and only our waiter hovering near by and eager to go home.

In the telling and listening to this compelling story, we hadn't realized that hours had passed. We could not even remember what we had ordered - much less what we had eaten. We apologized to our waiter. Andy insisted on picking up the check and he was grateful we had asked them to be our dinner companions. He no doubt remembered that in the Army, this dark-skinned soldier who always did his job, but was not always accepted by his fellow comrades.

We left the dining room and headed back to our reunion hospitality room hoping there were still people there. Indeed there was. I promptly introduced Andy and Linda, and the Angels were smiling as the long ago stowaway took center stage and told the rest of the fellows what he had been about all these years.

At the end of the reunion as we exchanged embraces and well wishes, we spoke of meeting again at our annual reunion wherever it would be. Andy told me that Linda and he would be going back to Manila the next summer and he wanted to send me a box of those good cigars from the Philippines. The following summer I indeed did receive those mild mellow wonderful cigars.

We kept in touch through the years by phone and letters. In a last letter from his wife Linda, she told me that Andy had passed away and she was returning to their home in Manila to be with the family. She thanked me for our long-standing friendship.

Ed Sammons
12/98

## WHAT GOES AROUND COMES AROUND

It really does happen - I remember a time during the war when we were pushing the Germans through France, Belgium and Holland to the German border at Aachen, the gateway for the 2nd Armored Division to the Weser, Rhine, Elbe and Berlin. Hitler gave orders to hold the line at all cost at the German border -- as no enemy soldier was to set foot on the soil of the Fatherland. We fought for three weeks in the November rain and cold to breach the line at Aachen, along side of the 30th Infantry Division as the 14th, 78th, & 92nd Field Artillery of our division fired 75 MM shells over our heads day and night into Aachen. We finally broke out of the mud and through Aachen which was completely destroyed, as it opened the gateway into Germany. We bridged the Weser, Rhine and Elbe rivers for our infantry and tanks on the road to Berlin.

Some 48 years later one of my grandsons was a college student at Haverford College in Pa., where he met a German Exchange Student from Aachen, Germany. They became good friends and my grandson, Chaon Garland, was invited to visit the family at Aachen the next summer during his travels in Europe. I told my grandson before he left for Europe - remember it would perhaps be best not to mention the war or the 2nd Armored Division, and especially not that his grandfather was a part of the division that leveled Aachen. - Chaon visited his friend in Aachen for a few days and they treated him royally. He did not mention the war. Aachen has been completely rebuilt and is a beautiful city in Germany.

Ed Sammons
8/97

## THE COLONEL AND THE CORPORAL

I first knew Lt.Col.Lewis W. Correll at Ft. Benning in 1941 when he was a Major, 2nd in Command of the 17th Armd. Engr. Bn., U.S. 2nd Armored Division. He was admired by the men of our battalion as an intelligent leader, knew his job as Engineer and treated his men with great respect. During the invasion of Sicily our Battalion Commander, Lt.Col.Hurley was killed by a land mine during the beach landing. Major Correll took over Command in England before "D" Day and guided us through five additional battle campaigns as Lt.Colonel.

On our race and rout of the Germans from "D" Day to Berlin, we over ran air fields, a concentration camp and small towns to get to the Rhine River. The Colonel's orders were to reach the Rhine River, remove the land mines, raft the infantry across and build a bridge for our tanks. We found a location and approach the night before, below a cow pasture that was the best site along the river bank. Our Company Commander, Captain McAdams proceeded to the bridge site in advance and with complete disregard for his own safety, he crossed the river with the first infantry assault forces under continuous small arms fire to check the far side bridge approach and exit roads. We struck before dawn to build the bridge. I located our Command half-track about fifty yards from the approach site. We dug into fox holes and maintained radio silence as the Germans were listening. The 142nd Signal Co. laid a telephone line from our half-track to more than a half mile up the hill to Battalion Headquarters, which was linked to the 78th Field Artillery who were to direct fire across the river to cover us, as the 88's and small arms fire were coming in.

It was at the Rhine River in March 1945, that I had my first close contact with the Colonel. In the midst of all the excitement, noise and dense fog the roving 88's were killing the cows in the pasture around us. Later we learned the 88's coming over were mounted on a track, firing four rounds then moving along a track to a different location to fire. One of our medics, Richard Kane, who was standing about thirty feet from me, was hit in his back with a large piece of shrapnel. The medics were busy. We were trying to get more fire power and air cover.

Shortly thereafter, the Colonel came rushing down to the site in his jeep to direct and check our progress. The Colonel told his driver to park the jeep behind the barn and wait. A few minutes later an 88 hit the barn and jeep killing the driver. The Colonel later told me that this was one of the toughest things he had to endure in the war. His driver had been with him for more than two years. Although the Germans hit the bridge twice blowing out a section each time, we managed to build the longest bridge across the Rhine, 1152 ft. in a record time of seven hours, under heavy fire for which our Company was awarded the Presidential Citation and decorated in person by President Harry S. Truman when we reached Berlin. We lost 21 men that day.

At our second meeting and first since war's end at our annual Army Reunion at Niagara Falls in 1978, the Colonel was our guest speaker and took us back through our travels of more than 1700 miles in combat and seven battle campaigns. He explained why we did certain things and the battle routes we travelled. We often wondered after a battle why certain Officers were suddenly transferred out. They just disappeared. The Colonel said - " They were not battle worthy ".

For the third time in 58 years, our lives crossed again in 1998. I met and spent the day with the Colonel at his home in Arizona. We had served together from 1941 to 1945 from Benning to Berlin. He was in charge of more than a thousand men and me - Corporal Sammons, in "E" Co., as radio operator, machine gunner and Command Half-track driver for our Company Commander, Captain James E. McAdams.

We spent the entire day and into the night reminiscing, and we both discovered we had survived many war incidents that the other one knew nothing about. There were some happy and funny experiences and many sad ones. After a lovely dinner and more talk we hugged each other, then bid each a farewell. What a wonderful day! We were no longer the Colonel and the Corporal - we were just Lou & Ed - two old World War II veterans that survived.

This is just one of the many war events in my life that I remember each day. Thank God for our Leader - Lewis W. Correll.

September 25, 1977

Dear friends of Company E,

Summer is over--everyone is settling down to jobs, old routines and schedules--the lazy days at the beach are gone. It is time to dig in for the winter. If that is a dreary thought, we would just like to remind you to think ahead to the 1978 Company E Reunion, for we are going to be in Niagara Falls! How about having an extra long weekend, or possibly an entire week of your vacation geared to being with your family and your old army buddies and their families at one of the top tourist attractions in this land of ours?

Walt and Doris Stewart will be your hosts for our annual get-together, and they are already making plans for your enjoyment. Make your individual plans now to include Niagara Falls!

We had a good turnout in Baltimore this past Labor Day Weekend thanks to the efforts of Leo and Ann Mecler. There were new faces, which pleased us all and many of the old faithful were there. However, there were also many old regulars missing, and we, indeed, missed their presence. Noel Whittington passed away as the Reunion was just getting under way, and we are also sad to report that Stanley Lipsey died in April. These two were especially loyal and true friends of Company E. Their absence will be sorely felt. It was a privilege to have known two such fine men.

Many could not attend this year's reunion because of ill health--those we heard from were Pete Zukow, T. A. Walker and Pete Foy. All are recovering nicely at this writing.

There are many good old New York buddies who will have no excuses for attending the 1978 affair. We hope, too, that Lil Kuppersmith, Clara Roberts, Polly Lipsey and Evelyn Rubin, all widows of Company E members will make a special effort to attend. We miss the pleasure of your company.

So there you have it in a nutshell--the one organization that is for, by and with you one hundred percent---is still alive and growing. Keep it that way. See you at the Falls next Labor Day Weekend! Walt and Doris will keep you posted throughout the year.

Sincerely your friends,

Ed and Bea Sammons

Bethesda, Maryland
September 25, 1979

Dear friends,

Another Labor Day weekend has come and gone, and you, who were unable to be present this year of 1979 in Spencer, Nebraska, missed the greatest one of all! It would take pages to tell you all the wonderful, fun-filled days and nights we had, all the interesting places we visited, and the genuine warmth and generous hospitality we encountered, not only by Martha and Joe Pfeifer, our hosts, and their wonderful family, but by all the people of Spencer--the ranchers, farmers, townspeople, the World War II Veterans of the local American Legion Post. It was something to behold!

We took notes for fear of being unable to recall something funny or important to relate in our letter to you. It is impossible to tell you all the experiences we had. We are sure Mac Atkins is still showing people in Harrisonburg his picture of the Nebraska Jack Rabbit! Undoubtedly, John Diederickson is still beguiling fellow gamblers in Atlantic City with the wonders of the wide-mouthed frog! Who can ever forget the ninety mile convoy trip we took on Friday? Russell Allen will never forget it--his car acted up more than a little bit, but a kindly Nebraska farmer gave it a lift and safe keeping at his farm while the convoy pushed onward through Fort Randall and the huge dam there. Remember the noon picnic in the park (Martha saw that the Chuck Wagon followed us everywhere we went, and always it was loaded down with food and beverage).

Who can forget our visit to the Sioux Indian Council Rooms--seeing the flags of the many Sioux tribes? Alas, the crossing of the wide Missouri on one of the last paddle boats still operating in America! The paddle boat carried four vehicles at a time, and one of the funniest incidents ever happened with the first four cars. Imagine if you will, these "boys" of Co. E., these Engineers who forged many a stream, built many a bridge, drove in countless convoys and parked endless vehicles--being <u>told</u>, <u>yelled at</u>, and <u>commanded</u> the proper way to park on the ferry--and by a mere snip of a boy at that! It was a volatile moment! But tempers held, and we crossed the Missouri in peace, waving to those who were left behind to make the next crossing!

Later we all met at the Two Rivers Bar in Niobrara, a restored Indian town, whose saloon was like something out of a western movie, player piano and all. This reporter will never forget the delicious pickled turkey gizzard. Gourmet eating at its finest! No kidding!

Oh, there is so much more--the pig roast, the square dancers, the mountains of food prepared by Martha and her ranch-house sweat team, as well as the people of the community who arrived with covered dishes, watermelons, cantaloupes, peaches, etc.; the successful auxiliary country store with the lovely homemade items our ladies brought or sent (as well as the beautiful hooked rugs made by Charlie Gnau), plus all the homemade crafts and homecanned gooods that the women of Spencer and community brought for us to sell! We made so much money that the current rumor making the rounds is that the men want to join the Auxiliary!

-2-

What about the picnic on Thursday night at the Pfeifer ranch? With all the good country food, tables full of chicken, beans, salads, pies, etc., however did that oh, so delectable Chesapeake Bay Crab Salad find its way on the groaning board? Now we know why Marion and Art Sigrist need that Air Stream--precious cargo that they haul!

We sat across the table at the picnic from Marshall Jackson, and discovered a mutual liking for cherry pie. Must say that Martha's pies rate an APLUS! This was Marshall's first reunion. His lovely wife brought numerous handmade items for our country store. We hope they will come next year, even if it takes a cherry pie to get him here from Waldo, Arkansas. Charlie Rose and his wife came from Pratt, Kansas, also first-timers, and we sincerely hope they will join us again.

Saturday Night Banquet--with Martha's "Seventieth Birthday-Girl" Mother presiding over the punch table--serving the finest Prairie Dew anywhere! The theme was country western, and the tables were covered with checked red and white cloths, printed menus and programs at each place as was a covered wagon with our insignia painted on it. On the tables were bundles of straw, guitars, and stagecoaches--all these favors to take home for remembrances. The feast of a banquet followed with the menu ranging from Chuckwagon Special (Windsor Smoked Loin) with cherry sauce to Buckshot (nuts and homemade mints). The blessing, the Lord's Prayer, was sung by a local girl, and the program that followed was just super entertainment, songs of the World War II era, and all this by local talent. The food was prepared and served by friends and relatives of the Pfeifers.....under Martha's direction. The Saturday night banquet was just a part of a Saturday that began with breakfast at Jake's Place (and another cold egg sandwich for Thelma Atkins)-- then on to Jerry and Gwen's hospitality rooms in their beautiful home. (Jerry, being the youngest son and youngest twin of Joe and Martha's). With the business affairs settled--back to the Skyview Motel (operated by Marcia, Oldest daughter)--and a change into our western evening togs for the banquet--then moving on to still another happening--the big country western dance at the Spencer Community Hall with the entire community invited!

How great it was! Meeting all those wonderful, warm, friendly people who were so gracious to us. It was a good feeling to know that those very ideals of American life which we fellows fought for and our fallen buddies died for, still exist in this country of ours, especially in Middle America--Spencer, Nebraska!

Joe, we will be super nice and not mention the size of the grass-hoppers nor the quantity thereof, for no one would believe us, but we hope that you will invite us again, so that we can renew our friendships made at Buff's Bar and all those other places in Spencer we visited, as well as in Gross, where we found that 5¢ cup of coffee still exists. Martha, you are something else--what a wonderful job you did in co-ordinating all the plans and making them work! Thanks a million to you both.

And now on to next year--our 35th anniversary reunion to be held in the Washington, D. C. area and to be hosted by yours truly. We will try our best to give you a good one, but do not expect the miracle of Spencer to be repeated. That happens once in a lifetime.

Mark your calendars. We'll be in touch. God love you each and everyone--keep well--see you in '80!

Sincerely, Bea and Ed Jemmens

ENCLOSURE: A copy of our "Thank You" letter sent to the local paper in Spencer.

Figure 28 Patton

Bethesda, Maryland
Sept. 20, 1980

Dear friends of Company E,

The reunion is over, but the memories linger on! We want to thank those of you who came and helped make this past Labor Day Weekend a fun-filled affair. It renews our hearts and spirits each year when we see old friends and buddies and wives greet each other with hugs and kisses (especially those we have not seen for some time); it is like family--in fact, we are a real family. It is a joy to be with one another and share the past, the present, and plan for our future outings.

The turn-out was excellent, with lots of old familiar faces, plus many whom we have not seen for some time. It was great to see three of the widows of our members, and we thank Lil Kuppersmith, Clara Roberts Dye and Evelyn Rubin for showing us they still are interested in Compnay E and all it stands for. We all love you and hope you will come again and bring your families. We also welcomed a new face, Bill Karr and his wife, Helen, from Ohio. We trust they will come again!

Our country store enjoyed its second successful year. We realized $382 from the sale of all the lovely hand-crafts and other things the ladies canned, made or brought in. The items went on sale and a good two-thirds were gone by business-meeting time on Saturday. After the meeting was concluded, the remainder of the items were sold at auction. Everyone enjoyed this so, especially the men, that we have decided to schedule the business meeting an hour earlier next year, and sell all the items at auction. We will try it and see how it works out....and what the results will be. Thanks to all the women who gave so generously of their time and talents to make the store so worth-while.

Now for the good news! There was much discussion about where the next reunion would be; several offers were made as well as suggestions, but it was voted to once again return to the valley of Virginia, in Harrisonburg, where we have had such great times before. Mac and Thelma Atkins will be our hosts, and you know that we will all have something to look forward to--for they know how to show everyone a good time. So keep this in mind when you are making vacation plans, and collecting and making your country store articles.

We would appreciate hearing from you if you know of new addresses for any of our members; for instance, all Geo. Hedges mail is returned to us with the Orchard Park, N. Y. address. Keep us informed on illnesses. We hope there will be no deaths, but if so, let us know. Have a good year, good health, and if we can be of service in any way, we will do whatever we can. Do get in touch. See you in 1981, if not before!

Your friends,

Bea and Ed Sammons

March 17, 1981

9514 Edgeley Road
Bethesda, Maryland 20014

Dear Members, Family & Friends;

A couple of weeks ago, Bea and I drove up to Valley Forge National Park in Penna., to the Freedoms Foundation to visit the site and see the almost completed "Alter of Battles", honoring the men of the 2nd. Armored Division World War II.

July 31, 1981 will be a day in history and a momentous occasion for you, the fighting soldiers and brave men of the 2nd. Armored Division. A day set aside to honor the living and dead by placement of this forever monument.

This dedication is in conjunction with the 27th. Annual Reunion of the 2nd. Armored Division Association, being held from July 29th thru August 1st, 1981. This reunion is a happy event and opportunity to once again meet many of our former comrades from all the different units of our division. -- I can understand if you are unable to attend the entire 4 day reunion, -- however, I urge you if at all possible to attend and be there for the all day dedication ceremonies on Friday July 31st, and perhaps the banquet and dance on Saturday.

There will be many former members of our Division representing every Company, Battalion, and Regiment at this great event, and we hope the 17th Engr. Bn., and Co."E" will lead the way in attendance just as they did at the 1976 Division Reunion in Philadelphia. I hope we can have at least 20 to 25 men of Company "E", plus their families to represent us. Enclosed is a reservation card for your registration, ( do it early to assure yourself of a choice room ) at a discount rate per room, which is almost 50% off the regular price. Please mail your reservation card directly to Stouffer's Valley Forge Hotel, and a note to me as to date of your arrival and departure in order I may co-ordinate the rooms of Co."E" as close together as possible.

This is a once in a life-time great event, to honor you, and permanent history for our children and grandchildren of the future to preserve our memory forever.

Please keep in touch - let me know how I can help. I look forward to seeing you for the all day dedication Friday morning July 31, 1981 at Valley Forge, and also Labor Day Weekend in the beautiful valley of Virginia.

Cordially yours,

Ed Sammons, Chairman

encl.

Palm Harbor, Florida
September 30, 1983

Dear friends of Company E,

Here we are home again after a month of travelling and attending the Company Reunion in Spencer, Nebraska.

How do we thank Martha and Joe and all of their family for the super wonderful effort in hosting this year's get-together? It was a lot of work and planning for the Pfeifers, and those 49 of us who were there can tell you that there was never a dull moment. Both the members and our several visitors all had the time of our lives.

It was a thrill to see so many of you. We filled Marcia's Motel; several couples and our Ramona were put up at Martha and Joe's, and we were houseguests of Jerry and Gwen (Martha and Joe's son and wife).

The welcome flags were flying and lined the streets as we drove into Spencer, and the hospitality of all those wonderful people warmed us our entire stay.

The picnic supper at the Fairgrounds on Thursday night hosted by Martha and Joe was a real smash! It was typical mid-western fare-- lots of fried chicken and all the fixins, plus Martha's homemade pies and very special homemade ice cream. We must add here that Art and Marian Sigrist added a special Chesapeake Bay touch to the menu with their homemade fresh backfin crabmeat salad! What a feast we all shared that evening!

On Friday morning a free continental breakfast was served at the motel by Marcia and crew. At noon we all met at the Senior Center for a delicious luncheon. All this was just a prelude to the Friday night Big Event! The Pig Roast and the Country store sale and auction! Needless to say that Friday was not a "be-kind-to-your Tummy day". Until you have experienced it, no one can tell you how delicious that roast pig, stuffed with sauerkraut, can be. Besides that there were tables laden with all kinds of goodies--salads, casseroles, breads, tons of sweets, gallons of iced tea and a barrel of cold beer. Man alive-- that's livin!

The Country Store and auction of the two paintings donated by Dorothy Powell and Lucille Rose brought a tidy sum into our fund. We have come to the conclusion that the fellows enjoy the country store and auction as much as the girls.

Saturday morning it was up and early--Butte, Nebraska Pancake Days! Company E rode a float in the parade, and were quite impressive riding down Main Street wearing complete (or nearly complete) uniforms of World War II, including General B. S. Barnes! After the parade all lined up for all the pancakes and sausage you could eat. As evidenced by the stacks of cakes devoured, we'd say that our guys proved they are still CHOW HOUNDS!

The business meeting was held at the Senior Center on Saturday afternoon. Messages from the T. A. Walkers, Pete Zukows, Louis Corrells and Gordon Ketchpaws were acknowledged. Next year's reunion takes place at Finger Lake, Canandaigua, N. Y., and will be hosted by Lorraine and Herbie Barnes. Herb has everything all set--the motel, food, as well as

## HELL ON WHEELS KEEPS ROLLING ALONG

A great happening is taking place in Orlando, Florida at the Wilson World Hotel, Oct. 23-27, 1985. At least it will be to members of Company "E" 17th Armd. Engr. Bn., 2nd Armored Division (Hell on Wheels) of World War II fame, who will be converging on the Walt Disney area from all parts of our Nation. They will bring their wives and families to attend the 40th annual reunion of their Company.

General George S. Patton, Jr. gave birth to this division, raised it, and took it into battle, and it became one of the greatest fighting and most decorated units of World War II. General Eisenhower, Field Marshall Montgomery, General Bradley, to name a few, all respected the courage and sagacity of this fighting outfit and paid great tribute to it. In 1945 at Berlin, Germany, President Harry S. Truman personally presented the Presidential Citation to the Division and cited them for extreme valor under enemy fire.

War correspondents such as Hal Boyle, Wes Gallagher, Tom Yarbrough, and many others of like caliber immortalized these GI's in many articles as they traveled with the Division as they saw action in North Africa, Sicily, Omaha Beach, Belgium, Holland and Berlin.

And so they come, the few remaining, to celebrate a reunion that has been an annual affair for 40 years. They come from all walks of life, - in our great Country - former Co. Commanders, Tough First Sergeants, Corporals, and GI Joe. Having seen and lived through many campaigns together, they look forward to meeting Ole Buddies and reliving their war experiences. Many a battle will be re-fought as Veterans of the 2nd Armored Division do their thing in 1985.

Authorized for Immediate Press Release :

*James E. Sammons*

James E. Sammons, Chairman

Co."E" Reunion Club
17th Armd. Engr. Bn.
2nd Armored Division

Palm Harbor, Florida

November 11, 1985

Co. "E" Reunion Club
17th Armd. Engr. Bn.
2nd Armored Division

Dear Members and Friends of Co."E",

    We want to thank you for coming to Orlando, Florida and making our 40th Anniversary Reunion a time to remember. It was great seeing the ole' friends who come year after year - and wonderful to meet the buddies we haven't seen since we came home from World War II - a salute to you all. We sincerely hope the newcomers will come again and join us at Reading, Pa. next year and at Lake Canandaiqua in New York in 1987.

    We were not only pleased with the large turnout, but we think the Wilson World Hotel did a most adequate job in tending to our needs, plus letting us use that lovely hospitality suite all week, and the mezzanine set-up for our country store. As usual, the Ladies did a wonderful job with the country store and the men bought and bought. We had some lovely and beautiful items, plus yummy jams, pickles, and jellies. So once again our country store and auction proved to be one of the highlights this year.

    Needless to say there were many bald heads who returned home with Minnie Mouse's kiss still intact - who wants to wash that away? How many hugged Donald Duck and were hugged in turn by Mickey and Pluto as well. The character breakfast was a real fun affair.

    Many sore feet were reported after a day at EPCOT, Sea World, and the Magic Kingdom - but no one complained too much. It was great being a kid again at Disney World and Sea World. A wonderful way to view our magnificient world at EPCOT. We learned that some of the gang found Rosie O'Gradys, Church Street Station and Cheyenne Saloon - a fun place to relax, eat, dance and enjoy the entertainment. Our former Co. Commander, Pete Zukow and his lovely wife, Jo, were our honored guests and we were delighted they could join us this year. Loren and Rosalee Guge, were also our guests. Loren is President of the 2nd Armored Division Assn., and he hosted the Division Reunion at Tampa last May. NOW he knows how we do things on a Company level. We really enjoyed their visit and sure hope they will do it again.

    So the party is over, that is until next year at Reading, Pa. - but the memories linger on. Ruth and Randy Gnau will host the '86 reunion and they are already planning a calender of events like you wouldn't believe. So keep early October 1986 reserved for Co."E" Reunion Time.

    Each reunion becomes more precious to us as veterans, for who knows, but God alone, how many more we will have the opportunity to enjoy.

    May God bless you. - See you at Reading '86.

Kindest Personal Regards,

*Ed Bea*

Ed and Bea Sammons

Co. "E" Reunion Club
17th Armd. Engr. Bn.
2nd Armored Division

TO ALL MEMBERS, FAMILIES, AND FRIENDS OF
CO."E" 17th ARMD. ENGR. BN. 2nd ARMD. DIV.

With great honor - CO."E" Reunion Club announces that our special guests for our 41st Annual Reunion at Reading, Pa., August 27 - 31, 1986, will be Capt. Jim Burt, Congressional Medal of Honor, 66th Armd. Regt., 2nd Armd. Div., and -- Lt/Col. Peter T. Sowa, Battalion Commander of the 17th Armd. Engr. Bn., 2nd Armd. Div.
You know or will know the incredible heroism of Jim Burt, CMH .
Col. Sowa will tell us how it is in the 17th, 45 years later. Could you hack it !
Be There -- We want a large turnout to meet, greet, and welcome these two outstanding men to our 41st reunion.

Cordially,

*Ed Sammons*

Ed Sammons, Chairman

2431 Grove Ridge Drive
Palm Harbor, Florida 33563

Palm Harbor, Florida
Sept. 17, 1986

DEAR MEMBERS AND FRIENDS OF CO. "E":

Back home again after a delightful trip to the northern states, the highlight of the trip being our 41st Annual Reunion at Reading, Pa.

Ruth & Randy Gnau were wonderful hosts and a great time was had by all. Their selection of hotel site was unsurpassed - and the dining was excellent. The staff of the Reading Motor Inn was most gracious in meeting our requirements. Attendance was great from our membership, and we were pleased that our dentist Art Marc and wife Lois joined us as well as Bernie & Rita Erstein and Andy & Linda Cortez from "B" Co. 17th. Fred Turner and his wife from "A" Co. 17th attended the Sat. night banquet.

The bargains were great at our Country Store. Thank you ladies for all your contributions and help, making it a great success again.

The bus trip to Atlantic City was fun - some of us lost some cash, and there were the lucky ones who cashed in on some winnings! They were the ones who almost missed the bus back to Reading! Many wives were able to get their husbands to the Outlet Malls on Friday. All reported bargains.

The Sat. night banquet was an enormous success - good, delicious Pa. Dutch Buffet, great musical entertainment, and two talented guest speakers. Jim Burt, recipient of the Congressional Medal of Honor, and his charming wife, Edie were presented first. Jim told us about his various encounters with the Engineers in WW II, all of which brought back many memories. Being the "certified teller of truth", that Jim proclaims himself to be, we firmly believed all the good things he said about our outfit, and how we won the war! Lt. Col. Pete Sowa, accompanied by his lovely wife, Maril, was our next speaker. Pete is the former Cmdr. of the 17th Engr. Bn. at Fort Hood, Texas and is presently studying at the Army War College at Carlisle Barracks, Pa. He spoke to us about the Engineers of today and what they are doing to be ready and on alert. Good to know the 17th Engrs., continue to have excellent leadership.

It was a memorable evening - and an honor to be with such outstanding men as Jim Burt and Pete Sowa, we thank them for joining us on this special occasion. We enjoyed the visit to the "Altar of Battles" at Valley Forge, even in the rain.

So we say goodbye to Reading for 1986 and a great reunion by Ruth & Randy. We have another good one to look forward to in Canandaigua, New York under the capable guidance of Herb & Lorranie Barnes. Please keep Labor Day Weekend 1987 reserved for our 42nd annual bash!

Each year some dear faces are missing. Who knows how much longer we can enjoy these wonderful get-togethers? God Bless, and we look forward to seeing you next year in Canandaigua.

With kindest personal regards,

Ed and Bea

Palm Harbor, Florida
September 19, 1987

DEAR MEMBERS AND FRIENDS OF CO."E";

All those Christmases of 1942,43,44 - that never were - somehow we knew someday it would come to pass - only it was at the American Legion Hall in Canandaigua, New York, and the date was Sept.5,1987! It was well worth waiting for!

Herb & Lorraine Barnes and the American Legion Post #256 of Canandaigua did a great job. The food, entertainment and program was a hit with all. From the Memorial Services to the Country Store - to the Banquet Speaker and Program - highlighted by Santa's visit and distribution of gifts, the 42nd Annual Reunion of Co."E"17th Armd. Engr. Bn. was another fun affair.

Dr. Marvin Rapp, noted Historian, recaptured the blazing glory of the 2nd Armored Division. Ed Young, local comedian tickled our ribs with his many stories. The sing-a-long directed by Doris Stewart was especially enjoyable - didn't realize we had so many good voices in our group. The sumptious banquet was excellent, Santa's visit, the gift exchange, the door prizes and 50/35/15 raffle capped a wonderful few days at Lake Canandaigua.

Next Year - it's Atlanta Georgia in October. Charlie and Dorothy Powell will be our Hosts. We are looking forward to that "Southern Hospitality". This year we raised over $700.00 at the Country Store and after all expenses we netted over $200.00 for next year. We sure missed our Country Store Manager this year, - Lee Mealer who passed away in August.

It was wonderful after 43 yrs. to see Orvell Simpson and his lovely wife Irmgard. We last saw Orvell at the loading docks in England, just before the invasion. Welcome back comrade!

Thanks to all of you for attending this year, our many guests, friends, and members of the other Companies of the 17th. You made our Christmas in September. REMEMBER ! ATLANTA IN '88 !

Our Best to You,

Ed & Bea Sammons

## HELL ON WHEELS KEEPS ROLLING ALONG

A great happening is taking place in Atlanta, Georgia at the Marriott Hotel Oct. 6 to 9 1988. At least it will be to members of Company "E" 17th Armd. Engr. Bn., 2nd Armored Division (Hell on Wheels) of World War II fame, who will be converging on the Atlanta area from all parts of our Nation. They will bring their wives and families to attend the 43rd annual reunion of their Company.

General George S. Patton, Jr. gave birth to this division raised it, and took it into battle, and it became one of the greatest fighting and most decorated units of World War II. Gen. Eisenhower, Field Marshall Montgomery, Gen. Bradley, to name a few, all respected the courage and sagacity of this fighting outfit and paid great tribute to it. In 1945 at Berlin, Germany, President Harry S. Truman personally presented the Presidential Citation to the Division and cited them for extreme valor under enemy fire.

War correspondents such as Hal Boyle, Was Gallagher, Tom Yarbrough, and many others of like caliber immortalized these GI's in many articles as they traveled with the Division as they saw action in North Africa, Sicily, Omaha Beach, Belgium, Holland and Berlin.

And so they come - the few remaining - to celebrate a reunion that has been an annual affair for 43 years. Having seen and lived through many campaigns together, they look forward to meetingOle Buddies and reliving their war experiences. Many a battle will be re-fought as Veterans of the 2nd Armored Division do their thing in 1988.

Authorized for Immediate Press Release :

---

James E. Sammons, Chairman

October 1988

DEAR MEMBERS AND FRIENDS OF CO."E" ;

What a wonderful Reunion we had this year - our 43rd. Atlanta provided us with some beautiful inspiring sights, but there was nothing like that SOUTHERN HOSPITALITY!, generated by our hosts Bill & Dorothy Powell and augmented by the assistance of their friends Harold (Radio) & Ruby Griggers. A lot of work and planning goes into hosting a reunion, and these four did a super great job. Thank you for a happy reunion. It was good to see all the ole' familiar faces, and it was so good to see Willie Scruggs who was able to be with us this year, as well as his wife Margaret. Hope to see them at Niagara Falls next year. Needless to say - our departed buddies and families were missed but their spirits were among us and the families that were present. Love ties are strong between our fellow G.I.'s and families. May it always remain!
Next year it is Niagara Falls, New York with Doris Stewart as hostess. Walt & Doris hosted two previous reunions and as you recall - we had some great times. So we are looking forward to the Falls and Canada - and know that Doris will be working and planning to have another great gathering in September -'89. We will be in touch,- as will Doris. Looking forward to being with you at Niagara in Sept.1989! Thanks again. Our best to each and everyone. God Bless!

Love,

*Ed & Bea*

Ed & Bea Sammons

Co. "E" Reunion Club
17th Armd. Engr. Bn.
2nd Armored Division

Palm Harbor, Florida

March '90

                                           Co. "E" REUNION CLUB
                                              17th Armd. Engr. Ba.
                                                2nd Armored Division
                                                    "Hell on Wheels"

<u>DEAR MEMBERS, FAMILY AND FRIENDS;</u>

    We are excited and delighted to inform you that our 45th Annual Reunion will be at the Sheridan Beach Resort, on Sand Key Island and beautiful Clearwater Beach on the Gulf of Mexico, Sept.6 to 9,1990. What a wonderful location to relax and enjoy on the beautiful Suncoast of Florida!

    Thursday, Sept.6th is Early Bird Day, and includes the Early Bird Dinner (freebee), which will be poolside at the beach in the evening.

    Friday is tour day - How about daytime sightseeing from island to island on a FREE trolley that stops at the Sheridan every 30 minutes with shopping along the way? It's waiting! THEN - Friday nite it may be dinner aboard the "Love Boat of Clearwater Beach", with sightseeing from 7 to 10 P.M. on Clearwater Bay. (We are working on this now).

    Saturday will be our usual business meeting and Country Store Auction. Due to the tremendous success of the auction, we are able to underwrite the entire cost of the Early Bird Dinner, Hospitality Room, food & drinks, plus other misc. expenses. Each person remember to bring a nice gift or two for this year's auction.

    Saturday nite we plan a delicious dinner, then entertainment and awarding the CASH attendance prizes and FREE Florida lottery tickets. These could pay your way!

    Each year we gather new faces, and that is what makes these past 44 happy reunions so worthwhile. Let's make this 45th a must year for everyone. If your friends want to come, and enjoy and many have through the years, they are always welcome to enjoy the good times. Gather up the kids, grand kids, friends and neighbors - for there is fun and relaxation waiting in Florida on the Suncoast.

    You cannot afford to miss this reunion! There will be sizable CASH attendance prizes, plus FREE lottery tickets with possible winnings up to $10,000.

    Make your plans now - it is later than you think - time is running out for our group. MORE LATER - in the meantime let me know if you plan to attend. Write or call me at - 813-787-4147.

All my best to you!

*Ed Sammons*

Ed Sammons
2431 Grove Ridge Drive
Palm Harbor, Fl. 34683-3220

October 1991

Dear Friends of Co. "E",

How sweet it was at our 46th Annual Reunion at Warner-Robins, Ga. which was hosted so graciously by the Powells and Griggers.

We enjoyed an Early Bird Dinner Thursday Evening. Friday we had an exciting bus trip back to Fort Benning, where we watched parachute jump classes in the morning, a class of 537 parachute soldiers with the 24th Airborne Infantry Division graduate, lunch in a mess hall for Generals to Privates, (no C or K rations if you please), then it was out to the Harmony Church area to inspect the big Motor Pool with tanks and vehicles returned from Saudi. Quite a change since 1942!

From Fort Benning we motored to Warm Springs, Ga. to visit the Little White House of F.D.R. Very memorable and nice to see.

Friday nite was story time and raffle at the Hospitality Room. Our Saturday morning was filled with 54 gifts to auction (including the girdle), plus our usual financial meeting and vote on next year's location. We voted to go to Lake Canandaigua, New York in '92 and to Winston Salem, N.C. in '93.

Saturday evening brought a delightful southern dinner, usual speeches, door prizes, great entertainment and singing and playing by Bill & Dottie's two daughters.

All in all we had a wonderful 46th Annual Reunion and were so delighted to see some members and wives we hadn't seen in a while - like Ed & Audrey Dudley from Saratoga, Calif., Bill & Helen Karn from Columbus, Ohio, Mel & Frieda Sorensen from Kitty Hawk, N.C., plus the many widows that continue to attend and represent our deceased comrades of Co. "E" 17th Armd. Engr. Bn.

Thanks again for the good times and we look forward to doing it all over again in '92 at Lake Canandaigua, New York in September.

God Bless! and the Best of Everything to You!

Love, Ed & Bea
Ed & Bea Sammons

Co. "E" REUNION CLUB
17th Armd. Engr. Bn.
2nd Armored Division
"Hell on Wheels"

P.S. Herbie & Lorraine Barnes will celebrate their 50th Wedding Anniv. Dec. 23, 1991. Please send them a card. Their address is - 37930 Bentley Dr., Wood Dale Park, Zephrhills, Florida 33541

OCTOBER ' 93

DEAR MEMBERS & FRIENDS OF CO. "E";

HOW SWEET IT WAS - OUR 48th ANNUAL REUNION AT WINSTON SALEM !

Beautiful North Carolina, perfect weather, and those beautiful fall leaves turning all colors. Many thanks to our Hosts Pete & Opal Foy, for a wonderful 3 day happy time and all the memories. From the Early Bird Dinner Thursday evening, to the N.C. style Bar-B-Q Friday nite, to the banquet and entertainment Saturday evening.

Everyone had a good time at the Saturday auction and luncheon. George, Herbie, Joe and Louie did a great job with the two hour auction. Emily French made those beautiful large life like dolls for the raffle again. We sure appreciate all the work involved. She must have worked all year. Thanks again Emily & Everett. It was happiness to see so many of the widows of our deceased members of CO."E" in attendance this year. Keep it up girls! We love you!

Bill Karr, the Artist, painted a great scene of "Ducks On Water", and presented everyone a large lithograph rendering. Thanks Bill, we sure enjoy you and Helen at our reunions.(Bill was an original member at Benning).

Twas good to see our "Ole Sarge" - Eddie Strickland and his wife Shirley again this year. Sgt. Dempsey of "C" Co. 17th Engrs. and his wife joined us this year. Hope to see you next year. We were happy to see our Bn. Dentist, Art Marc and his lovely wife once again. Many thanks to Buzz & Rita Erstein for all the professional pictures they take each year. This year they took special groups, like all the original members of Co."E" from Benning to Berlin. Also couples of all members in attendance and the widows. We sure appreciate all your great pictures. Buzz & Rita thanks again.

Herb Barnes made his usual Saturday Nite speech, to outlast all other speakers, if possible. He did! Then there was George Masch, the non-professional waiter, who took charge at the seafood dinner and showed the other waitresses how it was done! He received lots of tip money too!

We look forward to our 49th Annual Reunion next year, at the 'Ole Hickory Inn & Lodge in Lancaster, Pa. in October. Ruth & Randy have a great program of enjoyment for us and we hope everyone will be there to enjoy all the friendship, the Pa. Dutch Food, Dinner Theatre, Outlet Shops and Sightseeing in the heart of the Pennsylvania Dutch Country. Be there to enjoy with us!

God Bless You, with the best of everything!   Be in touch!

Love, *Ed & Bea*
Ed & Bea Sammons

DEAR MEMBERS & FRIENDS OF CO. "E":

Thanks for the memories of our 49th Annual Reunion at Lancaster, Pa., and the wonderful three days provided by the Olde Hickory Inn & Resort. A double thank you - Ruth & Randy Gnau for the great job you did in providing an enjoyable time with all our comrades and friends.

We enjoyed seeing Terrence Maguire - Hdqrs. Co. the 17th Engrs., and his wife Mary. We hope they join us at Clearwater Beach in '95.

The Bar-B-Que Thursday evening was delicious and more than one could eat, plus the fresh apple cider. WOW !

The dinner theatre Friday evening was great with all the excellent Pa. Dutch food and the entertaining 2 hr. "Sugar Babes" burlesque show.

Saturday the auction was exciting (Fire Chief Diederickson bid in the "Girdle") and Bea (my wife) won her first raffle in 49 years.

At the business meeting no one volunteered to Host the 1996 reunion, (our 51st), so no plans were made.

Saturday evening brought forth a beautiful banquet with tables set with Pa. apples and colorful Pa. fall decor. We heard two wonderful speakers in Col. Brown & Capt. Jim Burt (CMH 66th A.R.). Beautiful music of the 40's was provided by Soloist Don Bechtel (Ruth's Nephew) and accompanied by Doris Stewart. Great dinner music by - Wayne Expler.

Thanks to all the wonderful widows and guests in attendance. All in all, our 49th reunion at Lancaster was one of our finest and a happy 49th time was had by everyone.

As I reported at the business meeting, plans have been made for our 50th annual reunion at the same location that everyone enjoyed so much in 1990 - Sheraton Sand Key Resort on beautiful Sand Key Island at Clearwater Beach, Fl. We also have a signed agreement for a terrific 1 hour show by a nationally known man who portrays General Patton with his aid the Colonel (his wife). More on this great show later!

Plan now, for our 50th ANNUAL CELEBRATION REUNION AT THE SHERATON SAND KEY RESORT, SEPTEMBER 28, 29, 30, 1995.

Looking forward to seeing everyone for this ONCE IN A LIFETIME very special Golden Anniversary occasion. Keep in touch!

With Love - God Bless,

Ed & Bea

Ed & Bea Sammons

10/94

50th ANNUAL REUNION
CO. "E" 17th ARMD. ENGR. BN. 2nd ARMORED DIVISION
SHERATON SAND KEY RESORT
CLEARWATER BEACH, FLORIDA SEPT. 28, 29, 30, 1995

## HOW SWEET IT WAS !

It all started Thursday with welcome time at the Hospitality Suite followed by a picnic with all the trimmings.
Friday Night was down memory lane, going back to the songs we knew in the 40's - with great music and dancing after a delicious dinner. (We still have many excellent dancers.)
Saturday Morning brought on the Financial Report, Guest Speaker, Raffle and Fun Auction. Then the freebee lunch and then it was free time again.
Saturday Evening it was dinner, speeches and then the dynamic General Patton Show - "The General Shapes up His Troops". When the General went into his act - Senior Johnny Diederickson lost his teeth while saluting the General and Ziggy Seegmuller was speechless (for the first time), while standing at attention when the General asked for reimbursement of the boat and motor he sank at Ft. Benning while building a bridge. Lorranie Barnes found out from the General how Herbie received the title, B.S. The general shaped up George Masch, thanks to his old buddy Sgt. Taylor. The General then checked out Russ Allen for a girdle. Dwight Cooper reminded the General of the time we halted our half-track to regroup on orders from the Co. Commander and along came the General, (Patton) and demanded we move forward. He banged the side of our half-track with his swagger stick and said - "MOVE IT!" We did! I was that driver.
Merlin James, the Professional, as General Patton and his wife Barbara, (Colonel and Aide) brought back many memories of our close encounters with General Patton during WWII.
The Hershey Chocolate Co., joined in the celebration and gave everyone a Hershey Chocolate Bar in remembrance of Omaha Beach and our survival kit containing among other items - a Hershey Tropical Bar.
Then Planters Peanuts wished us a happy 50th and gave everyone a can of Planters Peanuts in memory of the case of peanuts they sent me in 1943 in North Africa when we were hungry and existing on "C" rations.
Everyone enjoyed the 3 days of food and drink in the Hospitality Suite, the video of past reunions, the pictures, letters and stories plus some rare pictures of General Patton in the War Room. Pete and Opal Foy from Winston Salem won the door prize - free weekend for two at the Sheraton Sand Key Resort. We are sorry many of our members and friends were unable to be with us, especially to enjoy the great performance by the General. We hope to see each of you next year. The auction and raffle fund will, "Pave The Way", for our 51st Annual Reunion at beautiful Lake Canandaigua, New York in '96. To be Hosted by Herbie & Lorraine Barnes and Doris Stewart.

**REMEMBER '96 AT CANANDAIGUA, NEW YORK !**

Many Thanks - for a happy reunion - All our best - See you next year!

*Ed & Bea*
Ed & Bea Sammons

10/95

Co. "E" REUNION CLUB
17th Armd. Engr. Bn.
2nd Armored Division
"Hell on Wheels"

Co. "E" REUNION CLUB
17th Armd. Engr. Bn.
2nd Armored Division
"Hell on Wheels"

DEAR MEMBERS, FAMILIES AND FRIENDS :

Twas a wonderful 51st reunion on the shores of Lake Canandaigua, New York at the Inn on the Lake. The Thursday picnic, the Friday night buffet with JUBILEE MUSIC GROUP to the exciting Saturday morning fun auction. We then topped it off with a Saturday night banquet and MAGIC SHOW.

Everyone enjoyed all the interesting places to visit in the area including the wineries. We look forward to our 52nd reunion next year.

I heard that fisherman Bill Karr caught two wide-mouth bass on the lake - that might be another fish story!

The group voted to change our reunion format next year, in order to make it easier for we seniors. I am working on a 3 day hotel package at Myrtle Beach to include rooms, breakfasts and 2 theatre shows. It will also include our usual hospitality suite, fun auction and 1 banquet.

We hope to have enough in our reunion fund to pay for the hospitality and major cost of the one banquet - so that the minor cost to each of us is the discounted 3 day package. Most of the hotels of interest are close to the Airport, so those that fly will have a courtesy van available to and from the hotel.

In order to get a feel as to how many will join us at Myrtle Beach in September or October '97, I am enclosing a form to be completed and returned to me **NOW** - before I reach an agreement with a hotel. On talking with some of the hotels we would desire, I find a few are booked for Sept.& Oct.'97, so I need your input as soon as possible!

I extend a special invitation to all you widows, members and friends that haven't joined us recently, to come and enjoy the people on canes and bring your wheelchair and join the fun!

KEEP ME INFORMED - MAIL THE INFORMATION TODAY!

All our best,

Ed & Bea

Ed and Bea
9/96

November 4, 1997

Dear Co."E" Members, Family & Friends;

    Thanks for making our 52nd Annual Reunion at Myrtle Beach a happy and enjoyable "Last Hurrah" cake, food, shows and friendship event. It has been an interesting and enjoyable 52 year journey with my wartime buddies, meeting, talking and remembering them each year as we travelled from Washington, D.C., to Va., to Pa., to Conn., to N.Y., to Nebraska, to Ga., to Carolina and Florida. I have a fond memory of each reunion. It all started one day in the Spring of 1946, when Bea and I visited with my buddy Charlie Gnau and wife Ruth. We looked at the Co."E" Roster I had from the war and decided to try to reach a few of the nearby fellows for a get-together to celebrate our return to civilian life.

    We held our first reunion on Labor Day Weekend in '46 at the hotel Hamilton in Washington, D.C. How great it was! It was then on to the World's Fair in New York in '64. It was Washington, D.C. again in '65, saluted in '65 by personal thank you letters from President Harry Truman and General Dwight Eisenhower. On to Gettysburg in '75, Disney World in '85, saluted again in '85 by a personal letter of thanks from President Ronald Reagan. In '95 it was Sand Key Island in Florida and a personal letter of thanks from President Bill Clinton, plus all the fun locations in between.

    We also endured the passing of many of our fellow soldiers and friends which was always difficult for our group. I feel they have been looking in on us and saying - well done. We are part of the "Passing Parade" in the history of men fighting for freedom. It is now time to pass this on to the next generation.

    We shall always be a part of military history as evidenced by the historic monument dedicated to the men of the 2nd Armored Division, along side General George Washington at Valley Forge. We plan to donate the balance of our reunion fund to the perpetual care of this beautiful monument that was dedicated in 1981. When in the area - stop and see a part of military history dedicated to you and your loved ones.

    I could write a book of all the characters and happy times we have shared together. Thanks for the memories - it has been a wonderful journey and as General MacArthur said in his farewell, "Old Soldiers Never Die They Just Fade Away". We plan to have mini-reunions as often as possible and meet for a weekend at a central location. May God Bless You!

Keep in touch!

Love Always,

*Ed & Bea*
Ed & Bea Sammons

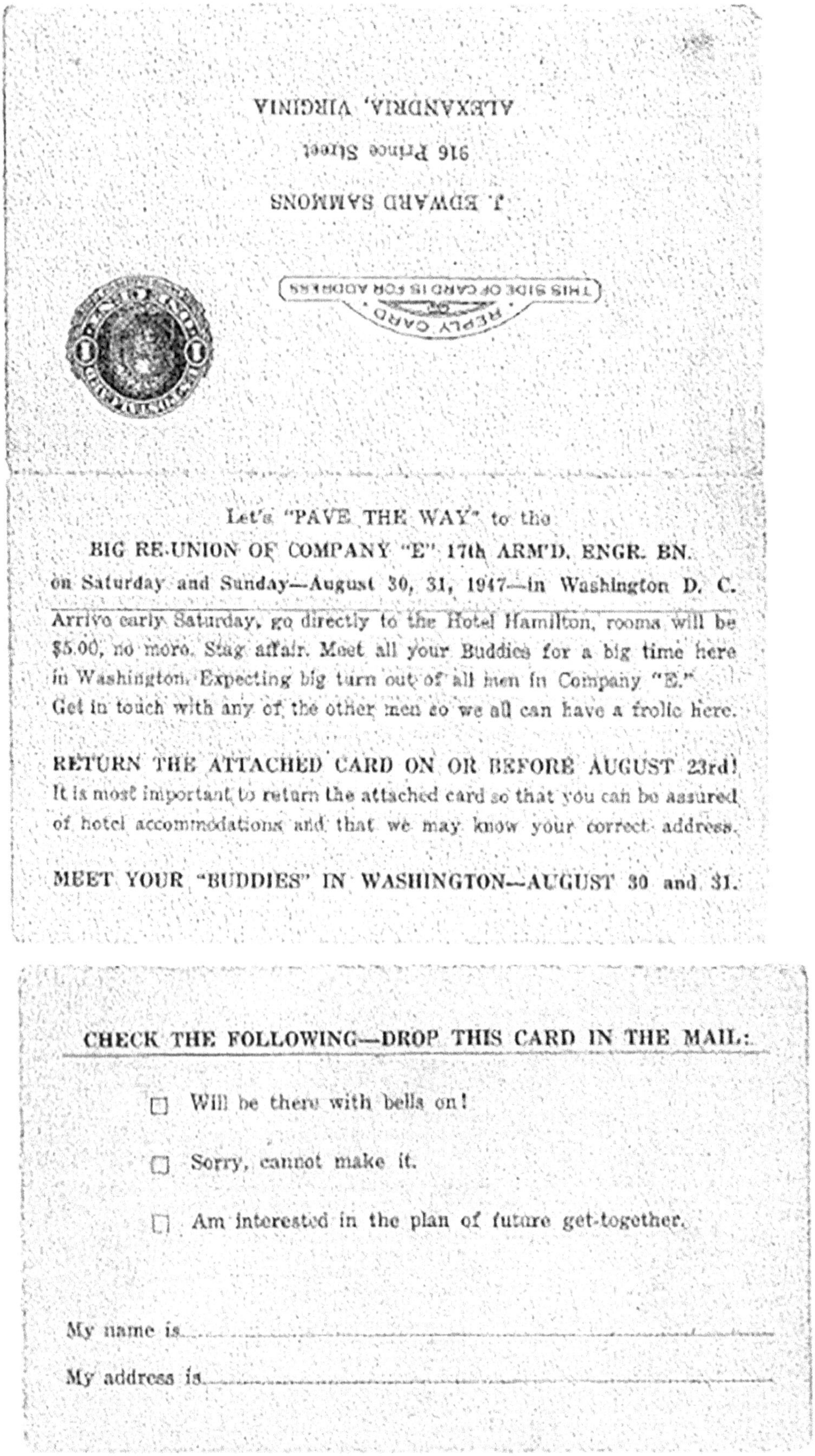

J. EDWARD SAMMONS

916 Prince Street

ALEXANDRIA, VIRGINIA

Let's "PAVE THE WAY" to the
BIG RE-UNION OF COMPANY "E" 17th ARM'D. ENGR. BN.
on Saturday and Sunday—August 30, 31, 1947—in Washington D. C.

Arrive early Saturday, go directly to the Hotel Hamilton, rooms will be $5.00, no more. Stag affair. Meet all your Buddies for a big time here in Washington. Expecting big turn out of all men in Company "E." Get in touch with any of the other men so we all can have a frolic here.

RETURN THE ATTACHED CARD ON OR BEFORE AUGUST 23rd!
It is most important to return the attached card so that you can be assured of hotel accommodations and that we may know your correct address.

MEET YOUR "BUDDIES" IN WASHINGTON—AUGUST 30 and 31.

---

CHECK THE FOLLOWING—DROP THIS CARD IN THE MAIL:

☐ Will be there with bells on!

☐ Sorry, cannot make it.

☐ Am interested in the plan of future get-together.

My name is............................................................

My address is..........................................................

Figure 29 Original Re-Union Card, 1947

## REUNIONS - 1946 - 1997

Charlie Gnau and I held our first reunion on Labor Day Weekend of 1946, at the Hamilton Hotel in Washington, D.C. with 8 men in attendance. We played poker, shot crap, drank beer, booze and talked a lot about our war experiences and returning home. We repeated this reunion again in 1947 at the same location with 14 men in attendance. In 1948 the wives and families joined us, which increased our attendance and began to insure our future reunions. In the fifties our reunions slowed a bit as everyone was busy raising families. At each reunion two fellows, usually George Whisenant and Harry (Curly) White were detailed to purchase two 30 gallon garbage cans from the nearest hardware store and keep them filled with beer and ice for the weekend. We would sit by the pool at night through the wee hours consuming cold beer and coke with a lot of conversation. We had reunions by Charlie Gnau in Pa., Art Sigrist in New Jersey, Eddie Strickland, Mac Atkins, Harry Young, and John Coughlin in Virginia. George Whisenant, T.A. Walker and Noel Whittington in North Carolina. Harry (Curly) White twice in Delaware. The 1964 reunion was Hosted by Harry and Lil Kuppersmith with a large turn-out. We attended the New York World's Fair and had a wonderful time. In 1965 Ed and Bea Sammons continued Hosting the annual reunions every five years through 1997 at many locations. In the seventies we had happy reunions thanks to Harry (Curly) White, James (Big Emma) Turner, T.A. Walker, Pete Foy, Jack Rico, Leo Mecler, Al (Curly) Provenzano, Walt STewart, Joe Pfeifer and Ed Sammons. We celebrated our 25th Annual Reunion again in Washington, D.C., our 30th in Gettysburg, Pa. My buddy of 59 years, George Masch, has been a great worker and joy at each reunion and a Trustee of our Reunion Club.

In the eighties we celebrated our 40th annual reunion at Walt Disney World in Orlando, then Niagara Falls with Walt and Doris Stewart, Spencer, Nebraska again and Herbie Barnes in Canadaigua, New York several times. Charlie Powell had a great reunion at Warner-Robbins, Ga. and Ed Sammons at Clearwater Beach, Florida for our 45th celebration. In the nineties it was Herbie Barnes in New York, Pete Foy in Winston Salem, N.C., Ruth and Randy Gnau in Pa. and Ed and Bea Sammons for our 50th at Clearwater Beach, Florida. At our banquet each year we had many Guest Speakers, including Col. Lewis W. Correll, Battalion Commander, Capt. Peter J. Zukow, Company Commander and Capt. Jim Burt, Congressional Medal of Honor recipient and Ed Sammons.

For further information of my war adventures and reunions listen to the 80 minute cassette tape of 1978. " War as I knew it ".

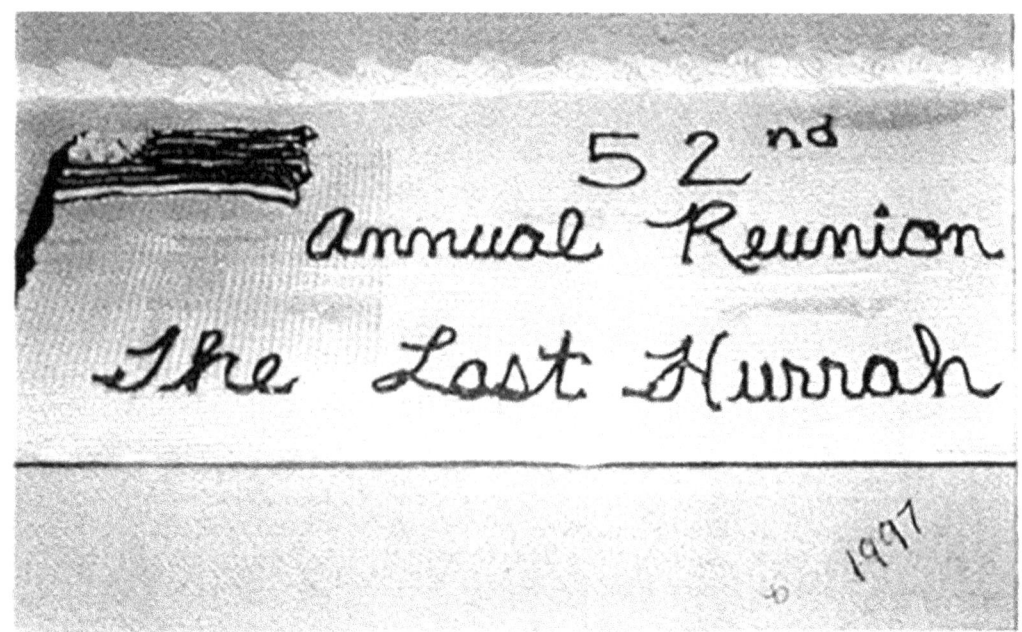

SPECIAL CAKE - FINAL ANNUAL REUNION MYRTLE BEACH, S. CAROLINA OCT. 1997

BELOW : FINAL ANNUAL REUNION MYRTLE BEACH, S. CAROLINA OCT. 1997
L/R CHARLIE POWELL, AL PROVENZANO, HERBIE BARNES, ED SAMMONS, CHARLES JACKSON, RUSS ALLEN

Figure 31 The Last Hurrah

HARRY S TRUMAN
INDEPENDENCE, MISSOURI

June 16, 1965

Dear Mr. Sammons:

Thank you for your invitation to Mrs. Truman and me to attend the Banquet on September 4, in Bethesda, Maryland, of Company E, 17th Armored Engineer Battalion of the 2nd Armored (Hell on Wheels) Division - during the Annual Reunion.

We appreciate the invitation most highly and sincerely wish we could be present but my schedule at that time prevents a trip to Washington. I am as sorry as I can be.

You have my best wishes for a big turn-out and a very happy reunion.

Sincerely yours,

Harry Truman

Mr. J. Edward Sammons, Chairman
Annual Reunion, Company E, 17th Armored
Engineer Battalion of the 2nd Armored Division
9514 Edgeley Road
Bethesda, Maryland 20014

OFFICE OF
DWIGHT D. EISENHOWER

Gettysburg, Pennsylvania
9 June 1965

Dear Mr. Sammons:

I have been directed to respond to your cordial letter, inviting General and Mrs. Eisenhower to attend the banquet of Company E, 17th Armored Engineer Battalion of the 2nd Armored Division in Bethesda on Saturday, September 4th.

I regret to advise you that they will be unable to accept your kind invitation as they are planning some extended trips during and surrounding the time of your celebration. I am sorry.

Nonetheless, General and Mrs. Eisenhower appreciate your thought of them and extend their very best wishes for an enjoyable and successful reunion.

Sincerely,

Robert L. Schulz

ROBERT L. SCHULZ
Brig. Gen. U.S.A. Ret.
Executive Assistant

Mr. J. Edward Sammons
9514 Edgeley Road
Bethesda, Maryland 20014

THE WHITE HOUSE

WASHINGTON

October 15, 1985

I am pleased and honored to send warm greetings to the officers and enlisted men of Company E, 17th Armored Engineer Battalion as you gather for your 40th reunion.

Throughout its involvement in World War II, your unit rallied to the cause of freedom with honor and distinction. You made a vital contribution to our final victory. I join all Americans in recognizing you and in paying tribute to the extraordinary service that you and your departed comrades rendered to flag and country.

Nancy and I salute you and send our best wishes for a happy and memorable 40th reunion. God bless you.

*Ronald Reagan*

THE WHITE HOUSE
WASHINGTON

September 12, 1995

Greetings to the veterans of Company E, 17th Armored Engineers, 2nd Armored Division, as you gather for your fiftieth annual reunion.

Your unit served the United States with honor and distinction during a crucial period in our history. We owe our liberties to the sacrifices of people who, like you, were willing to risk their lives for freedom. I know you join me in honoring your fallen comrades.

Each of you embodies the pride, professionalism, and accomplishment that make the United States Army one of the finest fighting forces the world has ever known. I salute you for your distinguished record of service, and I hope that you will enjoy your time together as you reflect on the bonds you share.

Best wishes for a memorable reunion.

*Bill Clinton*

# SIDEKICKS

### RANKS ARE THINNING IN THE VETERANS
### " PASSING PARADE "

One need look no further than the obituary pages of our nation's newspapers to see the " Passing Parade ". Our names are preceded by the replicas of the tiny Stars and Stripes.

We stormed the beaches at Sicily, Normandy, Iwo Jima, Anzio and other unpronounceable places around the world. We endured the cold "White Hell" of the Bulge in Belgium, chased the "Desert Fox" (Rommel) across the burning sands of the North African Desert and faced the blazing guns of enemy warships.

Yes, we were part of the " Passing Parade " of generations of American Military men and women who manned the ramparts to keep our country free; more will follow. Their ranks are thinning. Membership in their proud wartime fighting units have declined to the point that " Last Man " clubs have been established - - - fewer and fewer are there to answer - " Here " at annual reunions.

When we were young, an older generation told us - " We leave you a free and bountiful country. Die if you must, but keep it free ". We did what was asked of us, we fought for our freedom, and we kept it free.

Now, we ask of a younger generations of Americans - - " We leave you a free and prosperous country, if the need arises - - will you step forward to carry the torch of freedom ? Will you keep yourselves physically fit, morally strong and mentally alert to defend this freedom ? Or will you, in your pursuit of material things lose the value and true meaning of freedom ? Remember the words of Jefferson; " Material abundance without character is the surest way to destruction ".

BY FRANK HAILEY

Ed Sammons   8/97

COPY
#BROCHURE

Oct. 31, 2007

Dear Merle,

Thanks for the nice letter & picture of the cute boys. I know you and Dennis really enjoy them. The Sammons & Wilroys all had blue eyes. So what goes around - comes around. I remember London -

After the fighting in North Africa and Sicily we landed at LIverpool 2 weeks before Xmas 1943 and were stationed at Tidworth Barracks on the Salisbury Plain about 100 miles from London. The brick barracks at Tidworth were two floors high with 30 men on each floor, only heat was an old fireplace, bunk beds with straw mattress, 6 toilets and 6 wash basins - no showers. These barracks were built before WW I. This was like the Waldorf-Astoria compared to the next 2 yrs. after D Day. It was all down hilly. They had an old theatre at Tidworth and we were entertained by the great James Cagney and his Yankee-Doodle Show.

I had a weeks gun training shooting down air targets over the White Cliffs of Dover at gunnery school and qualified as expert gunner. We were given in groups of 6 R&R in London for six days. We stayed at the Reed Hotel near Picadilly Square and rode the thrilling subways to the end of each line (about 20 miles) and explored the town for food. For 2.00 I hired a London Cab (2 Pass.) their gas ration was 1 gal per day and you saw many along the way out of gas. The cab took us to all the historic places plus London China Town, where we saw a small building and the driver said 64 chinese live in the small bldg.

Four days after we checked out of the Reed Hotel a HItler bomb went down the elevator shaft. - Lucky again. We later went back to London and built a bridge across the Thames River for practice before the D Day invasion.

This is just one of the many events of my 4½ yrs of war.

All the best to you and family

Love, Uncle Ed

Ed

## AMERICAN RED CROSS
## 62 YEARS LATE

In my book "Grampa's War" I wrote several years ago, I told of during the Battle of the Bulge in January 1945 when I was up to my knees in ice and snow in 10 degree weather and a Red Cross truck offered me coffee and a donut for a dime. I did not have a dime and will never forget that day, as I was hungry, cold and war weary. Those who read about this incident in my book found it hard to believe the American Red Cross charged a dime for a coffee & donut to a fighting soldier in the Battle of the Bulge.

Now its confirmed - On this veterans day 2007, the American Red Cross has finally apologized for their money greed on soldiers that fought, died and saved our freedom by giving free donuts at the National D Day Memorial in Washington, D.C.

During our race from Omaha Beach by way of the battle at Saint Lo, Falaise Gap, bridge over the Seine, battle at each town across France, to being the first allied soldiers to free Belgium, bridge the Albert Canal, battle at Maastricht, to the freezing white cold at the battle of the bulge, battle at Aachen, to fighting our way onto Hitler's sacred Homeland, cracking the Siegfried Line and fighting to bridge our infantry and tanks across the Rhine.

All this and a G.I. would ask you for a dime - to buy an American Red Cross coffee & donut - to hear him say :

" Thanks you just contributed a dime to a yank that crossed
the Rhine - don't be an ass and begin to whine -
get your dime like I got mine "

I find it hard to accept this too late apology.

Ed Sammons
Co."E" 17th Armd. Combat Engr. Bn.
U.S. 2nd Armored Division 1944 - 1945

Dec. 7, 2009

Dear Ruth,

Thanks for your card and glad to know you were with friends on Thanksgiving.

I will try to explain the setup of Co. "E" ----

We were trained as Engineer and Infantry soldiers - no rivers to cross - no bridges to build we fought as Infantry - that is Co."E" command halftrack - along with 17th Engr Bn line companies (A.B.C.D.) of halftracks fought as Infantry. We brought up the Bridge Platoons as needed. This is the way we travelled from Benning to Berlin. Charlie and I were together all the way but different duties. I was up front with Command Halftrack and Charlie was in supply. I was sent to Radio Command School at Fort Knox, Ky. 6hrs a day, 6 days a week for 4 months and graduated in Aug. '41 as expert Morse Code Operator sending and receiving coded messages among 17th Engr Co. Commanders and Col. Correll at Bn. Hdqtrs. We had radio silence when the Germans were listening. Motorcycle messages were then delivered by Harry Young and George Hedges.

### ORDER OF SERVICE

COMPANY COMMAND: Capt. McAdams - Cooper - Sammons - Ellis - Boland
1st BRIDGE PLATOON: Lt. Coen - Strickland - Scruggs - T.A. Walker
2nd BRIDGE PLATOON: Lt. Thompson - Turner - G. Walker - Althouse
ENGR. SECTION: Lt. Coughlin - Raynor - Dudley - G. Miller - Bastile
KITCHEN TRUCKS: Worley - Hazen - Stewart - Tyson - Mecler Cannady
SUPPLY TRUCKS: Purtick - Gnau - Kuppersmith - Dodge
MAINT. MECHANICS: Taylor - Wiegman - Masch - Graham
MOTORCYCLE RIDERS: Young - Hedges

### 2nd ARMORED DIVISION – ORDER OF CASUALTIES
7089 - Killed - Wounded - Captured

\# 1 41st Infantry Regiment      \# 2 66th Light Tanks (Burt's Brigade)

\# 3 67th Medium Tank Bn.        \# 4 68th Heavy Tank Bn. and
                                     702nd Tank Destroyer Bn.

\# 5 17th Engr. bn.              \# 6 82nd Recon. Bn. (Spies & Scouts)

\# 7 14th - 78th - 92nd Field Artillery Bns.

\# 8 48th Medical Bn.

## WHEN I'M EIGHTY FOUR

Dear Lord, thanks to you I'm here at 84
There is much more I would like to explore
Unwrap each day like a precious gift from above
Enjoy each moment of his eternal love

I hope you let me live to 85 and endure the
never ending tide, into the sunset on Angels
Wings I would ride

This world is in a terrible fix
Let me stay and pray at 86

Bea is waiting for me in Heaven
I'm not sure I'm ready at 87

My move is slow and sometimes late
Let me be around at 88

I remember the happiness of family;
Ole' friends, the great depression, war & peace
It will be a great day at 89 if Bea I meet

When I reach 90 I will be glad
I will tell the things I remember as a lad
Model-T, Atwater-Kent, Amos & Andy, Maggie & Jiggs,
Ball-Point-Pen, Man-On-The-Moon, & sting of battle

At 91 I have told you things that number only seven
I just may be ready for the Golden Gate in Heaven

This world is not my home, I'm just passing thru
I hope to be around at 92

They say I'm just a pup and that may be true
I'll tell you about it at 102 - - Well-Maybe ?

Ed Sammons
9/12/03

ED SAMMONS
EIGHTY SIX YEARS YOUNG
9/12/05

This reminds me of the road I travelled from Benning to Berlin

## WE'VE DONE OUR HITCH IN HELL

I've been sitting here and thinking of the things I left behind
I'd hate to put on paper what is running through my mind
We've dug a thousand fox holes & liberated miles of enemy ground
A meaner place this side of hell is waiting to be found
But there's one consolation listen closely while I tell
When we die we'll go to heaven for we've done our hitch in hell
We've cleaned a thousand kitchens for the cooks to stew our beans
We've stood a hundred guard mounts & scrubbed the camp's latrines
We've washed a thousand mess kits and peeled a million spuds
We've rolled a hundred bed rolls and washed our dirty duds
The number of parades we've stood is very hard to tell
We won't parade in heaven for we've done our hitch in hell
We've picked up trash, butts & matches in our only Sunday pants
We've been bitten by mosquitoes and even flying ants
When our work on earth is done our friends behind will tell
They died & went to heaven for they did their hitch in hell
And when life's work is ended and we lay aside life's cares
We'll do our last parade up those golden shining stairs
The Angels all will welcome us and the harps will begin to play
We'll draw a million canteen books and spend them in a day
It is then we'll hear St. Peter say with a loud & husky yell ---
Take a front seat soldiers you've done your hitch in hell
G.I. Unknown

## I REMEMBER

Thank the LORD I'm here at 88
A little closer to heavens gate
I hope to live to 108
Hope is like the clouds in the sky
Some bring rain - others pass you by
Life is roaring down the way
I must do my best for another day

I remember Herbert Hoover & the great depression
Wearing Hoover badges on our pants was our expression
I remember Grampa and his life so grand
Gramma 8 children & beautiful Virginia farming land

My cousin Hilda is happy at 105
I can make it - - maybe 95
Life was great when I was eight
I learned my ABC's and to roller skate

Dixie Cream Donut Shoppe we loved so well
3 million donuts we did sell
Is another story yet to tell
As you travel down life's highway
and strive to reach your goal
Keep your eye upon the donut and not upon the hole

I have been put out to pasture to think and pray
To live with great memories each golden day
I have a great family I love each day
They make me so happy I must stay

Yesterday is gone
Tomorrow may never come
So I must enjoy this moment called Today


Ed Sammons
9/12/07

```
ALTAR  OF  BATTLES
2nd ARMORED DIVISION WWII
FREEDOMS FOUNDATION VALLEY FORGE, PA.
DEDICATED JULY 1981
FOUGHT IN - FRENCH MOROCCO, SICILY, OMAHA BEACH NORMANDY,
     FRANCE, BELGIUM, NETHERLANDS AND GERMANY
TRAVELED THRU - ALGERIA, TUNISIA AND ENGLAND
INVASIONS - NORTH AFRICA, SICILY AND OMAHA BEACH, NORMANDY
CAMPAIGNS - NORTH AFRICA, SICILY, NORMANDY, NORTHERN FRANCE,
     ARDENNES, RHINELAND AND CENTRAL EUROPE
```

```
THIS IS A BRIEF SUMMARY AND PICTURE OF THE ALTAR OF BATTLES AT VALLEY
FORGE. THE FLOOR IS MADE OF LARGE STONES FROM AND WITH NAMES OF EACH
STATE AND COUNTRY WE TRAVELED THRU FROM BENNING TO BERLIN. FROM THE
ALTAR THE LONG APPROACH WALKWAY HAS A BRASS PLAQUE ON EACH STEP NAMING
EACH BATTALION AND REGIMENT IN ORDER OF BATTLE CASUALTIES. THERE IS
A TREE PLANTED IN MEMORY OF EACH CONGRESSIONAL MEDAL OF HONOR RECEIPIENT.
THIS MEMORIAL IS A PERMANENT REMINDER TO FUTURE GENERATIONS AND A TRIBUTE
TO THOSE BRAVE MEN THAT GAVE THEIR ALL FOR FREEDOM. Co."E" REUNION CLUB
DONATED THE REMAINING REUNION FUND TO THIS HISTORIC MEMORIAL FOR PERPETUAL
CARE.   ED SAMMONS 1/98
```

Figure 32 Altar of Battles

Chapter VII | 123

Figure 33

**THE END GRAMPA'S WAR**

# PATTON'S HAND OF GOD

Figure 34 Sammons Family

The Hand of God surrounded many Soldiers during WWII especially those of the 17th Battalion, Co. E 2nd Armored Division under the training of General George S. Patton. These were a unique unit that was carefully selected and known as "Patton's Boy's". The men that "Paved the Way" to our freedoms we hold dear today. Going ahead of troops the brave men demolished and built roads and bridges in record time to get our troops to advance and win the battle with Hittler. These men were given one of the highest citations in WWII by President Truman for their outstanding commitment and record time building a bridge in just 7 hours to defeat the enemy.

**J. E. was one of these men—my dad and an American hero.**

# PART 1: MY HAND

## America's Great Depression

Figure 35 J.E.'s smiling face again with his sister Delane, Father, Mother, and Aunt Josephine

Discover a small-town boy, living in a small house and his large world of adventures in the 1920's and 1930's. J.E. gives humorous and vivid accounts of his childhood experiences, family, and friends.

Uncovering the discoveries and making of a real American hero. Go from his childhood scuffed boots to his worn-out boots as a soldier. These soles carried him through his missions of paving the way for the freedoms we hold today.

### Life As a Boy in Virginia

I know I probably painted a very bleak picture of America during the Great Depression, and how the Dust Bowl affected so much of the country's migration towards many of the larger cities during the 1930s, but, as you will see, weathering the storm of living through that historical period in time, as kids you remember that "special place"— the city we grew up in.

That special place, in one of those cities was Newport News, which provided the "growing up on the peninsula" for not only James Edward Sammons, "J.E." but also for other neighborhood kids such as Pearl Bailey, Ella Fitzgerald, and Ava Gardner.

Adding one more to the future famous bunch of kids, J.E. even had a cousin named Peggy— Peggy Hopkins Joyce. A starlet during the "Roaring Twenties, owning a glamorous flamboyant style. She was one of Charlie Chaplin's girls, and in Hollywood's inner circle of the famed "Roaring 20's" Hopefully soon, we will have Rita Sammons Harrell, provide us with her upcoming book, "Cousin Peggy", and reveal more of a true insight of what a "modern woman stuck in the past" had to endure to be as free, as women strive for to be today, a lay to rest the untruths, gossip, and misinformation of what already had been written about her family member.

It's only fitting that we start with a summary of recollections that J.E. vividly mapped out, of his early life growing up on the peninsula. Born over a century ago, on September 12th, 1919, these childhood memories were brought back to life during an interview conducted by columnist Parke Rouse of the Newport News Daily Press. Through each brief verbal comment that J.E. made during the interview, we can close our eyes and vividly imagine being there, in that sprawling Newport News during the 1920s and 1930s.

So, let's take a ride back in time, of these important recalls of memory flashes that remained so affectionately preserved in our Local American Hero, heartfelt memorable moments involving some the most noteworthy inhabitants of Newport News, while "Growing up on the Peninsula".

## GROWING UP ON THE PENINSULA

As I continue to be marveled by J.E. Sammons, an individual that had gone through the most intensive WWII battle campaigns in Europe, and having the ability, after so many years, to recall the most intimate of the sounds and smells of childhood, especially the Anderson cows' "Moos", the clatter of bottles, and the freshly milked sweet smell being delivered daily, so vividly described.

It was growing up on Jefferson Avenue in the 1930s that gave our young James Edward Sammons the chance to hear Cab Calloway, Lionel Hampton and other famous black musicians who seemed to flock towards Newport News, seemingly attracting these musical stars like a magnet, probably the best of jazz's talent, performing daily at the Dixie Theatre at Jefferson and 18th Street. He would fondly say during the interview that it wasn't only a childhood interest, but also a daring risk to chance, crossing from his predominantly white neighborhood section into that part of the city commonly known as "the blood fields". A label that needed no explanation due to the high crime rate, but also a section that boasted of other childhood neighbors of J.E., that grew up to be icons of America's rich musical talent… Pearl Bailey and Ella Fitzgerald.

It was during this interview, while recently retired and living with his family at Palm Harbor, Florida, that J.E. started opening his "letters and notes", written so long ago, with the intentions of completing a book to leave for his family, to remember him by the many experiences he seemed to have survived, but also how the fruits of those sacrifices made life so worthwhile to have lived.

He started the interview by opening up a letter, recalling his favorite hangout as a youth, which was Tony Koskino's Drugstore at 28th and Jefferson, where neighbor kids hung out. They were referred to as the "drugstore cowboys", and J.E. was seemingly proud of the notoriety that was attached to their kid group's name, as he continued the interview, but suddenly visually referring to a sudden flashback, much more forward in time, alluding from that sense of security we all seem to enjoy when we are kids, without a care in the world, to suddenly be thrust into a hell…with no beginning nor end, but knowing that if you didn't move forward, you would become part of the blood filled sand, soaking up a forgotten part in man's history, when the world's balance of good vs. evil, tipped ever so dangerously in peril.

J.E. was among the troops who landed early on Omaha Beach in the Allied invasion of France.

J.E. also mentions during the interview that he was born a few blocks from where singer Pearl Bailey was born, and roughly the same year in time as the famed "drugstore cowboys." You can almost hear the clop-clopping figure slowly approaching creating a dust filled cloud on every clopping sound made by Dr. Thomas Sims' horse and buggy, with absolutely no traffic in the day. He was heading to a dark-red brick row house at 2814 Jefferson to deliver J.E., on a fairly sunny Friday afternoon, the twelfth day of September 1919. Looking at it today, on Google the row house is still partly standing, but much else has changed.

J.E.'s letter seems to touch so many familiar subjects during that interview by the Daily Press reporter, and are "singular quote" that most of them, for those who recall the buildup years to World War II here on the Peninsula, it will seem very familiar.

**And, for those that might not know exactly what is meant by "the peninsula", well, it's simply this:**

*"We went fishing on Pier A and the Warwick Machine pier, catching mostly eels and toadfish. We went clamming in Hampton Roads, off Stuart Gardens, when it was the Old Dominion golf course. We sold the clams in the East End for 25 cents per dozen. We went crabbing at the Boat Harbor and bought crabmeat at Richardson's Crab House for 50 cents a pound.*

*I remember climbing the cliffs at the casino grounds, pretending we were Tom Mix, Hoot Gibson or Buck Jones after Saturday afternoon at the Olympic (later the James), watching the cowboys while eating a pound bag of peanut butter kisses we had bought for 10 cents across the street at Woolworth's.*

*I remember when they built the Paramount Theater and the pleasure of watching Gladys Lyle at the console of the mighty Hammond come up through the floor, playing beautiful music between movies. The Palace Theatre was owned by the Gordon brothers and had the best movies in town. For them, I hand-delivered movie flyers to half of Newport News to get a pass to see a movie. The first radio station in town was WGH. It was located between 28th and 29th streets on Washington, on the second floor. We climbed the long steps many times to see a man talk into a mike in a closed room with glass windows and a sign, "On the Air."*

*I remember the Great Depression of the '30s and how I worked at the A and P; on Jefferson each Friday after school till 9 and all-day Saturday for $2. Then I found a better job: Leon Boyd's Barber Shop. He said if I would build my own shoeshine stand and run all their errands, sweep and mop the floor each day, I could keep all the earnings from shining shoes at five cents a pair. On a good Saturday I would earn more than a buck, including tips.*

*I remember when a man named Hooper who lived in the East End was known as 'Walking Hooper.' Every weekend we would rush out to the 28th Street bridge to watch him. He claimed he walked the CandO; tracks to Richmond and back each weekend for his health. I remember when the First National Bank at 28th and Washington was the tallest building on the Peninsula.*

*Each summer my mother would take us three kids down to the CandO; Pier and catch the steamer Virginia to Norfolk. Then we would go on to Suffolk on the Edgerton Bus Line to my grandfather's farm and fish and crab every day in the Nansemond River.*

*I remember one story they used to tell between the First Baptist and Trinity Methodist churches on 29th Street. One Sunday Trinity was singing 'Will There Be Any Stars in my Crown?' and at the same time First Baptist was singing, 'No, Not One.' Once, I remember, the Rev. Mordecai Ham had a revival one summer on the casino and we had a bad rainstorm that blew his tent down three times in four days. He packed up and left town. Mr. and Mrs. Anderson operated a dairy in the 600 block of 29th Street, and behind their home they had a shed and two milk cows. (Heard the moo every day). Mrs. Anderson milked the two cows twice a day and he delivered the raw milk in bottles around our neighborhood. Whenever we kids walked by their house, we went 'moo.'*

*Who could forget Newport News High basketball coach Julie Conn and football coach Mike Byrne? I caddied at the Old Dominion course once for the pro, Jack Isaac, and watched another pro named Bobby Cruikshank play. I attended high school with Ava Gardner.*

*I recall the day they completed the James River Bridge. They had a grand opening, and cars could go over and back free. What a thrill. Dad and Wilroy got out the ole '24 Chevy and we waited to cross over and back, an all-day trip.*

*I recall the Yorktown Sesquicentennial and listening to President Hoover. My brother, Wilroy, and a couple of his friends were busy seating the then governor of New York, Franklin D. Roosevelt.*

*I remember the night Bruno Hauptmann was executed. As a newsboy, after waiting for hours at the loading dock of the Daily Press on 25th Street, I walked up and down Washington Avenue between the streetcar tracks, selling the extra for five cents.*

*When I came home from the war in 1945, I saw barbed wire enclosures on Mercury Boulevard near the James River bridge. The prisoners of war looked like some of the Germans we had captured in North Africa in 1943.*

With that, Ed Sammons' recollections end. He keeps up with Newport News through a niece in Hilton, the daughter of his brother Wilroy, who sends him clippings of this column. He says he still loves this "busy little city in Tidewater." A lot of people do.

Figure 36 We

*Time has not forgotten*

*Those faces of hardships and laughter Family of love and faith of hereafter Farm work for a small-town boy*

*Began his strength when he was deployed*

*In a place of shipbuilders and jazz singers who became renown Famous untold stories held in memories to now sound*

*Life then was grand just loving one another*

*As his big sister Delane took care of baby brother James Edward referred to his family as "WE"*

*His ability to characterize and remember lost moments we can all now see This courageous and comforting man*

*That would always lend his encouraging*

# THE DRUGSTORE COWBOYS

Figure 37 Drugstore Cowboys

Meet the Drugstore Cowboys hanging out with their friends at Tony Koskino's Drugstore and listen to many baseball games as they played over and over the Yankees and Washington Senators. Also getting the name from many watched silent movies of Tom Mix cowboy and jumping off trapped doors. A laugh from Dad was always about his older brother Wilroy jumping over a fence and ripping his pants. From then on they all called him "Rip Sammons". The discovery of radio was mostly static. Dad's first exposure to Radio was KDKA Pittsburgh and WLW Cincinnati. These Cowboys would climb the long dark wooden stairs to see a man in a glass enclosed room with a large microphone hanging from the ceiling and a sign that read: "Quiet On Air". Later this interest plays a vital role later in his Army life.
—**Rita Sammons Harrell**

A picture on a pony was the trend in those days, so up on the pony instead of saying cheese. Parents all were fascinated by a cowboy scene. Wilroy ready to steer holding the horse, J.E. upon the mane and held by hand on shoulder sister Delane.

# "NOW I LAY ME DOWN TO SLEEP... I PRAY THE LORD..."

Figure 38 J. E.'s boyhood wall hanging

"I pray the Lord my soul to keep". A family prayer said each night on bended knee. Dad felt blessed to have so little yet felt so much. A small sheet metal gas stove and some electric lights hanging from the ceiling in a small row house flat. The furnishings were poor, a mix of wood crates, scrap boards, and trashed furniture. Dad never felt deprived with such an abundance of family love. His older brother Wilroy and sister Delane referred to Dad as their "baby brother". I would hear that greeting for years to come whenever we all got together. The Great Depression made quite an impression on the important things in life.

—**Rita Sammons Harrell**

## Boyhood wall hanging

*Home The Place Where We Are Treated Best and Grumble Less*...this childhood boy-made plaque hung on dad's wall until he left for service. This was the core of faith and love his Newport News family instilled in him and he would recite to us at times...I never knew where it came from until I found it.

Figure 39 Sammons Family

Sammons Family, dressed with Sunday's best. A day when families would picnic and eat together with cousins. These were the times when J.E. remembered his dad in the summertime after Sunday school and church bringing out the wooden tub with the hand crank and spindle on the back porch. Mom would fill the tub with ice cream ingredients, Dad would pack the ice and start cranking and cranking until it became frozen.

Smiling Dad, eating homemade Sunday cookies with his happy family....Dad would always speak so kindly and lovingly of his mother, father big brother, Wilroy and big sister, Delane. Dad would always refer to his dad as a "great marine," and Daisy, his mom, as the household strength that would say prayers with him at night.

# GRAMPA'S FARM ON THE NANSEMOND RIVER

## Steamboat Farmer

GRAMPA Wilroy's Farm is where J.E. and his family all moved to during the "Great Depression." During this time farming the crops were in demand and the Riverboat would take these crops of vegetables, produce and seafood up the river to distribute in many cities and towns. Living in the city of Newport News with the industrial shipbuilding and many shops and stores and then moving to a lifestyle of plowing and seeding, became humbling for J.E. — he was so thankful and grateful. Dad liked fishing, but never liked eating the fish. His favorite was peanut picking rather than shining shoes. Lessons of the land quickly learned by J.E from relocating to GRAMPA's farm during the "Great Depression." Plenty of wild turkeys, potatoes, spinach, squash, sweet corn, green beans, and watermelons J.E. help to load on the boats to Baltimore from the Nansemond River. Later J.E. recognizes the value of this experience that proves to be crucial to his wartime survival.

## Pier A in Newport News & the Nansemond Ferry

Where young J.E. would come with his brother to drop off produce to market on other boats to ports up the Nansemond River and take the Nansemond Ferry Boat to GRAMPA's Farm from Newport News, VA.

# MOVIE STARS

Great Stars and Jazz singers were born or raised in Newport News. Pearl Bailey and Ella Fitzgerald were born just blocks from Dad's birthplace. The famous Dixie Theatre where many famous jazz musicians played.

Dad always looked up to his older brother Wilroy who Dad recalled the Yorktown Sesquicentennial and listening to President Hoover while Wilroy and friends were seating then Governor Franklin D. Roosevelt.

**—Rita Sammons Harrell**

# TEENAGER AVA GARDNER

When J.E. was a freshman at Newport News High School, he remembered that a beautiful girl became the talk of football and basketball stars. Her name was Ava Gardner, as she attended Newport News High where she and her family moved from a small rural town in NC. They left their home during the Great Depression to come to the Shipbuilding town of Newport News where work was ample and her mom could run a boarding house. I do remember Dad telling us how pretty her eyes were. After graduation, she went off to NC then Hollywood and ended up marrying Frank Sinatra.

# J.E.'S FAMOUS "COUSIN PEGGY"

## Cousin Peggy

Our Cousin Peggy….I can still hear Dad saying—"you have a very famous actress in our family" never took him serious until I researched and found….so much not mentioned on this troubled soul that she could not feel right in a small town…A Kardashian of the 1920's—but truly a soul that brought gossip, humor, and glamour to our country… Read more to come on Peggy's best, so she can finally rest!

## Cousin Peggy as a Girl

Before there was Peggy Joyce Hopkins there was Marguerite (Peggy) Upton. Her Grandmother was Margaret Wilroy. Her biographical stories maybe only tell that her 'diamonds" were her best friend. My dad heard the stories of another little girl in the buggy his aunt Josephine would babysit at GRAMPA Wilroy's farm.

## A "Ziegfield Follies Girl"

During the roaring 20's Peggy Hopkins Joyce became a Ziegfield Follies girl, as Dad would mention after she had left boarding school.

## Cousin Peggy... A Shining Star

Cousin Peggy ran off with a vaudeville cyclist and became the "most popular girl in America" in the twenties and by the thirties less publicized in her most trying years where many say she had a great heart and a wonderful sense of humor and loved to laugh. Her family back in Virginia never spoke ill of all her marrying men but rather passed down to little J. E. that his cousin was a shining star. Some of the photos taken of Peggy on a certain sailboat…on the sail ship's mast, smiling with one of her "many friends", none other than the legendary ***Charlie Chaplin.***

# PART 2—PATTON'S HAND

## Blindly Following Patton's Hell On Wheels…thru Hell

Figure 40 J.E. sitting on top of a tank

# FROM BENNING TO BERLIN: INTRODUCTION TO HELL

As we follow J.E.'s path from his early days in Virginia growing up, surviving the American Great Depression, the air of war that is brewing in Europe is felt in the United States. It was the start of a new decade, the 1940's, leaving behind 5 years of a German build up, that has to be fully explained, in order to grasp the reason why Hitler was so successful inciting an entire country into a second World War.

Already, in Newport News, ship building preparations are being made, and enlistments are the order of the day. Young James Edward Sammons, was willing, able, and ready to serve, as he waved goodbye to his family, enroute to Ft. Benning, GA., where one of the greatest generals in military history, Major General George S. Patton, awaited the inexperienced J.E., along with many unsuspecting 20 year olds, to provide a brief taste of the hell that awaited them. The newly formed armored division would be perfectly constructed with the experienced Patton, that had built a career leading up to, and, destined for this moment in time. Patton's "Hell On Wheels" was a perfect name

And J.E.'s engineering technical experience acquired in (school in GA), allowed him to be in the forefront, preparing the way for Patton's fast-moving tanks…. Rightfully being called, "We Pave the Way", it was J.E.'s group that allowed Patton to speed towards battle front destinations, in record breaking time, and even acquiring the name from Hitler's divisions as "Roosevelt's Butchers".

# WHO WERE THESE MEN OF BATTALION 17, COMPANY E, 2ND ARMORED DIVISION?

They were wheels that moved through mountains, demolished and rebuilt roads to lead our troops to Victory! Known as Patton's "HELL ON WHEELS" these men became the machine non stoppable to succeed in 7 battle campaigns! Many of these brave and strong men were handpicked and selected for their mission to make a way to overcome the Germans. Special recognition came to this unique group by President Truman with a citation for their efforts to win the great battle against the Nazi forces that won the freedoms. "These men were welded into a solid fighting unit by General Patton", J.E. would say. For over 4 years, this highly trained group these men were not only buds but also great friends who just could not let their friendships end. Now knowing after seeing these men and families for 52 reunions I understand why the unit so tight and devoted to one another. Patton needed these kinds of men specialized in each position to quickly deliver and not quiver to achieve their highly difficult mission. J.E.'s final speech says it all.

—Rita Sammons Harrell

Figure 41. J.E. leaving for Army Basic Training

J.E. ready to go off to training at FT Benning.
A picture at his sister Delane's house in Newport News.

Figure 42 J.E. at Fort Benning, 1941

J.E. in 1941 with Mustache in training at Ft Benning GA.

Figure 42 J. E. at Headquarters - The Armored Force School

Figure 43 Radio School, 1941, Ft. Knox, KY.

Figure 44 J.E. at Fort Knox

J.E. at Ft Knox while in Radio School learning MORSE CODE—Little did he ever know then, how it would all end. A road map of his life consisted of learning, training, and being the spark in his unit to ignite the flame of hope and helping them cope.

Figure 45 J.E. with truck

J.E. Driver of the Half-track always remembering "Patton" yelling "MOVE IT"! Frist started learning Morse code at the Army Radio School in Ft. Knox KY. Then his driving skills were discovered, and became the lead driver in the half-tracks, motorcycle and later jeep driving some commanders.

Figure 46 J. E. Driving a truck at Ft. Benning

At FT Benning, becoming "the" Jeep Driver for Commanders later in the Battle Campaigns Go Daddy! As he went and drove every kind of vehicle in WWII. I don't know which driver's seat he liked best.

## Who were these men of Battalion 17, Company E, 2nd Armored Division? | 157

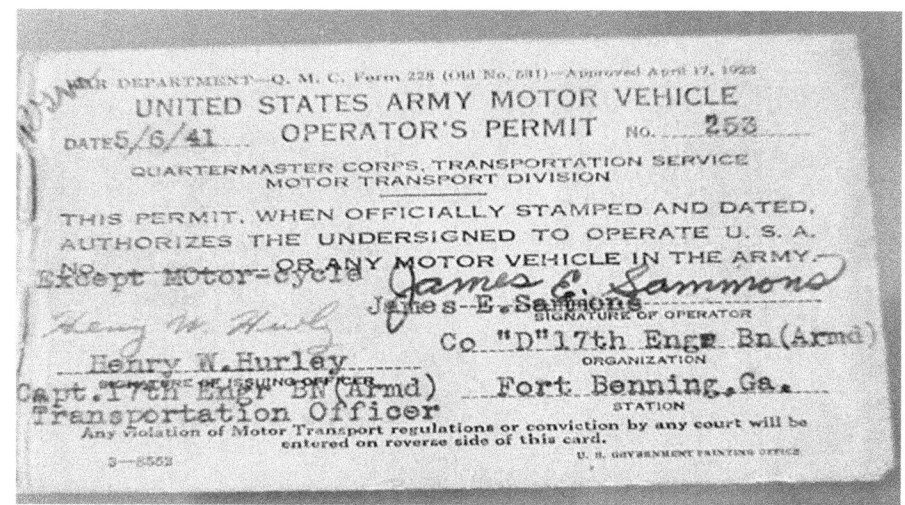

Figure 47 J. E. Army motor vehicle license

Figure 48 We Pave the Way patch

Figure 49 Hell on Wheels patch

Figure 50 J.E. on his motorcycle at Ft Benning.

Oh how he loved the ride and drive. He also had a great sense of adventure. I remember when all of us six kids climbed into the station wagon and dad drove down to Menomonee Falls, WI in freezing cold weather and drove us on ice! He loved racing cars too, and his cars were his joy later in life.

Figure 51 J.E. posed during maneuvers.

Posed during maneuvers, J.E. reminds me in this picture of my grandson Brayden, who has his blue eyes, long arms and hands with a smile such pride.

Figure 52 J. E. on motorcycle with buddies

Figure 53 J.E. shows his skill as a driver, getting out of a tough situation.

Figure 54 J.E. at Ft Benning with his FORD GPW Jeep.

A military workhorse for the 2nd Armored Division designed to help assist in moving troops, helping with casualties, and getting around quickly no matter what the terrain was. These jeeps carried the name known to many soldiers as the "Blitz Buggy". Over 200,000 were built during WWII.

The "G" in GPW stood for "Government", the "P" stood for passenger vehicle with an 80" wheelbase, and the "W" stood for "Willys" licensed design.

Figure 55 J.E. in a half-track truck

J.E. at Ft Benning in his half-track. The M-2 with anti-ditching front roller made this highly used vehicle for the 17th Battalion greatly used by the engineers.

Figure 56 The J.E. stance

Proud J.E. and his wonderful confident stance, I could always pick out Dad though many 17th Battalion picture sites just by the way he held himself with such pride. He just stood out to me and maybe the other children of soldiers also felt the same. Something felt when you recognize a certain characteristic way of him that is genetic in our brains that always remains.

Figure 57 Hitch a Ride

Dad's funny side. Funny times, with his pals, J.E. had a humorous side that he loved a good joke and tell many himself that would have you in stiches. J.E. was a character himself and sized up everyone else—gave them a funny name that carried on lifelong. J.E. refers to these great Sidekicks with remarks of all. Some that I remember well are Buttermilk—who loved to dance at the Reunions. Mac who was the biggest tease, Herbie Barns, Kid Walker, Ziggy, Coop, TA, Russ, Strick, Ziggy and Charlie. Charlie was small but full of muscles and so strong. I remember Dad telling me he could carry a refrigerator on his head. This was happy Dad at Radio School in Ft. Knox KY. Little did he know then how his war path would change.

Figure 58 Latrine Duty

Both being a staple routine in a soldier's daily training chores, quickly becomes second nature. J.E. took it in great strive and knew this was just a part of the service. He would recall, laugh, and say, "thank goodness it didn't last too many days."

BASIC INFANTRY SOLDIER TRAINING WITH GENERAL PATTON – JAN. 1941
(NOTE PRE-WAR EQUIPMENT)

Figure 59  J. E. on Guard Duty

Figure 60 Two soldiers on a wall

Two soldiers taking a break from training. J.E. had so many pals and buddies in the Army…He so enjoyed hearing stories and knowing about each soldier's life. This was the start of keeping these true friends together for over 50 years after the war. So hospitable J.E. became the motivator of many of these men and in their future family lives.

The 17th Battalion, 2nd Armored Division, Co E had training maneuvers during real infantry and combat training thus creating real life danger for these engineers. It worked to their advantage, and these types of bridges became the pathway to victory for our troops.

Figure 61 Bridge building, Ft. Benning, 1941

Fort Benning to Berlin grueling maneuvers demolishing and re-building. Paving and clearing terrain. Some of the hardest engineering skills required for a job to "pave the way" to Freedom days.

*...and under "combat conditions" below bridge building, Pee Dee River*

Figure 62 Combat Conditions

Who were these men of Battalion 17, Company E, 2nd Armored Division? | 171

Figure 63 Bridge across the Chat-a-hoo-chi River, 1942

Across the European countryside, they built the bridges for freedom and demolished the ones that caused our enemy troops to run. "Paving the Way" as these strong, stable engineers were able to accomplish building bridges in less than seven hours. A handpicked bunch with unique skills and powers.

Figure 64 J.E. the Soldier on a bridge

J.E. and one of his best buds, Eddie Strickland, worked on this road together in the training maneuvers. I can only imagine the hard labor. The tracks over the years of blood, sweat and tears, are now just a few memories left to a few soldiers left.

Figure 65 J. E building bridges and roads

Figure 66 North and South Carolina maneuvers

Dad would say later after I moved to South Carolina, Hey I maneuvered there in Cheraw, SC, in a swampy land. We had to learn how to plow thru the muddy and rough terrain. Dad would remark how this land was close to his family roots long ago. He was a Virginian then, but most of his family migrated from Camden County, NC.

Figure 67 J.E. at the half-track gun

Steady Eddie at aim in training maneuvers. M3 Half-track designed to withstand rugged country areas. The Sherman tank was the most used in WW2 and became the combat tank for J.E. in North Africa in 1943. The Sherman tanks were for many soldiers called "Ronsons" after a slogan of a lighter at that time. "Lights every time".

Figure 68 J.E. with group on Patton's Tanks

J.E. Center top—his picture is that same serious look as in many others. The 17th Battalion were his band of brothers. Many times dad would say to me "he could write a book of all the characters of Co. E". J.E. loved as if all were brothers. Hell on Wheels—Patton Boys…they were rough and ready.

Figure 69 J. E. ready for action on one of Patton's tractor monsters.

Demolishing and building bridges... Live maneuver trainings made the 17th aware of live fire combat, bombings, to enable them to victory in real live time of war.

Figure 70. Patton addressing soldiers at Ft. Benning, GA picture taken by J. E.

Figure 71. General Patton

The 17th Battalion Company "E" received the "GENERAL PATTON AWARD" The soldiers in the 17th referred to themselves "AS ONE OF THE PATTON BOYS". Patton Trained these fine strong engineers in "real live maneuvers" while in the swamps of Louisiana, Tennessee, North and South Carolina. Patton commanded major combat units in North Africa. I remember the "Swaddle Stick" hit on Dad's half-track as a driver. "MOVE IT" Dad would mimic his stern and forceful yell. Patton the unit said got them through hell.

"Move It" Patton yelled, and he hit his swaddle stick upon J.E.'s half-track. J.E. was the driver, and he pressed the pedal as hard as he could. From that encounter with Patton, J.E. knew the expectation and the realization of the making of a soldier for Co. E.

Figure 72 2nd Armored Division panoramic view

Panoramic view of the 2nd Armored Division, known as "Hell on Wheels"! They were the units that made it possible for our troops to invade and take out our enemy. J.E. was so proud of his country and just as proud of the 17th Battalion, Co. E.

Figure 73 Chow Time

Dad said you have to make friends with all the cook leaders of each battle station—
that way you can get seconds and fill your belly up.

# Who were these men of Battalion 17, Company E, 2nd Armored Division?

Figure 74 The Engineers of the 17th

Dad labeled "his buddies" I see some familiar faces I saw as a child at many reunions. God Bless these strong and bonded buds who worked so hard.

Figure 75 Company E 17th Engineers, J.E. circled

I see a soldier with the straightest shoulders and a determined proud face. Smack in the center of all these young soldiers where it was his destiny place. Later I met most of these men and families as dad gathered them together each year for remembrance and cheer with stories, funny pranks, and lots of beer!

Who is that soldier smack in the middle? The one with the stance for firm 7 committal. It must be my dad, who stood tall and would tell of so many Great War stories to all!

I knew most of these great men and their families. I do believe Patton personally selected these strong and courageous men to "Pave the Way" for our troops to invade and conquer the enemy. Dad loved the movie the "Great Escape" and "Patton" but said "Band of Brothers" and "Sgt. Ryan" were too close to home for him to watch.

Figure 76 Riverside Bar and Grill, Madison Ave, NYC Nov 9th 1942

The last supper for 5 pals ready to head out to sea. Above left to right—J.E., Ray Ellis, Geo Miller, Herman Feldman (captured at Battle of the Bulge).

# NEXT STOP...NORTH AFRICA

Figure 77 J. E. French Morocco 1943

British Prime Minister Sir Winston S. Churchill in 1943 met with President Franklin D. Roosevelt and senior military advisors in Casablanca and Morocco to devise the military strategy for the United States Army for the coming year. This was about the timeframe that J.E. was headed there with the 2nd Armored Divisions.

Figure 78. J. E. on a Camel in Rabat French Morocco

Figure 79 Morocco side street

# SUDDENLY, ONE OF OUR OWN... GONE

Figure 80 Lt. Col. Hurley

Dad recalled the death of Lt. Col. Hurley in a minefield where he was driving a jeep in Sicily in action. The 17th Battalion, Dad said, had a sad day when they found out. Not a dry eye in the unit. "We all respected him greatly". Dad would always tell the story of the mine hitting Hurley, how it made them feel even more determined and focused to keep "paving the way" to victory.

Thanks to Capt. Burt, for saving P.O.W.s, not quitting, fighting, until victorious & winning the Battle of Aachen, and a dagger to Hitler … Allied closing the "Aachen Gap"

Figure 81 Uncle Welly

Figure 82 Capt. Burt

## Uncle Welly

Dad knew of my Uncle Welly's capture and prisoner of war and wrote in "GRAMPA'S WAR", in honor of my Uncle Welly who I remember who loved his black coffee and bowl of ice cream.

One of my mother's older brother Henry Wellington Chaon was held prisoner in 1944. With the victory of Captain Burt's great commanding skills with closing the Aachen Gap many prisoners escaped as my Uncle Welly did. Dad was nearby at the time fighting while demolishing and building bridges. This was the intersection of history where many of my cousins would not be here if not for the extraordinary bravery and infantry skills under Burt's command. So thankful, so many wonderful cousins that would not be here without the fortitude of all the units to succeed.

Figure 83 President Truman and Capt. Burt

President Harry S. Truman awarded the Congressional Medal of Honor, to Capt. Burt for saving P.O.W.s, including Uncle Welly, a dear member of our Sammons family; in later years Capt. Burt would be invited as the honored guest at one of J.E.'s 52 "We Pave the Way" Co. E Reunions.

# UNCLE WELLY POW STORY

CIRCUMSTANCES SURROUNDING PRISONER OF WAR
HENRY WELLINGTON CHAON
117th INFANTRY REGIMENT
U.S 30th INFANTRY DIVISION
WORLD WAR II
OCTOBER - 1944

Researched & Compiled by : Ed Sammons 17th Armd. Engr. Bn.
U.S 2nd Armored Division
Reference : "Hell on Wheels" Book by : Donald E. Houston, Historian

After the battle at Maastricht, the 2nd Armored Division fought it's way toward the city of Aachen, Germany. Hitler's orders were to stop us at all costs - "No allied soldier is to set foot on the soil of the Fatherland". In October 1944, the weather turned cold with continuous rain and the 2nd Armored Division was pinned down for more than 3 weeks near the town of Heerleen. The 29th Infantry Division was on our left flank and on our right was the 30th Infantry Division. The 2nd Armored Division was the Spearhead. General Hobbs, Commander of the 30th Infantry Division, told General Harmon, Commander of the 2nd Armored Division that the 117th Infantry Regiment could take the towns of Schaufenberg and Wurselen with the help of a 2nd Armored Tank Regiment. General Harmon volunteered a medium tank regiment to support the 117th Infantry Regiment. A fierce battle raged for 4 days, with many killed, wounded and captured on both sides. The 3 Divisions later routed the Germans and captured the city of Aachen. Captain James M. Burt, Commander "B" Co.66th Armored Tank Regiment, 2nd Armored Division, was later awarded the Congressional Medal of Honor by the President at the White House with the following
#CITATION
Captain James M. Burt was in command of Company "B" 66th Armored Regiment on the outskirts of Wurselen, Germany, on 13 October 1944 when his organization participated in a coordinated infantry-tank attack designed to isolate the large German Garrison which was tenaciously defending the city of Aachen. In the first day's action, when infnatrymen ran into murderous small-arms and mortor fire, Captain Burt dismounted from his tank about 200 yards to the rear and moved forward on foot beyond the infantry positions, where as the enemy concentrated a tremendous volume of fire upon him, he calmly motioned his tanks into good firing positions. As our ground attack gained momentum, he climbed aboard his tank and directed the action from the rear deck, exposed to hostile volleys which finally wounded him painfully in the face and neck. He maintained his dangerous post despite point-blank gunfire until friendly artillery knocked out the enemy weapons, and then proceeded to the advanced scout's position to deploy his tanks for the defense of the gains which had been made. The next day, when the enemy counter-attacked, he left cover and went 75 yards through heavy fire to assist the 30th Infantry Commander who was seriously wounded. For the next 8 days, through rainy, miserable weather, and under constant heavy shelling, Captain Burt held the combined forces together dominating and controlling the critical situation through the sheer force of his heroic example.
(CONTINUED)

(CONTINUED)

To direct artillery fire, on 15 October, He took his tank 300 yards into enemy lines where he dismounted and remained for 1 hour giving accurate data to friendly gunners. twice more that day he went into enemy territory under deadly fire on reconnaissance. In succeeding days he never faltered in his determination to defeat the strong German forces opposing him. Twice the tank in which he was riding was knocked out by enemy action and each time he climbed aboard another vehicle and continued to fight. He took great risks to rescue wounded comrades and inflicted prodigious destruction on enemy personnel and material even though suffering from the wounds he received in the battle's opening phase. Captain Burt's intrepidity and disregard of personal safety was so complete that his own men and the infantry who attached themselves to him were inspired to overcome the wretched and extremly hazardous conditions which accompanied one of the most bitter local actions of the war. The victory achieved closed the Aachen Gap.

NOTE : HENRY WELLINGTON CHAON WAS THE BROTHER OF MY WIFE –
       BEATRICE VERONICA CHAON SAMMONS

# AND THE BIG ONE... J.E. WAS THERE... THE "BATTLE OF THE BULGE"

Figure 84 Battle of the Bulge veteran certificate

Dad hung this "Battle of the Bulge" certificate on his wall, as reminder of this was a very trying battle to overcome, and many horrific stories of comrades and how they finally won.

# "WE PAVE THE WAY" ...MAKING PATTON'S TANKS MOVE AT LIGHTNING SPEED!

As we follow J.E.'s path from his early days in Virginia growing up, surviving the American Great Depression, the air of war that is brewing in Europe is felt in the United States. It was the start of a new decade, the 1940's, leaving behind 5 years of a German build up, that has to be fully explained, in order to grasp the reason why Hitler was so successful inciting an entire country into a second World War.

Already, in Newport News, ship building preparations are being made, and enlistments are the order of the day. Young James Edward Sammons was willing, able, and ready to serve, as he waved goodbye to his family, enroute to Ft. Benning, GA., where one of the greatest generals in military history, Major General George S. Patton, awaited the inexperienced J.E., along with many unsuspecting 20 year olds, to provide a brief taste of the hell that awaited them. The newly formed armored division would be perfectly constructed with the experienced Patton, that had built a career leading up to, and, destined for this moment in time. Patton's "Hell on Wheels" was a perfect name.

And J.E.'s engineering technical experience acquired in (school in GA), allowed him to be in the forefront, preparing the way for Patton's fast-moving tanks…. Rightfully being called, "We Pave the Way", it was J.E.'s group that allowed Patton to speed towards battle front destinations, in record breaking time, and even acquiring the name from Hitler's divisions as "Roosevelt's Butchers".

Figure 85 We Pave the Way patch

The 17th Battalion, 2nd Armored Division, Company E. "WE PAVE THE WAY" who received a special citation from President Truman on their completion of extraordinary measures to insure a successful completion of their mission in record time. A Unit so strong and resilient that it literally became the foundation of winning WWII.

# PLATOON PICTURES

J.E. wrote on the backs of these platoon pictures of the 17th Battalion. These were the great engineering soldiers who engaged in enemy fire while constructing, demolishing, and re- building, they led the pathway to freedom.

Figure 86  Platoon Picture

> 1st PLATOON
> THE NEW FACE IN THE GROUP IS
> T-4 ROSELEE. THE NEW ENGINEER SECT. SGT.
> HE'S SITTING BEHIND SAYCE AND BROWN.
> YOU CAN SEE HOW CPL JONES MADE OUT
> IN LAST NIGHTS POKER GAME. "THERE
> GOES THAT NEW HEN HOUSE." ZOMBIE
> WANTED TO SHOOT THE PHOTOGRAPHER.
> SGT JOHN HAS COUNTED HIS POINTS AND
> FEELS LIKE A CIVILIAN ALREADY.
> FROM THE LOOKS OF THINGS, P.W. SMITH AND
> ATKINS AGREE WITH ZOMBIE. GRASIK SEEMS
> HAPPY FISH HAS GONE TO SLEEP.

1st PLATOON

Figure 87 1st Platoon Picture

Figure 88 2nd Platoon Picture

> NOTE THE NEW OFFICER. REMEMBER HIM? WE STILL HAVE BLUE EYES THOUGH. PECK ALMOST SAT ON BASTILLE'S LAP. CHIEF SAYS THAT HE BELIEVES WE OUGHT TO ALL GET DRUNK THEN HAVE OUR PICTURES TAKEN. "WE LOOK BETTER." I THINK THAT TENNIS IS EYEING A T.S.P. IT'S A LONG WAY TO TIDDLY WINKS SO SPIKE HAS NO BOTTLE ON THE HIP. ANDY TOOK IT AWAY FROM HIM.
>
> ENGR, SECTION

# Engineering Platoon

Figure 89 Engineering Platoon

> KUPPERSMITH BEING DIFFERENT HQR. SECTION
> HOLT TRYING TO APPEAR INTELLIGENT
> NOTE THE COL. STILL CUSSING.
> WAIT EVEN WASHED HIS FACE
> DELAHOUSSAYE DID'NT EVEN HAVE A GUN ON.
> C.B. SITS APART FROM THE DIT DA GANG.
> GINSBERG POSES. WHILE LT. ARNONE MOST SEE
> CORRAL 10 MILES OFF. CANADY IS DREAMING
> OF THAT STEW HE LEFT ON THE STOVE.
> MARKEY IS TRYING TO CONVINCE GRAHAM THAT THE
> POINT SYSTEM IS RUN BY DEMOCRATS.
> FORTICK IS HIDING A BLACK EYE. HE MUST HAVE
> SALVAGED THE WRONG PR. OF JOCK'S.

Headquarters section

# LETTERS NOT FORGOTTEN

## Written to honor and remember those that accompanied J.E. from Benning to Berlin

J.E.'s Radio School Buddy Bob Pryor last note to dad. He says he thought the French Morocco was the most dangerous time of all the battles.

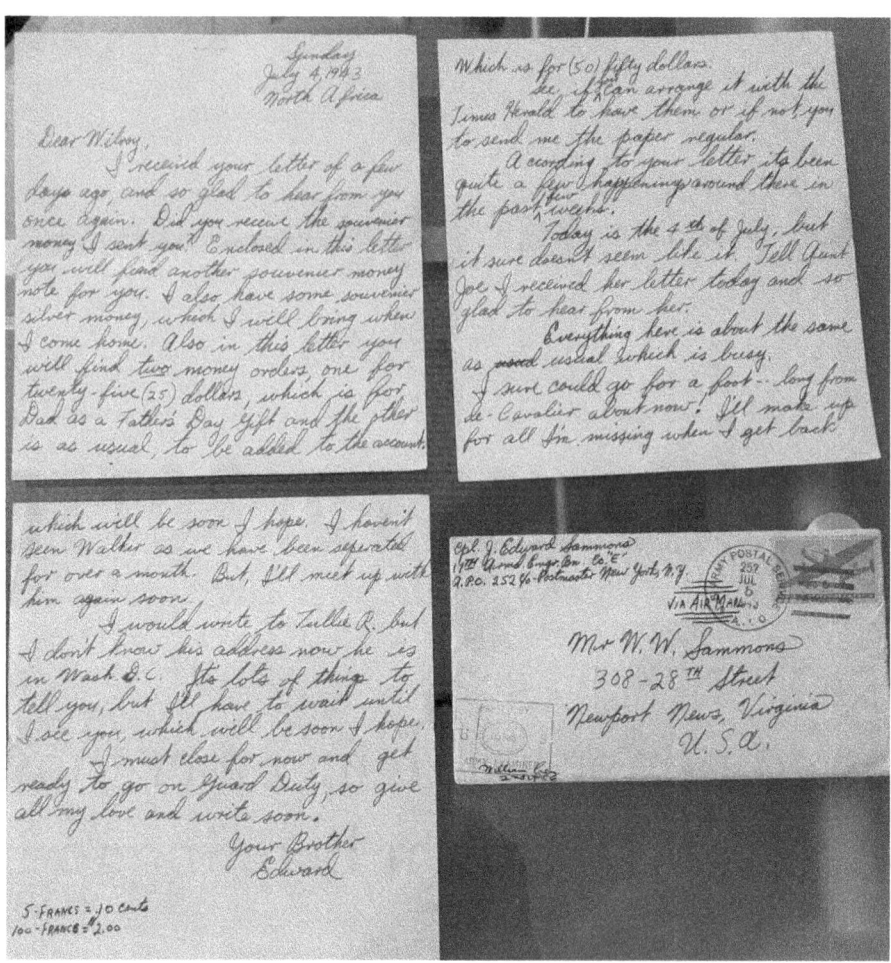

## Letters to Wilroy, and of course to Bea

What a great brother and son J.E. had become. He wrote and cared about all his family with many letters of love.

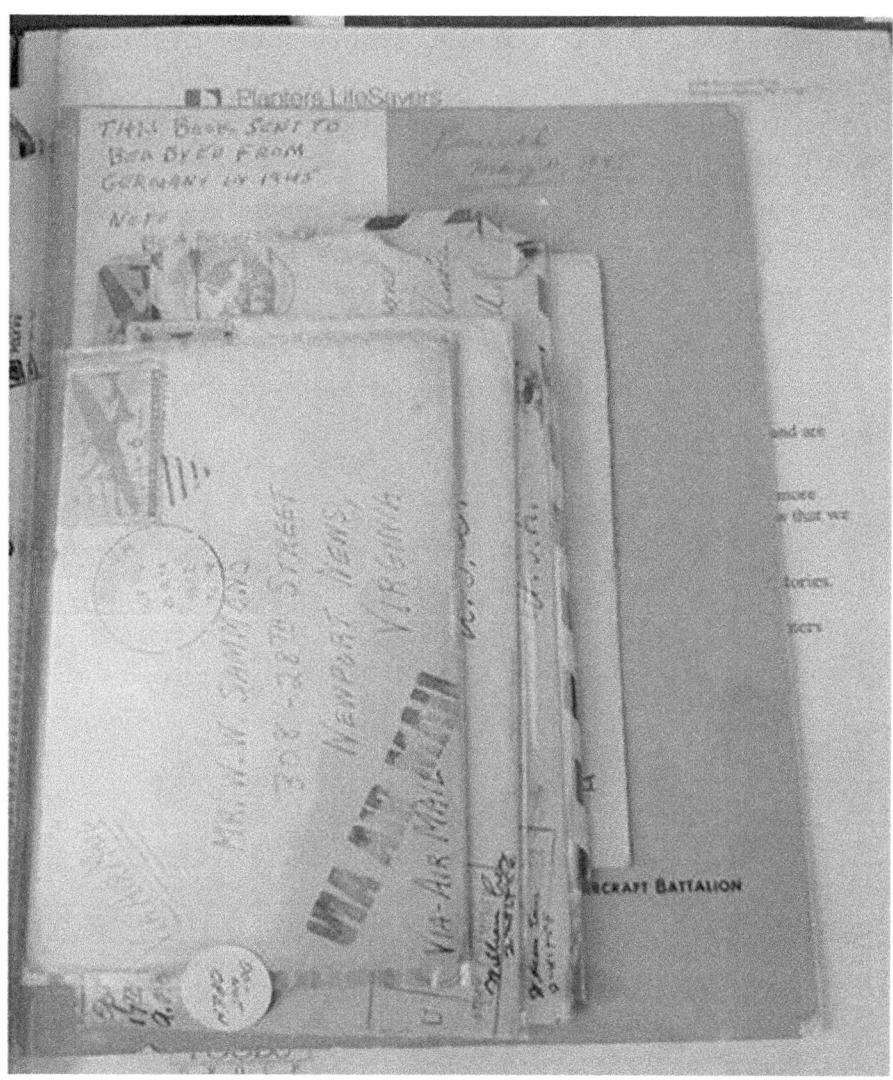

## War Letters

Dad saved all his letters sent to him during the war. Some letters from him back to his family in Newport News Virginia actually discovered several years ago by my cousins Joan and Merle at a yard sale in Newport News. How coincidental was that? They quickly sent them off to dad and he was thrilled. Now he had all of the letters he had sent back. These letters were saved in a dresser or something. Then found in the HAND OF DAD'S NIECE and given to J.E.

I read these letters and found out more about life than any history book could tell me. The love of a family – so devoted and hard working. His older brother needed to apprentice at a printing company to help provide for the family. So much on a soldier's mind at that time.

## Presidential Citation 1945

**Presidential Citation to the 2nd Armored Division, 17th Battalion for their bravery and commitment to their successes in "Paving the Way" to our Freedom we hold today.**

Special Awarded Citation to the 17th Battalion Company E from President Truman for their outstanding performance of duty in action against the enemy during the period of March 8 through April 13, 1945. In preparation to and during the advance of the 2nd Armored Division from the

RHINE RIVER to the ELBE RIVER. Company "E" 17th Armored Engineers Battalion for utilizing their—valued experience accumulated in assault operations and numerous battle campaigns. This Army Unit developed and maintained an "esprit de corps" and high state of training and professional skill that enabled their unit to bridge the troops on the RHINE RIVER. This was and still is the most notable water barrier encountered by the Allied Forces on the European Continent! This construction of 1153 feet of treadway bridging in only SEVEN HOURS, in the face of enemy fire, a speed unparalleled in military service.

Figure 90 James Edward Sammons '

# "My name is James Edward Sammons, and I am writing these memories down so that my grandchildren and their grandchildren can know and understand the battles of great sacrifices to have our freedoms we hold today."

Historians someday will know of a soldier who by spirt and hand of God, Patton, Family and Friends remembered this history to the victory end! He taught his battalion the ways of love from his devoted hand he lent every man and his family to know about the story of "Who Were These Men? From Benning to Belin.

Figure 91 J.E.'s medals, & Catalog of medals

J.E. received many unit awards, bronze stars, and President's citation. All the seven battle campaigns the 17th Battalion succeeded to "pave the way" for the troops to invade. An engineering group of men that when I think of them, I just say AMEN.

INDENTIFICATION CHART

James E. Sammons - U.S.Army Serial # 33040248

U.S. Military Service Jan.10, 1941 to May 26, 1945

WORLD WAR II

READING TOP TO BOTTOM LEFT TO RIGHT

| ROW 1 | ROW 2 | ROW 3 |
|---|---|---|
| Good Conduct Medal | 2nd Armored Division Insigna First American Army Division to be personally decorated with the Presidential Citation and presented in person by Harry S. Truman, President of U.S., 1945 | Victory Medal World War II |
| American Defense Service Medal | 17th Armored Engineer Battalion Insigna | National Service Medal |
| Qualification Badge Half Track - Tank Company Command Unit Driver, Radio Operator, Machine Gunner 30-50 | European African Middle Eastern Campaign Medal with Silver Star, Bronze Star, & Invasion Arrowhead<br><br>Battle Campaigns<br><br>North African - 1942 - 43<br>Normandy - Omaha Beach D day Invasion June 1944<br>Battle of St.Lo France - July 1944<br>Holland - Liberation Oct.& Nov.1944<br>Belgium - Battle of Bulge - Dec.1944<br>Germany - Battle of the Rhine, Roer, and Berlin - 1945 | Qualified as - Expert Thompson Sub- Machine Gun |

Surrounding Shoulder Rope Medal

BELGIAN FOURRAGERE - Awarded to 2nd Armored Division for being First Allied Soldiers to reach and enter Belgian Soil and liberation from the Germans.
VICTORY BATTLE OF THE BULGE

## Catalog of Medals

Figure 92 J. E.'s original dog tags, worn from start to finish

J.E.'s original Military dog tags worn through the seven battles until the very end of the War. When I hold them, I get the chills—just thinking of all the miles these tags traveled and all the seen battles.

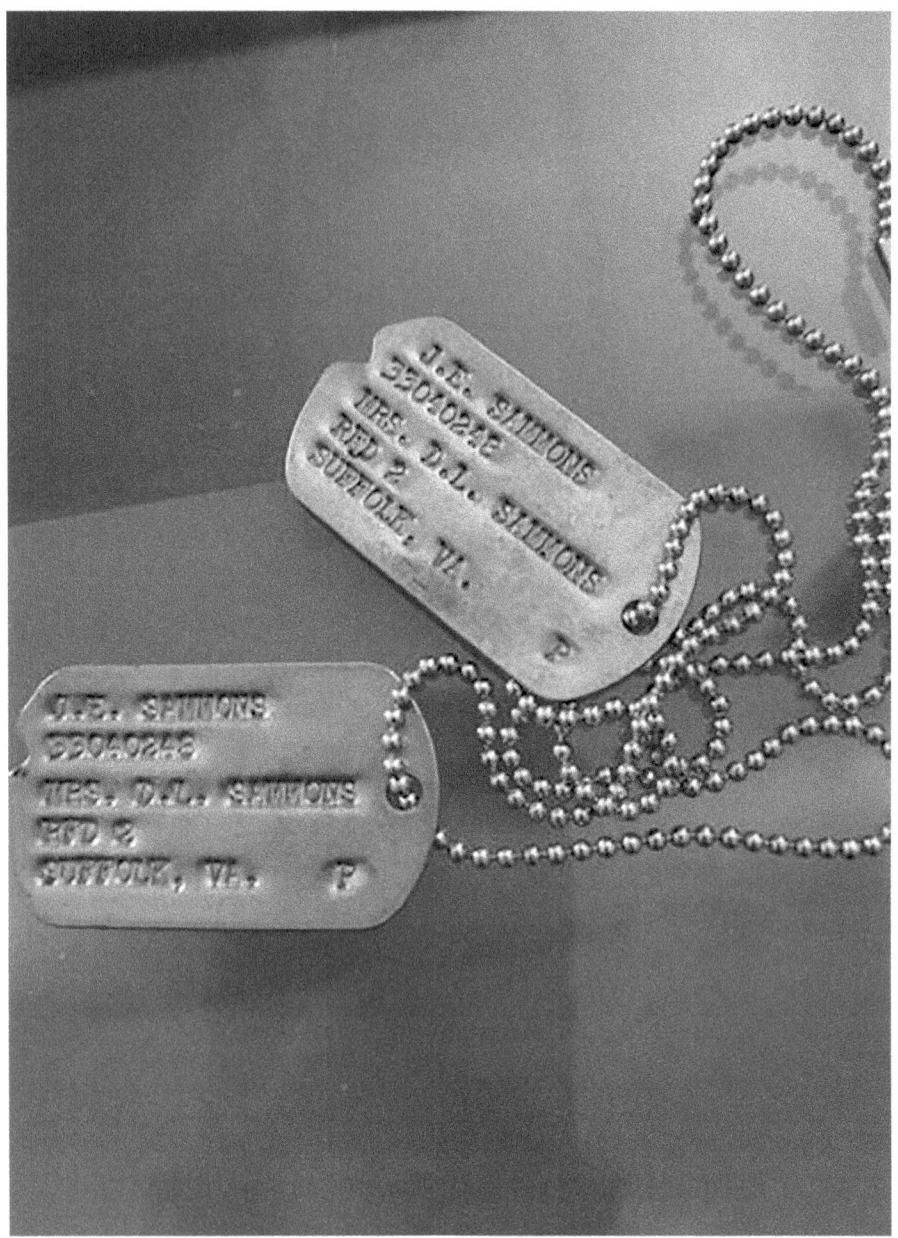

Figure 93 J.E. backup dog tags

J.E. had a second back up set of dog tags. These were extra tags and kept inside his safety kit. Dad said he had in his safety kit: Hershey candy bar, Cyanide pill. Eatable map of route of invasion, Cigarettes, Aspirin, Bandage and Gum.

# J.E. IN NORTHERN AFRICA, FRENCH MOROCCO, TUNISIA, AND SICILY"

A duffle bag in hand, with a prayer in his head J.E. is bound for the first of many battles. He departs on a ship with his Unit Co E and the Division in the middle of the night to avoid later any German U-boats in sight. Many scary and fearful moments as air raids and bombs nearly missed their ship. These soldiers did not know where they were going and took 13 days to reach Casablanca. Nearly escaping, J.E. knew these bombings were not the worst to come.

When arrived in North Africa the Division was welcomed with Arab chanting "an eye for an eye and one for you." Then on to the European battles in Morocco, Tunisia, and Sicily. Where Company E was and 2 Armored Division was in vigilant action in fighting and making the passageways for tanks, and infantry forces to advance and succeed in their mission.

**—Rita Sammons Harrell**

# FROM SICILY, ORDERED BACK TO THE UK...

## The Tidworth training and waiting for "D-DAY"

### It started with a British ship nightmare...

Dad's recall of his ride out of homeport to join with his fellow soldiers to begin a journey of SEVEN battles. That would be his testament of his lifetime in remembering the soul values and virtues that he nurtured with an overabundance of love and friendships to all his comrades through his entire life.

### GELA TO PALERMO
### WITH
### GENERAL PATTON

In July '43 the 2nd Armored Division invaded the island of Sicily. We landed at Gela and fought our way around the left side of the coast toward our target Palermo. Our first encounter with the Italian Army and their pre-war guns was no match for the 2nd Armored Division. However, our Battalion Commander, Col. Hurley was killed at Gela. We encountered the German Herman Goering Panzer Division on our way to Palermo. Gen. Montgomery with British forces landed at the same time to clear the right side of the island and fight the German 15th Panzer Division on their way to Palermo. Gen. Patton was heard to say - we will beat Montgomery to Palermo if it takes a truck load of dead G.I. dog tags. We beat Gen. Montgomery and the British to Palermo. There the fighting ended. After a few weeks we were loaded on an English Ship with a commando group of British Rangers returning to England as hero's for their invasion of Italy.

That boat ride to England dodging German U Boats was another rough and exciting war event.

Ed Sammons

## BRITISH SHIP NIGHTMARE
## TO ENGLAND

In Nov.'43 on the British Ship we travelled was out of home port more than 18 months. Was low on food and the flour in the hole was quite damp and moldy. The British Commando Rangers were in the next compartment. The bread we were eating was heavy and soggy. After eating this bread for two days we wondered if the British Commando's were eating this bread - Yes - only after beating it on the table - holding it up to the porthole light to make sure all the bugs were out. They served us dried lima beans cooked in water for breakfast and other horrible food. After that we ate our "C" rations.

We continued thru the Mediterranean to the Strait of Gibraltar going thru in blackout about midnight. We encountered German U Boats along the lower coast of France. The ship quickly turned Northwest - full speed ahead. Then came the general alarm - secure life jackets and prepare to abandon ship. The ship was rocking & vibrating for hours as we headed Northwest in the Atlantic. After 14 days dodging German U Boats we landed at Liverpool, England, Lucky Again! As the British Rangers came down the gangplank a British Brass Band was playing homecoming music and continued as we came down. After that ride - I could understand why the Germans were winning the war.

Ed Sammons

## Tidworth, England, 1944

Figure 94 J. E. in Tidworth, England, 1944

Figure 95 J. E. in Tidworth, England, 1944

Figure 96 "Sidekicks" and long-lasting friendships

Oct. 31, 2007

Dear Merle,

    Thanks for the nice letter & picture of the cute boys. I know you and Dennis really enjoy them. The Sammons & Wilroys all had blue eyes. So what goes around - comes around. I remember London -

    After the fighting in North Africa and Sicily we landed at LIverpool 2 weeks before Xmas 1943 and were stationed at Tidworth Barracks on the Salisbury Plain about 100 miles from London. The brick barracks at Tidworth were two floors high with 30 men on each floor, only heat was an old fireplace, bunk beds with straw mattress, 6 toilets and 6 wash basins - no showers. These barracks were built before WW I. This was like the Waldorf-Astor compared to the next 2 yrs. after D Day. It was all down hilly. They had an old theatre at Tidworth and we were entertained by the great James Cagney and his Yankee-Doodle Show.

    I had a weeks gun training shooting down air targets over the White Cliffs of Dover at gunnery school and qualified as expert gunner. We were given in groups of 6 R&R in London for six days. We stayed at the Reed Hotel near Picadilly Square and rode the thrilling subways to the end of each line (about 20 miles) and explored the town for food. For 2.00 I hired a London Cab (2 Pass.) their gas ration was 1 gal per day and you saw many along the way out of gas. The cab took us to all the historic places plus London China Town, where we saw a small building and the driver said 64 chinese live in the small bldg.

    Four days after we checked out of the Reed Hotel a HItler bomb went down the elevator shaft. - Lucky again. We later went back to London and built a bridge across the Thames River for practice before the D Day invasion.

    This is just one of the many events of my 4½ yrs of war.
              All the best to you and family
                    Love, Uncle Ed

Tidworth letter

This letter back to my cousin Merle Sammons Ivey from dad explains the reference to Tidworth.

Figure 97 Full Field Inspection at Tidworth Barracks, West of London

## Many stories of Tidworth

J.E. was full of stories as he developed so many friends. All of Co. E was his family for 4 ½ years. Dad would always shed a tear when telling sad heartwarming stories and funny ones. Dad enjoyed his laughter and jokes and loved seeing people having fun. I guess the hospitality of a solider was a quality that bonded his unit together and made a strength machine of engineers that focused and were determined that: "Paved the way"—for freedom.

# FINALLY D-DAY + 1

## God Speed thru Hell!

*"We were behind schedule by half a day already…we could see miles of our ships returning to our POD Southampton from Normandy with the wounded…the unloading of the wounded was a tangled butchery…vomiting, crying, praying, even dead silence after lame jokes, & off we were…finally."*
--- **James Edward Sammons** (Loaded aboard LST with our
3 halftracks, two jeeps, and 1 truck) J.E. at D-Day+1, first stop…
Omaha Beach, Normandy, and then to the Battle of Saint-Lô

The Division landed in Normandy operated in the Cotentin Peninsula and formed the right flank of the Operation Cobra assault. D Day at Omaha Beach J.E. called a "NIGHTMARE" Ships offshore bombardment of US Ships and bombs dropping overhead while J.E. drop the lead half- track into water and winding narrow paths until he reached the top of the ridge. So many challenges J.E. faces and resolves.
—**Rita Sammons Harrell**

## 'I spent the night in a foxhole reciting the 23rd Psalm'

Behind Omaha Beach the ground rose into what some soldiers remember as a "hill" or a "ridge," and others who climbed steeper areas call a "bluff." Beside the bluff are the rocky cliffs leading to Pointe du Hoc.

The debris of battle was still evident when Cpl. James Sammons drove his half-track up a narrow, winding path. "I saw signs that said, '*Achtung Minen*,' and when I got to the road on the ridge, there were dead Germans scattered about the top of the hill.

"By this time, the heat gauge on the dashboard of my half-track was in the red zone, but I had to keep moving so the vehicles coming up behind me could clear the ridge. Then we all stopped long enough to put on elbow-length asbestos gloves and remove the waterproofing from the engine and other parts.

"We dug in that night, and German planes dropped flares and breadbasket bombs. I spent the night in a foxhole reciting the 23rd Psalm."

J.E.'s name featured in an unknown Newspaper clipping (2nd paragraph)—23rd Psalm

## HEDGEROW HELL IN NORMANDY

For 3 weeks after we landed at Omaha Beach we were pinned down in the hedgerows of Normandy, as we had no help from the 8th Air Force in England due to the bad weather and fog over the channel.

We were strafed early morning and before dark every night by German fighter planes and then came the night bombers dropping lighted flares then circle and drop 500 # bread basket bombs filled with hot sharp pieces of steel skimming the ground. To survive you had to be under ground. They say there are no atheists in fox holes, not true, we had one soldier in our company an atheists, Charles Walling who was among the first in a fox hole. We lost several men each day and night. One morning after the nightmare in a fox hole we found our medical doctor, Capt. Kelly dead from a concussion from a bomb explosion near his fox hole. Sgt. Cooper and I were detailed to put his G.I. blanket wrapped body into the back seat of a jeep and take him back to a hospital tent near Omaha Beach. On arrival we saw many 2nd Armored Division soldiers on the ground covered with blankets near the hospital tent. The medic that accepted Capt. Kelly's body told us they had more than 50 bodies from the previous days and nights. I spent many nights in a fox hole saying the 23rd Psalm, Lucky again on help from above.

One morning the sun came out over the channel and soon the sky was filled with more than 500 B-17 and other bombers coming to our rescue and then we broke out of the hedgerows toward Saint Lo.

The bombers opened the path ahead, but a few bombs fell short of their mark, Saint Lo and killed more than 200 men of the 2nd Armored and 29th Infantry Divisions. They called it the price of war.

We made our way through Saint Lo which was completely destroyed and on to our next battle with the German 2nd Panzer Division at the Falaise Gap.

Ed Sammons
Co."E" 17th Armd. Combat Engr. Bn.
2nd Armored Division ( "HELL ON WHEELS" )

Omaha Beach and J.E.'s recollection and reflection in the foxhole.

FIGHTER PILOT BOOTS

After landing in Normandy at Omaha Beach D-2 we attacked the 2nd German Panzer Division that had the 101st Airborne Division trapped near Carentan After 3 weeks of battle we finally broke thru Saint Lo and continued to chase the 2nd Panzer Division across France. One afternoon on a hot July day there was a dog fight overhead by the German Messerschmidt planes and the U.S. 8th Army Air Force P-51 fighters. During the fight the German planes downed two P-51's and the others retreated back to England. One of the P-51 pilots ejected and landed by my half-track. We became friends and he stayed with us until a way back to England. When he left he gave me his fleece lined leather vest and fleeced lined leather boots and said - "Where you are going you will need them - Where I'm going they have plenty of them". When we finally reached Belgium still fighting the 2nd Panzer Division we entered the Battle of the Bulge and - the pilot was so right. In our fight in 10 degree ice & snow the boots were the difference between frozen feet & not frozen feet.

    Just one of the many life saving events.

Ed Sammons

# "THE MAP"

## Operation Overlord Map

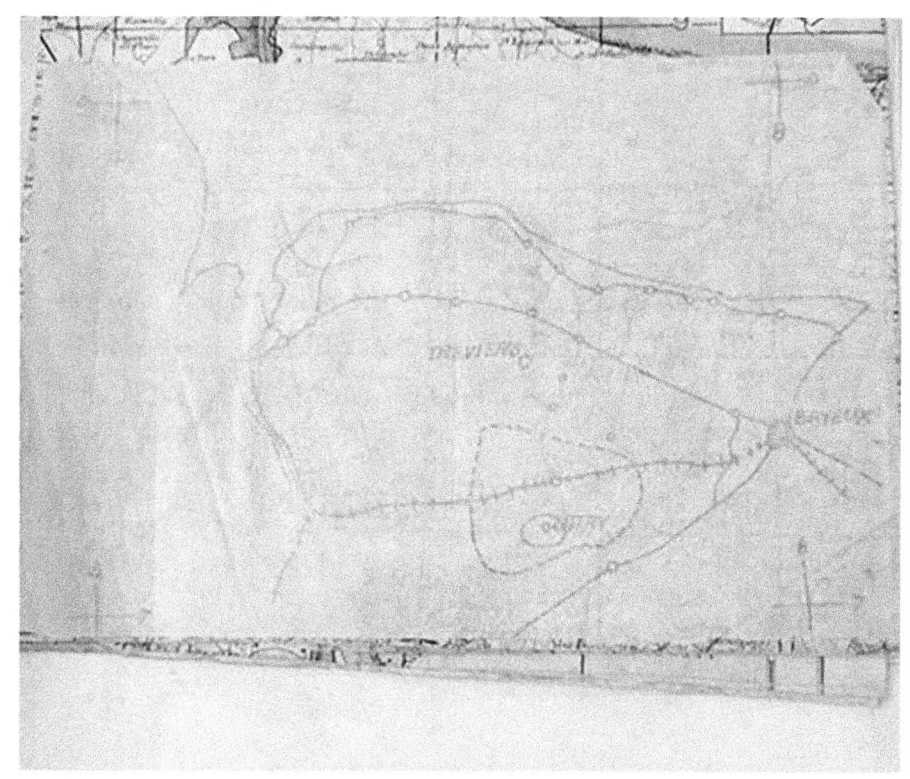

"D" Day Map and Overlay: JUNE 6, 1944—Landed—D +1

THE MAP ISSUED TO EACH "D" DAY SOLDIER PRIOR TO INVASION, SHOWS EXACT LOCATION OF OUR LANDING ON OVERLAY MAP. OVERLAY MAP WAS TO BE—EATEN IN THE EVENT OF CAPTURE. WE WERE TO PENETRATE 2 MILES INLAND TO THE DeMolay -LITTRY AREA.

HEADQUARTERS 2D ARMORED DIVISION
Office of the Division Commander

To Officers and Soldiers of All Ranks:

As we start on our great adventure, participation in the liberation of Europe from the tyranny of the Nazi, I would like to be able to talk to each soldier under my command individually. Since that is not possible, I am writing this personal message to you.

In the spring of 1940, Dunkirk took place. At that time our gallant Allies equipped with a few obsolescent weapons were driven from the continent by a superbly equipped, well trained and vicious enemy vastly superior in numbers. That was FOUR years ago.

Today we are back. The picture has changed. We and our Allies are superior numerically. This time we are well equipped and well trained and we go in with the solid backing of our country and its people.

According to the papers a false invasion report was broadcast in America last Saturday. It was denied within five minutes. But in that five minutes, "there were cheers and tears among the crowds at street corners", "church bells began to ring", and "tens of thousands at a baseball game stood bareheaded for a moment's silent prayer". With the invasion of liberation, such scenes are constantly duplicated in all the lands where righteous people everywhere pray for you, for our Allies, for the success of this invasion.

Its success lies in your hands - in the hands of every Allied soldier - and those hands are capable.

At this moment our troops are driving inland. Our job is to give impetus to that drive - and to drive deeper still.

On then, to battle - find the enemy - smoke him out - kill him, for that is the road to victory.

EDWARD H. BROOKS,
Major General, U.S.A.,
Commanding.

## FIGHTING ACROSS FRANCE – HITLER JACKPOT

After D day, Omaha Beach, Normandy & Battle at Saint LO we the 2nd Armored "Hell on Wheels" Division moved from town to town fighting German Panzer Divisions. We were told that the Liberation and Glory to free Paris was for the French Army. So we turned and moved across Central France and brought freedom to the suffering people of France, Belgium and Netherlands. The French Underground wearing the CROSS OF LORRAINE was always there to take control. In each town they killed all the French Officials that worked for the NAZI and shaved the heads of their women friends.

After our rapid drive to clear one town of German resistance we pulled into a field beyond the town for a couple hours to check our fuel and eat another can of C rations as we were tired, dirty and hungry. Ray Ellis of our halftrack crew, George Miller jeep driver and medic Gene Geneski decided to take Miller's jeep and go back to town for eggs & french bread. On their way they were flagged by a Frenchman and told that German soldiers were ahead in a small wooded area. Ray decided to go around the back side of the woods and George would enter from this side and meet in the middle. Gene would wait at the jeep and if he heard shots come with medical aid. The 3 German soldiers surrendered without a fight. They now had 2 lugars, 1 rifle and a briefcase from the Officer, Sargeant & Private (a bodyguard). They put the 3 prisoners on the front of the jeep and drove into town and turned them over to the French Underground.

In the meantime we received orders to move forward missing one halftrack gunner, jeep driver and medic. We came to a stop about 2AM for rest and while I was sleeping on the ground next to my halftrack the 3 missing comrades showed up with 3 guns and a briefcase. The next day on checking the briefcase, it was filled with french francs of 50 & 100 notes (Made in Germany) about 20,000 U.S. dollars. They divided the money and George stuffed his share in his glove compartment of the jeep.

We moved through France and became the first Allied Soldiers to enter Belgium. In Belgium we over-ran the Belsen-Olsen concentration camp which was empty as the Germans had fled before we arrived. A few days later Sgt. Cooper of our halftrack crew was putting a map into Miller's glove compartment and french francs hit the floorboard. No one knew how they got there when asked by Sgt. Cooper. He played by the book and we were afraid he would report it.(At our 50th Annual Reunion in 1995 we told Dwight Cooper the story of the french francs.)

We fought our way through Belgium & Netherlands to near the German border at Aachen. Gen. Eisenhower said we had won the war and were to have R & R in Paris. Ray, George & Gene became the bank for comrades going to Paris loaning until payday (bogus french francs) to me and members of our company. The military in Washington became wise after they sent us 2 million payroll and we returned 3 million to the States. After 5 days in Paris (and my first bath in 2 yrs) all hell broke loose --- the cold and bloody Battle of the Bulge.

Ed Sammons  6/15/10

## BATTLE OF THE BULGE AT HOUFFALIZE

After fighting to bridge the Albert Canal in Belgium and our battle for Maastricht we re-grouped in the Nov.1944 wet & cold then moved near the German border and the City of Aachen for assault.

The German Army broke thru the line about 100 miles to our South at Bastogne. We backed tracked with the entire division about 75 miles in blackout at night to meet head-on and stop the German 2nd Panzer Division & 560 Volks Grenadier Division at Houffalize, in it's drive to split the Allies and cut off our supply.

The pick & shovel platoon of our Company in 10 degree weather cleared a path over the steep hills of blacktop roads covered with 10" of snow over 2" of ice for our tanks to engage in battle.

I was driver and Morse Code radio operator of Command halftrack for the Company Commander. After 4 days of battle the 2nd Armored Division completely destroyed the 560 Panzer Division. Hitler's SS Storm Troopers called the 2nd Armored Division - " Roosevelt's Butchers ".

A night later (the password was Geronimo) we continued to pursue the Germans and after daylight the next morning one of our halftracks with 12 men on board came to a bridge in the road. Before they could check the bridge for explosives a German 88 bullet crossed the bridge and hit the center of the armored windshield - went thru and out the rear door. Not a soldier was hurt.

IT WAS CHRISTMAS MORNING

Ed Sammons
Co."E"17th Armd Combat Engr Bn
2nd Armored Division
" HELL ON WHEELS "

# FINAL VICTORY

## Crossing The Rhine

Figure 98 J.E. at the Rhine River March 1945

Figure 99 J. E. standing in front of a truck on Hell Day

Figure 100 J. E. sitting on a German Pillbox

## HELL DAY ON THE RHINE

Mar.'45 on our race and route of the German Panzer Divisions from D day, France, Belgium, Holland, Battle of the Bulge to Berlin we overran air fields, Belsen-Olsen concentration camp small towns and battle at Hamelin to get to the town of Wesel on the Rhine. At the Rhine the orders were to remove land mines, raft the infantry assault forces across and build a bridge for our infantry & tanks. We found a good location the night before below a cow pasture. Before dawn we started. I located our half-track about 50 yrds. from the approach site with our crew. We dug fox-holes and maintained Morse Code radio silence as the Germans were listening. Our 142nd Signal Co. laid a telephone line from our half-track to Battalion Command, half mile away which was linked by wire to the 78th field artillery who were to direct fire across the river to cover us from small arms fire and 88's coming in. We were in constant contact by telephone from the fox-hole with Battalion Command. After daylight the Rhine was fogged in and the Piper Cub planes of the 78th were grounded and of little help to the 17th Engr. Bn.

Our Battalion Commander - Col. Correll came in his jeep to direct and check our progress. His driver parked the jeep behind a barn. Afew minutes later an 88 hit the barn and jeep killing Col. Correll's driver. In the midst of all the excitement, noise and dense fog the 88's were killing cows in the pasture and several of us. Later we learned the 88's were mounted on a track firing 4 rounds and moving up and down the Rhine. Richard Kane, one of our medics was helping the wounded by me when hit in his back by a large piece of shrapnel. Lucky Again!

Although the Germans hit the bridge twice blowing out a section each time and 7 comrades we managed to build the longest bridge (1152 Ft. in 7 hrs.) under heavy fire (a record) for our infantry and tanks to cross. Company "E" was decorated with the Presidenti Citation in person by President Harry S, Truman when we reached Berlin. We lost 21 comrades that day.

Ed Sammons
Co."E" 17th Armd. Combat Engr. Bn.
2nd Armored Division

Figure 101 Laundry Service during Hell on Wheels ...battle towards the Rhine River

Notice how there is a difference from the clean uniforms they had when they first landed in Northern Africa!

Figure 102 Crossing the Rhine Courtesy of E Co. 17th Armored Engr Bn

The Rhine River bridge was constructed in record time of 7 hours to defeat the enemy. First picture taken as soon as finished; Co. E. Engineers finished "the inspect-walk" allowing J.E. to take "first picture after constructed".

Figure 103 KRUP Iron Works, Germany, March 1945

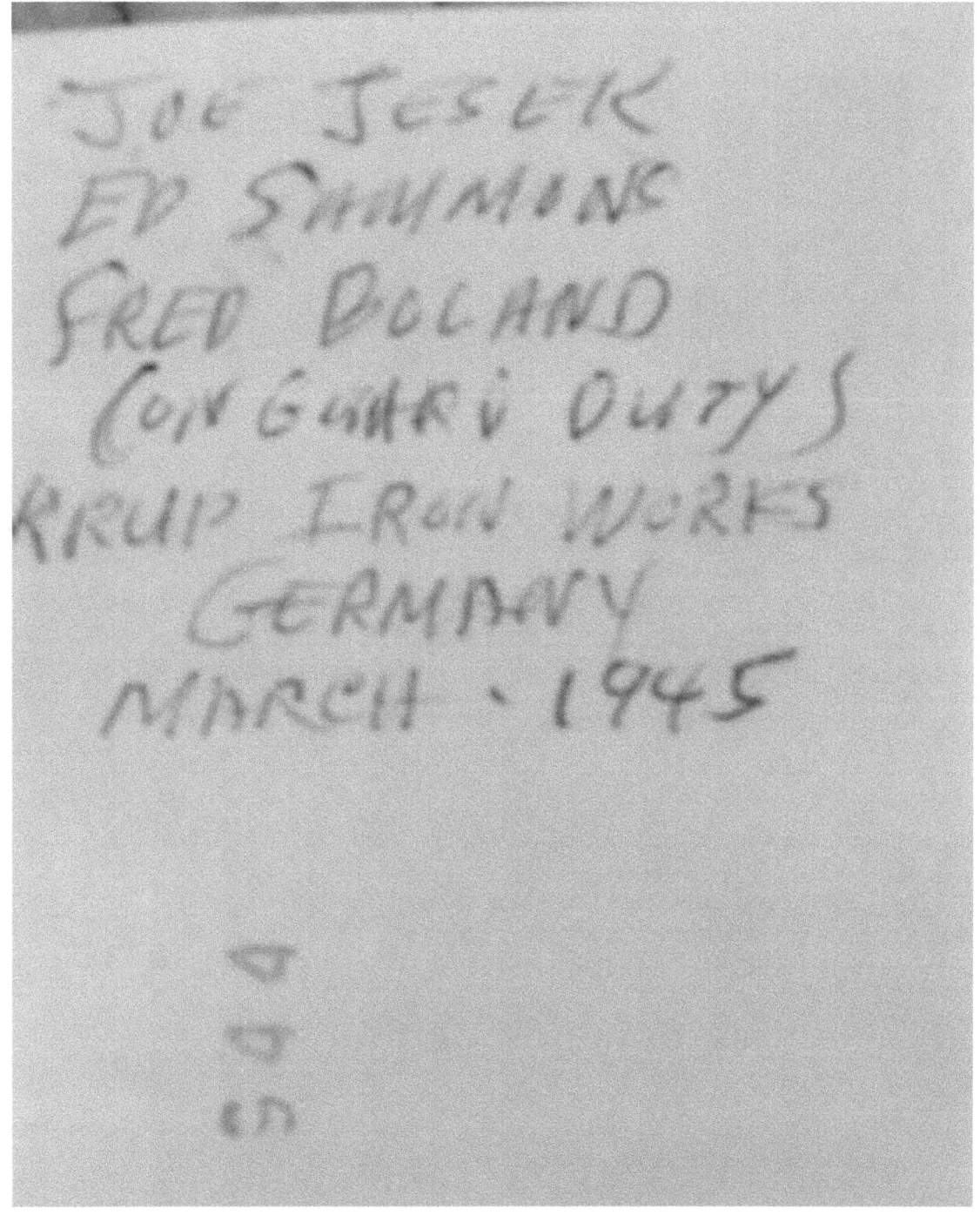

Figure 104  Notes on the back of KRUP Iron Works picture: Joe Jesek, Ed Sammons, Fred Boland (on guard duty) KRUP Iron Works, Germany March 1945

# "THE NOTE"

This note accompanied J.E. in the Rhineland, Siegfried Line, Magdeburg, and the Battle of Aachen

Out of food, gas, water and stripped of supplies, the final assault against the Nazi homeland began in Rhineland and ended in Aachen. Company E completed construction of pontoon bridge with structures to cross in 7 hours. J.E. and his family Unit Company E crossed the ELB River, and the 2nd Armored Division started with 15,000 men, with only 4,000 returning home. This is what J.E. believed… In helping, loving, caring, and fighting for those in need.

Sad but glorious, J.E. said they all were tired and worn out, hungry and filthy in smelly clothes, but each of us soldiers couldn't wait to see the "Ole Girl" in the harbor once again.

—**Rita Sammons Harrell**

# "A life not lived for others …is not worth living"

This is what J.E. believed… In helping, loving, caring, and fighting for those in need. A real life worth living for those of the soldier's life giving….I found the note he kept in his GI cap one day in some of dad's papers. His belief in people was so great of each soldier only positives he could ever relate.

# THE AMERICAN RED CROSS

The following is J.E.'s story of what happened after the Battle of the Bulge… hungry, frozen, nothing could be better than a hot cup of coffee, with a donut to dip into it, and have something inside their empty stomachs after weeks of shelling. But the American Red Cross charged a nominal fee for coffee and donuts, During WWII allied troops could not afford to give away similar items so as not to demoralize allied troops — a dime was charged. The American Red cross sold items at or below cost and did not make a profit from the sale.

Aligning with her father's gratitude to the Red Cross in **GRAMPA'S WAR** for finally *never again charging military personnel.*

"My father, after 77 years, is smiling from Heaven, and reminding us, and all future generations, to remember what he always said, coincidentally as owner of Dixie Cream Donuts in the 1960's, … "Keep your eye upon the doughnut and not upon the hole."

"Thank You again, to the American Red Cross, for their lasting commitment to honor such men, like "J.E." Sammons, our American Hero in PATTON'S HAND OF GOD."

ARC WWII Patch

CPL James E Sammons, my dad if alive today would be sending out his letter of this accomplishment to all of Company E and its wives. With an expression of joy and completeness I know the relief and peace it would have brought the unit of Company E today. The cause of this effect of no dime at the Rhine for these men wore on their minds. I'm sure Dad would have also written a couple poems, sent a nice response and something like this:

*"My Coffee is hot and my doughnut is warm Battling sand and snowy chilly WWII storms*

*A soldier's soul replenishment of spirit returns*

*To complete the battle combat every soldier greatly earned"* *Thank You Again, ARC.*

European African Middle Eastern Campaign medal

This Medal J.E. received from his Algeria-French Morocco, Tunisia, Sicily, Northern Apennines, Rhineland, Ardennes-Alsace, and Central Europe battle campaigns. Dad cherished his awards in remembering those times—***when coffee and a doughnut just cost a dime!!***

### A SALUTE TO HERBIE - THE HERBIE I KNEW

Herbie was there when we were training for war with General Patton at Ft. Benning in 1941.

He was there when we received our first 3 day pass together and hitch-hiked from Ft. Benning to Tallahassee, Fl. and back for a free weekend.

Herbie was there when we built many bridges from Georgia to Texas to North and South Carolina - and later across Europe.

He was there when we crossed the Atlantic through the German U Boats and helped silence the French in French Morocco.

Herbie was there with me in the African Desert when it was 110 degrees in the shade and there was no shade.

He was with me dodging the German U Boats in the Mediterranean and the English Channel on our way to England to prepare for D day.

Herbie was there when we trained for war over the White Cliffs of Dover in England.

He was there when we landed "D" plus 2 at Omaha Beach in Normandy.

Herbie was with me through thick and thin in France, Belgium, Holland, to Berlin.

He was there the night we shoveled sand and dirt all night on the icy hills in the bitter cold and snow for our tanks to hit head-on and defeat the German 1st SS Panzer Division at Houffalize during the Battle of the Bulge.

Herbie was thereand did a great job Hosting many of our reunions from New York to Florida and more.

Herbie always smiled when I called him "DAD". (I'm a little younger).

HERBERT JESSE BARNES was an honorable soldier and one of my best friends and comrade for 60 years.

I miss him - and will always remember the tough times and the many happy times we shared together.

Ed Sammons 1/21/01
"E" Company 17th Armd. Engr. Bn.
2nd Armored division

Dad wept so often for his dear friend and comrade Herbie Barnes. Herbie and his family attended so many Reunions and was a great inspiration of a solider, as dad would say.

## THE GHOST OF A SOLDIER

Visualize if you will the ghost of a GI somewhere in Belgium on Christmas Eve of 1944 as he clutches his M-1 rifle with frostbitten fingers. He stands with frozen feet knee-deep in the snow, weak from lack of food, fatally wounded by constant enemy artillery and heart-broken from the eternity away from his loved-ones.

He is sickened by the death and carnage of war. He looks at us through clenched teeth :

I died for your birthright bestowed by your forefathers in the Constitution and now you allow school boards to graduate your children too illiterate to comprehend its meaning.

I fought in the freezing hell of the Ardennes for your freedom to vote and you stay home because the line is too long or the weather is bad.

I left my family alone and heart-broken to guarantee your feeedom of speech and you remain silent on controversial issues because you're afraid to offend.

I orphaned my children to ensure you a government of the people, by the people, and for the people and now you have allowed it to steal your democracy from you.

It is I, the soldier, not the President who tolerates your freedom to choose your soul-mate.

It is I, the soldier, not your Congressman, who grants you freedom of expression.

It is I, the soldier, not the Attorney General who demands that your protection granted by the Bill of Rights be honored.

It is I, the soldier, not the Priest or Rabbi who provides your right to worship whomever and however you wish.

It is I, the soldier, not the political activist, who allows you the right to demonstrate.

And it is I, the soldier, who follows the flag, who fights for the flag and whose dead body is embraced by the flag, who permits the protester to burn the beloved flag.

**And it is, for damn sure, about time someone did something about it**

Veterans - Battle of The Bulge

Note : This could have been one of my comrades.
       I survived - James Ed Sammons

The Ghost of a Soldier

```
              COMRADES  OF  COMPANY  "E"


                 I'm thinking today at 92
My comrades of co."E" are very few
From Casablanca we did fight
"Hell on Wheels" showed it's might
My Comrades of Co."E"
We took Palermo Sicily in four weeks
General Patton paraded in the streets
D-Day training at White Cliffs of Dover
To Omaha Beach we went over
We rolled through France like "Hell on Wheels"
In Belgium we knocked the Germans on their heels
My Comrades of Co."E"
In Holland they sang with glee
My comrades made them free
Battle of the Bulge in freezing snow
From Bastogne to Houffalize the Germans had to go
March on the Rhineland was our last big fight
We crossed the Rhine fighting day and night
My Comrades of Co."E"
Our war ended at Magdeberg - we were tired
Co."E" & "Hell on Wheels" soon to be retired
Our Monument at Valley Forge is here to stay
Stop and see Co."E" - it will never move away

Ed Sammons   9/12/11
```

Comrades of Company E (poem)

Dad delivered these two, especially the "Ghost of A Soldier" story in many reunion receptions.

Dad would recite the "Comrades of Co. E" poem, many times, and again one of the last ones before he died, and we cried. As dad would always sit in an armchair—but came and sat beside me on our sofa. With hankie in hand, he placed his hand on my knee and shook his head in gratefulness that he survived and had such a wonderful family life.

# Reunion Poem

## – by Rita Sammons Harrell

J.E. pals and buds gather here above; he knows what really matters

To J.E. the relation with each and every SOULdier to grow together older

J.E. started his first Reunion of all his buds and families started in 1946 It became a time of releasing by telling stories and pics

Soon the Reunions became quite a family affair Every year, a solider hosted his hometown place

A release of stress from a soldier's face as all would embrace

# STORIES WRITTEN ABOUT D-DAY

## J.E. and Co. E

### Because they were right there...

J.E. Stories and Material Notes from an article (unknown source) provided by: Rita Sammons Harrell

*Cpl. James E. Sammons was accustomed to going places where he was not welcomed. He had fought his way into North Africa with the U.S. 2nd Armored Division, invaded Tunisia and charged up the beaches of Sicily.*

*Normandy was next. His outfit was waiting inside a barbed-wire enclosure near Portsmouth on the coast of England. It was the evening of June 5, 1944.*

*"They trotted out the best dinner we'd had since leaving home _ steak, fresh vegetables, fresh fruit. We were being fattened up before the kill."*

*Behind Omaha Beach the ground rose into what some soldiers remember as a "hill" or a "ridge," and others who climbed steeper areas call a "bluff." Beside the bluff are the rocky cliffs leading to Pointe du Hoc. The debris of battle was still evident (which included a description of body parts being collected by the medics, which we have decided not to include in this writing) when Cpl. James Sammons drove his half-track up a narrow, winding path. "I saw signs that said, "Achtung Minen,' and when I got to the road on the ridge, there were dead Germans scattered about the top of the hill. "By this time, the heat gauge on the dashboard of my half-track was in the red zone, but I had to keep moving so the vehicles coming up behind me could clear the ridge. Then we all stopped long enough to put on elbow-length asbestos gloves and remove the waterproofing from the engine and other parts. "We dug in that night, and German planes dropped flares and breadbasket bombs. I spent the night in a foxhole reciting the 23rd Psalm.*

Figure 106 Cpl. James Edward Sammons wearing his stripes and the most important battle theatre ribbon..."Battle of the Bulge"

STORIES WRITTEN about D-DAY | 253

Figure 107 Rita and J. E.

# PART 3: "GOD'S HAND"

My Hospitable Dad… and America's Hero

## Finally, Home... to my Love, Bea!!!

Figure 108 J.E. and Bea

This book would not be possible without the strength and love of my mom who wrote daily letters to my Dad J.E. during all his battles. They met at the USO before Dad's deployment into the Army. J.E. saved many of my mom's encouraging letters while in foxholes, and thru the trenches. These letters and Dad's pocket bible gave J.E. the strength to look forward to another day, as many bombs were near misses to him.

J.E. saved everything from WWII. I just could not list all the wonderful stories he told, and all the Army wives and buddies he helped over all his living years. He had a gift of perception, recollection, and dedication. This is not like any soldier story, but the story of how a young boy became the spiritual strength of the 17th Company E. One day long after my dad had passed, I drove to my sister's house and picked up all Dad's boxes of love.

Figure 109 J.E. and Bea in front of Dad's new car after the war

Figure 110 J.E., Bea, J.E.'s mom

Figure 111 J.E. and his mother

J.E., and his mom Daisy Lee Wilroy Sammons…I didn't get to meet them until I was three. The other family picture is of my mom, Joan, and little Wilroy. Both Joan, little Wilroy and Merle (not pictured) were all a vital part of J.E.'s close family. All of them played a vital part in contributing to J.E.'s stories.

Figure 112 Hell on Wheels collage, mounted on cardboard

This photograph mounted on a thick cardboard backing and displayed on the table for every— 2nd Armored Division 17th Battalion Co. E, "HELL ON WHEELS" Reunions. Memories that carried J.E. physically and mentally from 1941 thru 2012. J.E. was an American Hero in servicing his fellow soldiers and families the rest of the days of his life. He remains in many hearts today as the example of true love, hospitality, and faith.

# PRESIDENT HARRY S. TRUMAN

"President Harry S. Truman" …U.S. President Truman personally decorated the men of Co. E 17th Battalion Engineers of the 2nd Armored Division—HELL ON WHEELS! For the first time on German soil, Truman awarded a "Presidential Citation." The "Hell on Wheels" demolished and built bridges in record time to defeat the Nazi's. This citation was a heartfelt monumental moment in history for these "Patton Boys". Present at the citation was Gen. George S. Patton, Jr. who had tears in his eyes….and J.E.'s good friend Lt. Col. Correll as head of the formation etc.

Later J.E. would invite President Truman in 1965 to be their guest at their Annual Reunion. President Truman sent a letter back to J.E. of regret that he and Bess could not attend and saluted J.E. and his Reunion Group for their great service to our country.

**—Rita Sammons Harrell**

HARRY S TRUMAN
INDEPENDENCE, MISSOURI

June 16, 1965

Dear Mr. Sammons:

Thank you for your invitation to Mrs. Truman and me to attend the Banquet on September 4, in Bethesda, Maryland, of Company E, 17th Armored Engineer Battalion of the 2nd Armored (Hell on Wheels) Division - during the Annual Reunion.

We appreciate the invitation most highly and sincerely wish we could be present but my schedule at that time prevents a trip to Washington. I am as sorry as I can be.

You have my best wishes for a big turn-out and a very happy reunion.

Sincerely yours,

Harry Truman

Mr. J. Edward Sammons, Chairman
Annual Reunion, Company E, 17th Armored
Engineer Battalion of the 2nd Armored Division
9514 Edgeley Road
Bethesda, Maryland 20014

# PRESIDENT EISENHOWER AND MRS. EISENHOWER

President Eisenhower and Mrs. Eisenhower…June 9th, 1965 from the office of General Dwight D. Eisenhower, J.E. received a response in regards to the Company E, 17th Battalion 2nd Armored Division Reunion banquet. Dwight was a big part of the Invasion of North Africa, directed the invasion of Sicily, spearheaded the beaches maneuvers of Normandy and won battle for freedoms WWII. J.E. always had such high respect and regards towards Eisenhower, and the General and Mrs. Eisenhower appreciated J.E.'s thoughtful invite in regret and wishes the best for an enjoyable reunion celebration. —Rita Sammons Harrell

OFFICE OF
DWIGHT D. EISENHOWER

Gettysburg, Pennsylvania
9 June 1965

Dear Mr. Sammons:

I have been directed to respond to your cordial letter, inviting General and Mrs. Eisenhower to attend the banquet of Company E, 17th Armored Engineer Battalion of the 2nd Armored Division in Bethesda on Saturday, September 4th.

I regret to advise you that they will be unable to accept your kind invitation as they are planning some extended trips during and surrounding the time of your celebration. I am sorry.

Nonetheless, General and Mrs. Eisenhower appreciate your thought of them and extend their very best wishes for an enjoyable and successful reunion.

Sincerely,

ROBERT L. SCHULZ
Brig. Gen. U.S.A. Ret.
Executive Assistant

Mr. J. Edward Sammons
9514 Edgeley Road
Bethesda, Maryland 20014

# PRESIDENT RONALD REAGAN

"President Ronald Reagan"…Hail to the Chief—In 1985 President Ronald Reagan salutes J.E. and the men of Company E. 17 Battalion for their vital contribution that gained our freedoms today. Always a positive and one of the most optimistic and humorous presidents, Reagan also fought in WWII in the Army Reserve.

Ron was one of J.E.'s favorite Presidents, loved his acting years and his economic push for our country. J.E. was thrilled to have President Reagan's acknowledgement to him and his Reunion Club. J.E. was so proud at this time to be an American and rally around the flag of freedom from their victories in combat engineering for the United States!

**—Rita Sammons Harrell**

THE WHITE HOUSE
WASHINGTON

October 15, 1985

I am pleased and honored to send warm greetings to the officers and enlisted men of Company E, 17th Armored Engineer Battalion as you gather for your 40th reunion.

Throughout its involvement in World War II, your unit rallied to the cause of freedom with honor and distinction. You made a vital contribution to our final victory. I join all Americans in recognizing you and in paying tribute to the extraordinary service that you and your departed comrades rendered to flag and country.

Nancy and I salute you and send our best wishes for a happy and memorable 40th reunion. God bless you.

*Ronald Reagan*

# PRESIDENT BILL CLINTON

"President Bill Clinton"...On September 12th 1995 and ironically J.E.'s birthday, President Bill Clinton sent J.E. a greeting to him and Company E, 17th Battalion Engineers of the 2nd Armored Division. President Clinton acknowledged the great sacrifices of the unit as great heroes during our crucial period in history. J.E. actually talked with an accent like Clinton and used his thumb press as President Clinton to make a point. Bill Clinton had a great sense of humor and was such an entertainer. Clinton saluted the unit with their distinguished record of service in the Army with well wishes for all the bonding and memories at their Annual Reunions.
—**Rita Sammons Harrell**

THE WHITE HOUSE

WASHINGTON

September 12, 1995

Greetings to the veterans of Company E, 17th Armored Engineers, 2nd Armored Division, as you gather for your fiftieth annual reunion.

Your unit served the United States with honor and distinction during a crucial period in our history. We owe our liberties to the sacrifices of people who, like you, were willing to risk their lives for freedom. I know you join me in honoring your fallen comrades.

Each of you embodies the pride, professionalism, and accomplishment that make the United States Army one of the finest fighting forces the world has ever known. I salute you for your distinguished record of service, and I hope that you will enjoy your time together as you reflect on the bonds you share.

Best wishes for a memorable reunion.

*Bill Clinton*

# J.E.'S CORRESPONDENCES

## Sharing History

### Letter to Stephen Ambrose

What inspired Dr. Ambrose to suddenly show up at a reunion of an "Easy Company" in 1988, and prompt him to collect their stories turning them into "Band of Brothers, E Company, 506th Regiment, 101st Airborne: From Normandy to Hitler's Nest (1992). D-Day (1994). All of Stephen Ambrose's material was based on "oral historical accounts", by veterans that had experienced the same specific moments in history that found them in these epic battles… the same as J.E. !

The following "J.E. letters" to Stephen Ambrose represent actual "oral historical experiences" that Dr. Ambrose used to comprise his first best seller.

Christopher Lehman-Haupt, writing for the New York Times proclaimed the following: "Reading this history, you can understand why for so many of its participants, despite all the death surrounding them, life revealed itself, in that moment, at that particular place".

### And … also Letters to & from Tom Brokaw

*"When I wrote about the men and women who came out of the Depression, who won great victories and made lasting sacrifices in World War II and then returned home to begin building the world we have*

*today—the people I called the Greatest Generation—it was my way of saying thank you. But I was not prepared for the avalanche of letters and responses touched off by that book. I had written a book about America, and now America was writing back."*
—**Tom Brokaw**

July 21, 1987

Dr. Stephen E. Ambrose, Director
Eisenhower Center
University of New Orleans
New Orleans, Louisiana 70148

Dear Dr. Ambrose,

Enclosed is my personal view of what happened to me as an overall picture of the situation before, during and immediately after D day.

There are many ugly details I could include, such as who was killed, wounded, how, why, and during. However, these details remain in my memory and not yet on recall.

I hope these thoughts will be of interest to future historians concerning that sad day, yet a day of liberation in a fight for our freedom.

I am looking forward to the 50th Anniversary in remembrance of D day and hope to join you and others on that historic day.

If I can be of further assistance in this matter, please advise.

Sincerely,

*James E. Sammons*

James E. Sammons
2431 Grove Ridge Drive
Palm Harbor, Florida 34683

JES/bm

Ambrose letter

The response I have received to The Greatest Generation and The Greatest Generation Speaks has been overwhelming and most gratifying. I appreciate your letter and kind words.

Thank you for sharing your story and perspective on this era with me. This is testimony to the lasting effects of these memorable times.

Thank you again for thinking of me.

All best,

Tom Brokaw

2/9/01

Tom Brokaw letter reply to J.E.

January 28, 1999

Mr. Tom Brokaw
NBC 20 Rockefeller Plaza
New York, N.Y. 10112

Dear Mr. Brokaw,

    Congratulations to you on your best selling book about our Great Generation of World War II veterans.

    I watched the Larry King Show and the interview with you and happy to learn a newsman with your credentials has finally told it like it was. We veterans who served are grateful to you. We did what we had to do in order to preserve our Freedom.

    Let me tell you about a comrade in arms during World War II - Captain James M. Burt, Congressional Medal of Honor recipient - a REAL HERO to me and the men of our Division he led into battle. Perhaps you have heard of him - if not, you might want to investigate him for your next book and show the tremendous sacrifices this wonderful soldier made for our Liberty and Freedom.

    He lives in a suburb of Reading, Pa. Last Fall his home town in South Lee, Mass., dedicated a monument to him. This humble American's life is worth a book in itself.

    In October 1944, we were fighting to capture Aachen, Germany and Hitler had given orders that no allied soldier was to enter the soil of the Fatherland. The fighting raged for four days with the ferocity revealed in the citation which accompanied the Medal of Honor awarded by President Harry S. Truman to Captain James M. Burt.

    REFERENCE : "HELL ON WHEELS" - THE 2nd ARMORED DIVISION
               BY: DONALD E. HOUSTON
               CHAPTER 14 - BREACHING THE SIEGFRIED LINE
               LIBRARY OF CONGRESS CATALOG # 76-58757

    This was but a small part of our journey from Benning to Berlin that we have celebrated the past 50 years at our annual reunions.

Sincerely,

*James E. Sammons*

James E. Sammons U.S. Army Ser. # 33040248
The Landings at Sea Forest
4522 Seagull Dr. # 217
New Port Richey, Florida 34652-2069
ENCL. Part of speech by me at our 52nd Annual Reunion October '97 to my comrades of Co."E" 17th Armored Combat Engineer Bn., U.S. 2nd Armored Division

J.E. letter to Tom Brokaw

3 February 1999

Dear Mr. Sammons,

The response I have received to THE GREATEST GENERATION, book and documentary, has been overwhelming and most gratifying. I appreciate your letter and kind words.

Thank you for writing and sharing your experience of that era. I look forward to looking into the reference you sent about Captain James Burt.

All best,

Tom Brokaw

James E. Sammons
The Landings at Sea Forest
4522 Seagull Drive #217
New Port Richey FL 34652 – 2069

Tom Brokaw's second letter to J.E.

## The National World War II Museum

"The National WWII Museum"…A video contribution was recorded and taped by a historian of the National WWII Museum in 2010 of J.E.'s seven campaign battles. J.E. was proud and spoke without any prompting or papers. J.E. seemed clear of each battle campaign and spoke with sensitivity and feeling as if he were reliving it. J.E. wanted so much to share this vital info for his children and grandchildren.

**—Rita Sammons Harrell**

Oral History Interview discs

THE NATIONAL WORLD WAR II MUSEUM has 2 recorded interview Disc's with 2 sides of Part 1 and Part 2 on display at the museum in New Orleans, LA. Shortly before J.E.'s passing the museum contacted dad to hear his side of the 7 Battle Campaigns he fought. These are descriptive, and his memory, humor, humbleness, and depth of love of his country is way beyond patriotic. It is astounding, fascinating on the recollections and the hospitable manner he showed his unit.

These 2-sided video discs are really dramatizations of recollected accounts of the 7 campaign battles with the 17th Battalion, 2nd Armored Division. Have a tissue ready for Uncle Eddie as he goes into detail on what the soldiers went through.

An honored and excited Dad to receive the copies of his video discs. He gave all of us girls a copy for keepsake.

Figure 113 35th Anniversary Reunion Program

## Patton's son attends the 35th reunion

What a thrill it was to have Patton's son Major General George S. Patton attend their 35th Reunion at Pooks Hill Marriott! It was a great turnout and dad was so happy to open arms to the son of the General that had led them to victory. J.E. pulled out no stops when it came to being the "hospitality guru."

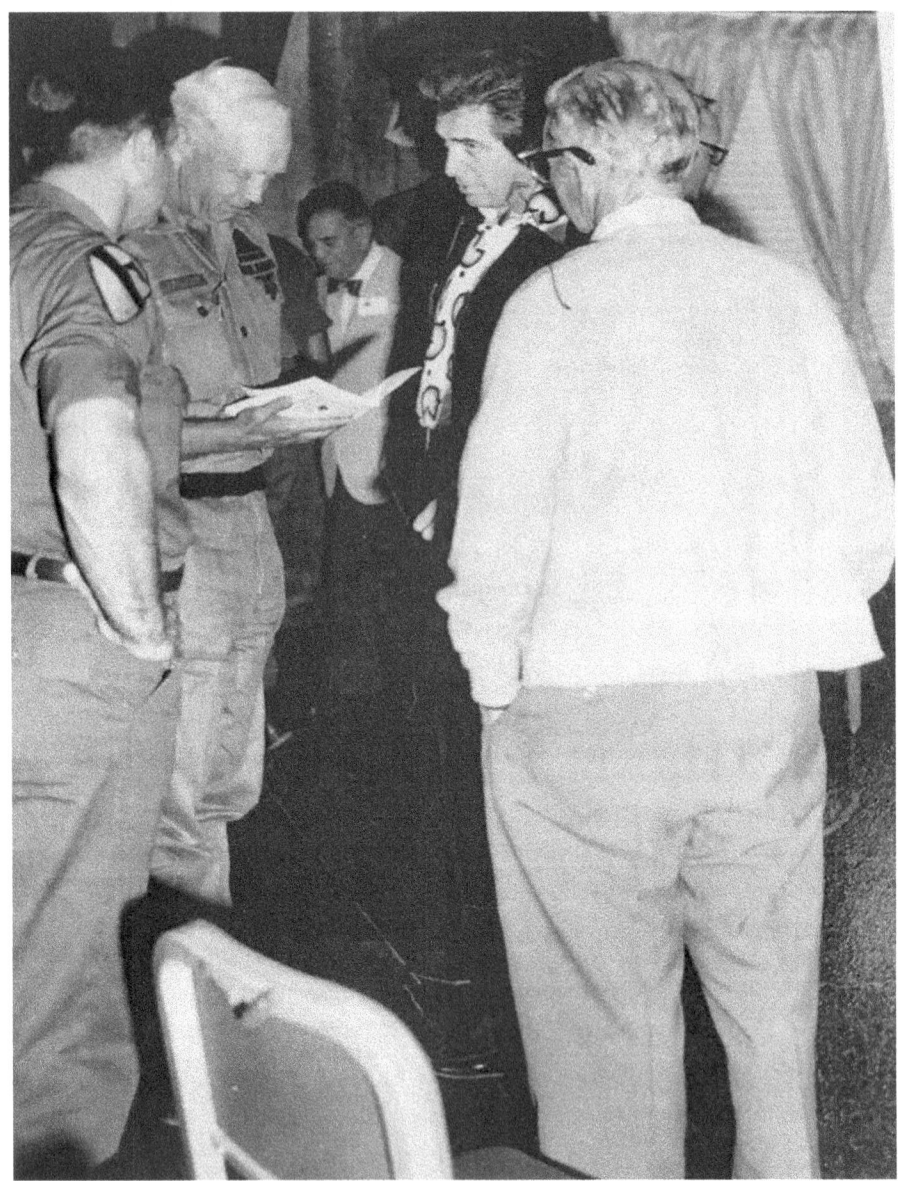

Figure 114 Robert Pryor interviews Patton

Robert Pryor interviewing General George S Patton. Bob was J.E.'s Radio School Buddy and a good friend. Robert took on the Reunions of the 2nd Armored Division and also came to the 17th Reunions.

General George S. Patton was a complex commander and general with a personality driven by his belief on this earth in combating the evil enemy in WWII. From real live maneuvers, hitting J.E.'s half-track with his swaddle tick to "MOVE IT" in his gruff demanding voice—soldiers of the 17th Battalion, 2nd Armored Division, Company E, gained their respect knowing that this was the leadership needed to be successful.

GENERAL GEORGE S. PATTON JR. In charge of "HELL ON WHEELS"

## THE LEGACY CONTINUES...

Figure 115 J. E.'s Granddaughter, Carrie

My patriotic daughter, Carrie receiving her certificate from the US Air Force for her part in assisting in the Iraqi Freeman operation. Following in her grandfather's footsteps in engineering and drove a 5 Ton-6x6 Truck in Iraq.

Figure 116 J. E. and Bea at the head reunion table

Mom and Dad at the head reunion table as always. Then Dad would get on the microphone and start welcoming every single family, and usually say something funny about each soldier attending.

Figure 117 40th reunion cake, 1985

Always had a Reunion cake every year. Plenty of sweetness and beer.

Figure 118 1989 Reunion Gun Salute

Figure 119 Spencer, Nebraska, J. E. on float

Who's the man in the center!! He —who stands afloat so tall and stern, must be my dad never self-concerned. Fun times in Spencer, Nebraska for a reunion of finger licking hog picking.

Figure 120 Dad with his granddaughter, Carrie at her wedding 2006.

Figure 121 Dad and Carrie dancing at her wedding.

He loved being with all the family and held tight Carrie's hand as he knew she too, was a driver of a half-track and crew engineer in Iraqi Freedom Operation War.

Figure 122 Welcome to Canadaigua, Reunion of 1992

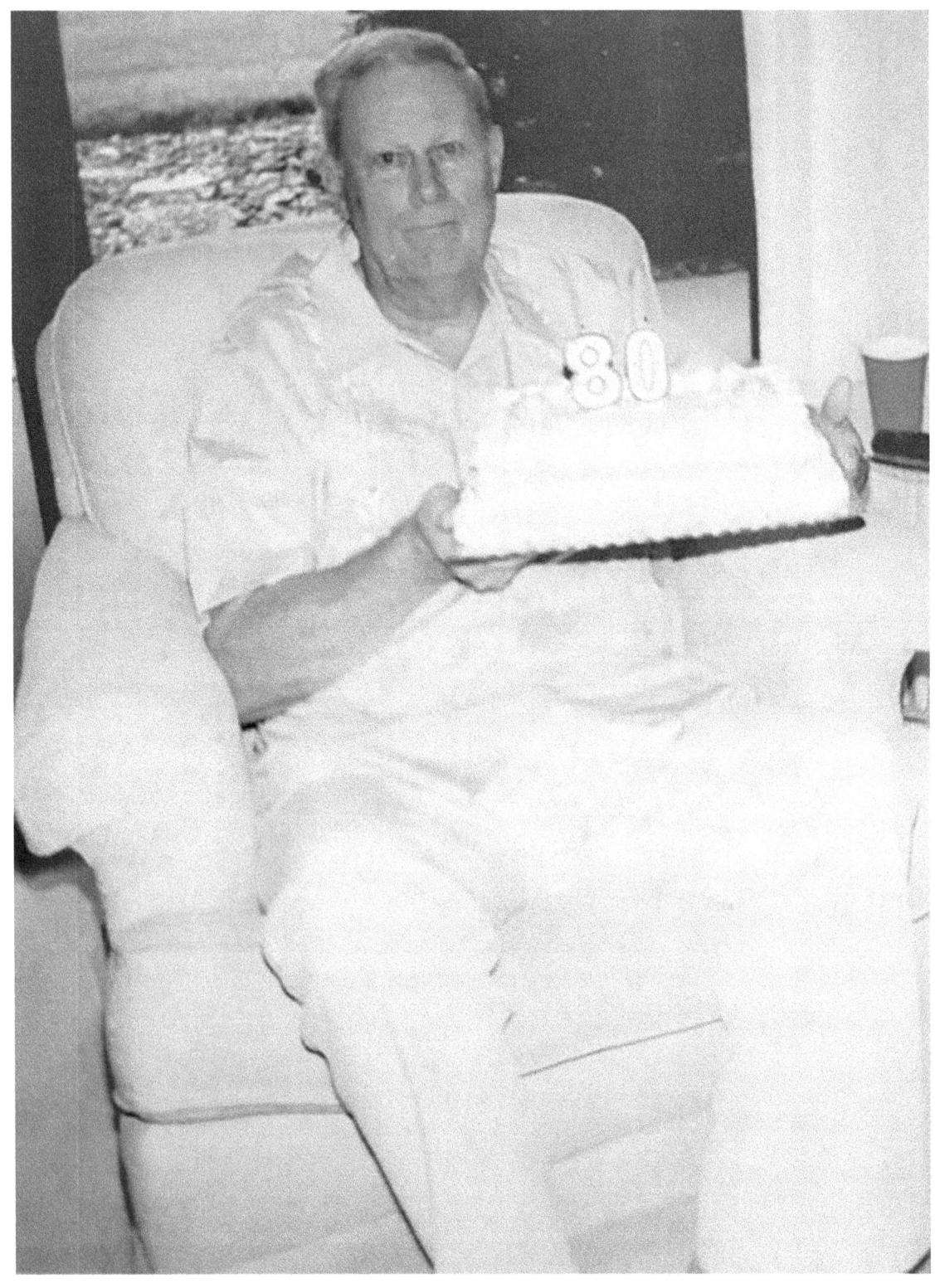

Figure 123 Dad's 80th in Palm Harbor

# Crossing the Bar

Sunset and evening star

And one clear call for me !

And may there be no moaning of the bar, When I put out to sea,

But such a tide as moving seems asleep, Too full for sound and foam,

When that which drew from out the boundless deep

Turns again home. Twilight and evening bell,

And after that the dark!

And may there be no sadness of farewell, When I embark;

For tho' from out our bourne of Time and Place

The flood may bear me far,

I hope to see my Pilot face to face When I have crossed the bar.

**- Tennyson**

*Crossing the Bar (Dad's favorite poet, and poem)*

Dad's favorite poem that he carried around in his briefcase from Mel's house to mine during his monthly stays at a time.

Figure 124 J.E.'s 3 beautiful granddaughters and cousin Julie Harris celebrating

Figure 125 My husband, Blaine

**Rita...**

Your Dad, and his Brave Division,
fought, sacrificed, and 'built the bridges'
that helped win WWII.

It is your love, respect and perseverance,
that now guarantees his memories of the War
will never be forgotten.

I, and all of your family...
Now, past and future...
Will aways be in awe of the hours and years of hard work you spent in preserving his memories, by creating this wonderful book.

A book, and legacy, that will be read and studied for generations to come!

**Thank you, to my husband Blaine, for your advice, editing and consistency in getting PHOG done.**

Figure 126 J.E and his blonde little girl, Rita

I was always "Daddy's Girl" and could hardly wait to sit upon his lap. As you can see in this picture of my mom's family—GRAMPA Chaon at the head—Mom next to dad with her hand. Dad stretching his hand towards me. This picture brings back so many wonderful memories!

Figure 127 Our family in Milwaukee WI. Six kids. I'm on Dad's lap. The only blonde!

Figure 128 J. E. and Rita (Palm Harbor)

Dad relaxing with me at Palm Harbor Florida before they moved to Newport Richey. I came to help with a yard sale. We ate dinner at dad's favorite restaurant and had our favorite crab cocktail etc.

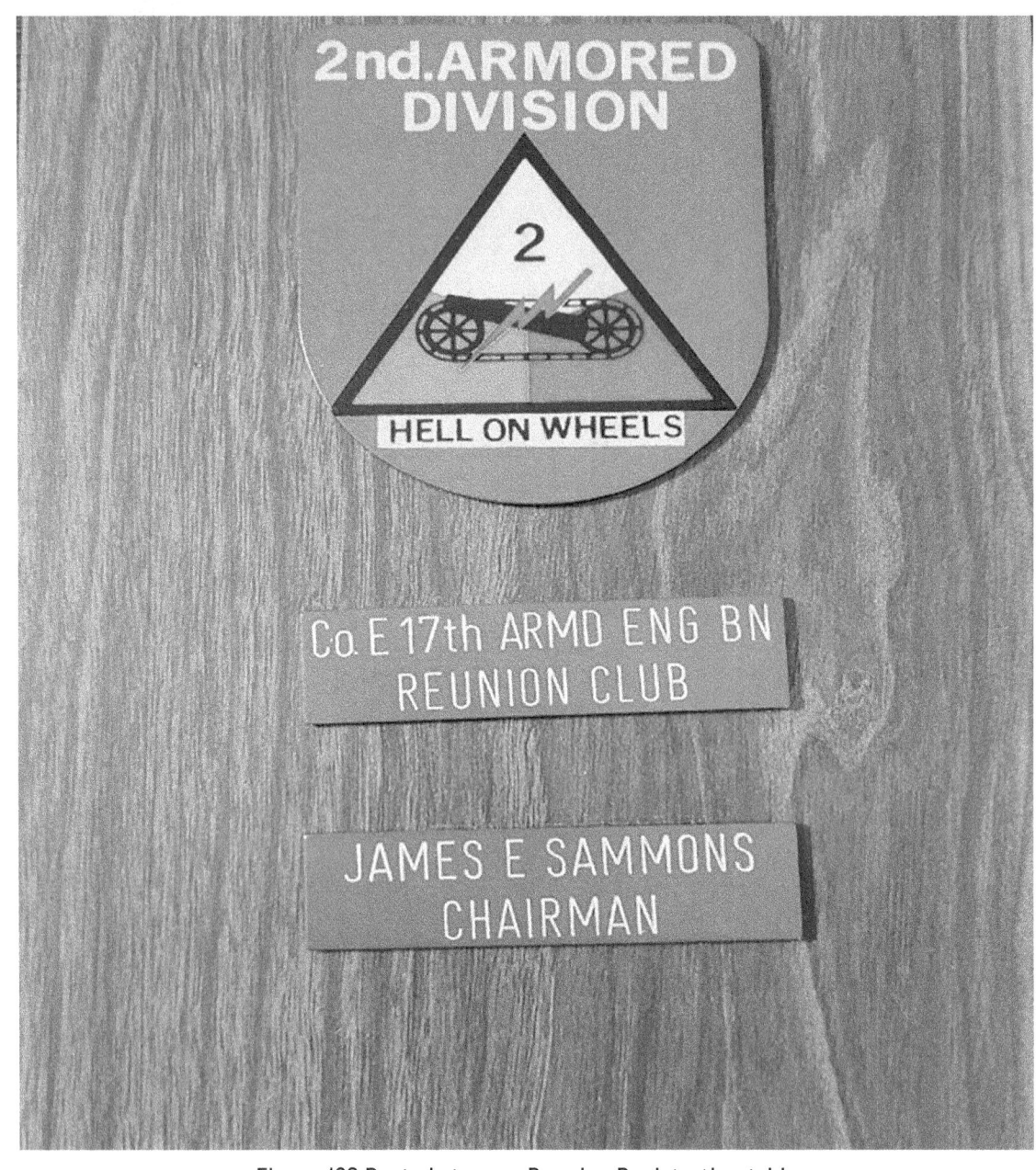
Figure 129 Posted at every Reunion Registration table

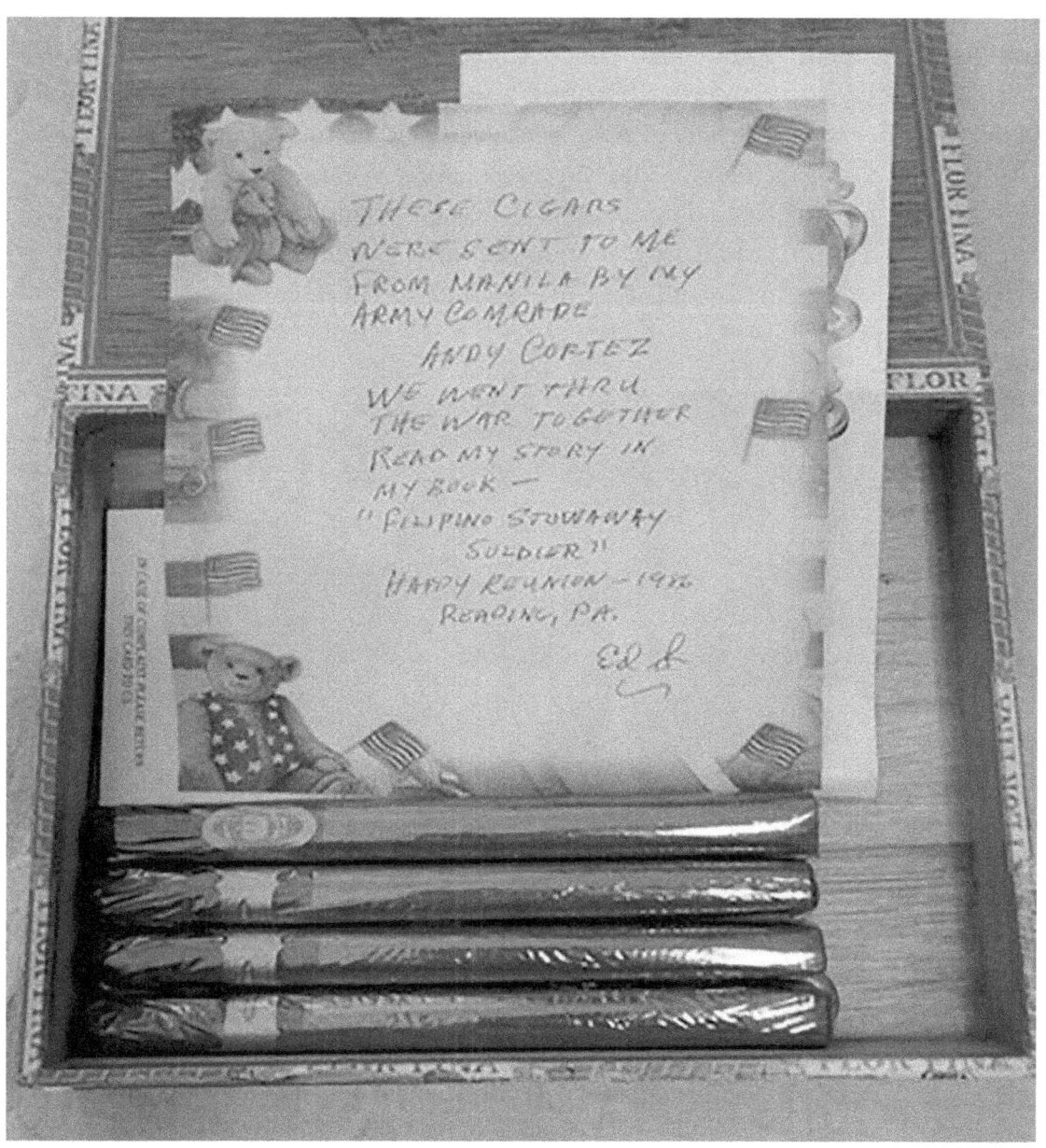

Figure 130. Box of Cigars with note

## Hospitable "Filipino Stowaway Story" in J.E.'s "GRAMPA'S WAR"

Is so much of the emotion and devotion of Co. E and Andy, a stowaway refugee and how he survived by the hospitality of a Captain, and crew. A lesson of love, faith, and "great hospitality" towards our fellow man.

J.E. wrote this story about Andre Cortez. How he strived and literally, starved himself, going after his childhood dream of "going to America". The story is with heavy heart and such great respect and admiration for this stowaway, who becomes a soldier in J.E.'s unit. His determination, dedication and sacrifices were never-ending. Andre received the Silver Star, 2 Bronze Stars, 2 Invasion Arrowheads, Belgian Croix de Guerre and the Presidential Citation. Andy became the beacon of light that ignited all those in attendance at the 41st Reunion Banquet. There was not a dry eye in the house. After 41 years, Andre and his wife entered the hotel dining room and walked in with a cane as his unbelievable story begins.... (full story in "Grampa's War").

Figure 131 48th Reunion picture

J.E. was so proud to be at this reunion. Many could not attend, as some wives came on their own. To still fill the hospitality room with handmade gifts and girdles. (the story of the famous "girdle" in Grampa's War).

Figure 132 J. E.

Figure 133 Carrie

J.E. in uniform and granddaughter Carrie just graduated from the United States Air Force. So Ironic that she was stationed in Balade, Iraq driving the Half-Track thru the sandy dirt roads at the Army base during Operation Iraqi Freedom war.

Figure 134 J. E.'s Lucky Strike Cigarettes and note

Lucky Strike went to war!! J.E saved all his first cigarettes and everything he could keep to someday tell and show his story of war.

## LUCKY STRIKE WENT TO WAR

This carton of Lucky Strike cigarettes was purchased by Ed Sammons at the Fort Dix, N.J. PX in October 1942. Total cost of $1.70. I was taking these along in my duffle bag for emergency cigarettes.

These LUcky Strike cigarettes travelled with me in combat for more than 1700 miles - to NOrth Africa, Sicily, England, Omaha Beach D day, Normandy, Northern France, Belgium, across the Rhine to Berlin. (Cigarettes were in our rations so I never needed them).

Lucky Strike green was needed for the war, so all future cartons were white.

I gave away a few packs to cigarette lovers and one pack to Esther Chaon as this was her favorite brand.

# "Patton was right" ...
## said J.E.'s buddies in WWII, Melchior Lascola and Al Provenzano

Figure 134 J. E.'s buddies

*"Patton was right"…reminded us that "time will tell…when the Russians will strike against the Allies!* On the left, Melchior Lascola, and Al Provenzano recall the days as General Patton's combat engineers; and two of J.E.'s frequent Co. E. Reunion attendees.

Recent events by the Russians in Ukraine proved that not stopping the Russians in 1945, proved a risk of not stopping their ultimate goal…. Now being Putin's world domination… starting with an invasion on an innocent country

## "Patton was right..."

"Awwright…let's get this party started", yelled J.E. at the crowd, now starting to settle down after hearing the typical three gavel banging.

Those sitting at the 22 tables registered were the veterans from Company "E" 17th Armored Engineer Battalion of the 2nd Armored Division…General George S, Patton's famed "Hell On Wheels".

It was their 32 Annual Reunion being held at a local resort in Glen burnie, Maryland, hosted by Cpl. J.E. (James Edward) Sammons, and his lovely wife, Bea, always smiling and greeting everyone from her seat at the front of the room, alongside her forever partner, now standing at the podium.

"Awwwwwright….now, where were we…oh yes. Now then… many of you may not have heard the complete stories from our New Jersey and Connecticut representatives, Pvt. Melchior Mascola, and Cpl. Al Provenzano…..So without further adieu…. Here's Mel…."

"Thanks J.E.", started Melchior, taking hold of the microphone with his right hand, and using his left hand to flip the connecting cord away from him as he started to stand. "In Oran, Algeria, after we were dropped off in Northern Africa, there were three of us… I'd sell shoes to the Ay-rabs".

Then his other two buddies, posing as MPs, Military Policemen, would confiscate the shoes, further along the way. This way, they would have them back for a "resale" to other new customers.

"And, you can imagine…that by the time we sold the same pair 30 times…we had made a few dollars", laughing so hard, he practically fell over to the table, still hanging on to the cord and the mike.

"But…but no, we didn't stop there…no sir!!!", exclaimed Mel pointing now with one finger, while still holding the mike.

"When we were in that cork forest….yes, (as he pointed to Leo Mecler, who had been one of the cooks)….in Mo-rocco… we would cut pieces of cork, and disguise them with empty wrappers, and sell them as cartons of cigarettes. It was quite a money-maker since the Ay-rabs were paying $100 a carton… and I guess now, they're getting' even with us with the oil!!! **(note: this was 1977, when the Carter administration was dealing with the national gasoline shortage crisis!)**

As the applause started to wind down, you could hear the comments by a couple in the back saying, "Same old…same old", which was immediately disputed by a sharp…"No, they do tend to change their stories, just a little…year after year!!!", laughed Norma Seegmuller.

"And this convention", joked her tall and burly husband, Frank, "was sponsored by the money left over from the loot we received in Berlin !!!".

"Ohhh yeah…I love to listen to 'em goin' on year after year," exclaimed Marian Proven- zano, whose stocky husband, Al, was a corporal under Patton.

J.E. again stood up and read from the podium:
"Awright….I would like to mention a couple of things…first, that Noel Whittington, did not make it this year to show the motion pictures that he took of every reunion. Noel passed last Friday, in Winston-Salem, and according to a couple of buddies who stayed to take care of Noel's arrangements…he fought to the very end".

In the Co. "E" Reunion notes it further mentioned how much the majority of the men respected General Patton. Mr. Mascola was in the minority, saying that Patton found GI's altogether "too expendable". He could never forget, he said, Patton's assertion that "he was going to take a town…even if it took a truckload of dog-tags".

But in the end of the reunion, both, Pvt. Melchior Mascola, and Cpl. Al Provenzano agreed and insisted that "Patton was right". The general had maintained that if Roosevelt had not stopped him , the general would have gone in and "cleaned up the Russians, and we wouldn't have this problem with communism today".

***Special Note:** The above article was put together from J.E. notes, and newspaper clippings from the late 1970's.

**\*Disclaimer:** *The characters and their comments are presented to provide a perspective on the historical events and do not reflect the personal views, beliefs, or values of the author and publisher. The content is based on historical records and interpretations prevalent at the time of writing and should be understood in the context of the era in which these articles were created.*

# FIFTY-TWO YEARS OF REUNIONS

"52 Years of Reunions" …How sweet it was—fifty-two years of rare heartfelt stories of men of Co E 17th Battalion 2nd Armored Division Annual Reunions. Known as "the Patton Boys" these men remembered and relieved historic moments until the "last hurrah" in 1997; as many of the sidekicks already made it to heaven.

The years ahead were the hardest battle for J.E., as he lost so many of his dear friends, their wives and families. Concentrating on his book and poems kept J.E. motivated on his smith corona typewriter and 1975-word processor to finish his book. J.E. was the vital link for all his war buds to communicate, release and relate their worn-out memories. J.E. was the keeper, observer and mediator to each soldier.

**—Rita Sammons Harrell**

FIFTY-TWO YEARS OF REUNIONS

Members - Family - Friends :

   Thanks for making our 52nd Annual Reunion at Myrtle Beach a happy and enjoyable " LAST HURRAH " with cake, food, stage shows and friendship event. It has been an interesting and enjoyable 52 year journey with my wartime buddies, meeting, talking and remembering them each year as we travelled from Wash. D.C. to Va., Md. Pa. N.J. Ohio and to the New York World's Fair in '64 then Gettysburg, the Carolina's to the Nebraska Ranch to and Florida. I have fond memories of each reunion.

   It all started one day in Spring of 1946, when Bea and I visited my buddy Charles Gnau and wife Ruth. We looked at the Co.:E: Roster I had from the war and decided to try to reach a few of the nearby fellows for a great get-together to celebrate return to civilian life. We held our first reunion on Labor Day Weekend in '46 at the hoel Hamilton in Wash. D.C. How Great it was ! It was then on to the World's Fair, D.C. again in '65, saluted in '65 by personnel thank you letters from President Harry Truman and Gen. Dwight Eisenhower. On to Gettysburg in '75, Disney World in '85, saluted again in '85 by personnel letter of thanks from President Ronald Reagan. In '95 it was Sand Key Island in Florida and a personnel letter of thanks from President Bill Clinton, plus all the fun locations in between.

   We also endured the passing of many of our fellow soldiers and friends which was always difficult for our group. I feel they have been looking in on us and saying - Well done. We are part of the " Passing Parade in the history of men fighting for freedom. It is now time to pass this on to the next generation. We shall always be a part of military history as evidenced by the historic monument dedicated to the men of the 2nd Armored Division, along side General George Washington at Valley Forge. This beautiful monument was dedicated in 1981. when in the area - Stop and see a part of military history dedicated to you and your loved ones.

   I could write a book of all the characters and happy times we have shared together. It has been a wonderful journey and as Gen.MacArthur said in his farewell - 'OLD SOLDIERS NEVER DIE - THEY JUST FADE AWAY"

   Thanks for the memories     May God Bless


Ed Sammons, Chairman
Co."E" Reunion Club
17th Armd. Combat Engr. Bn.
2nd Armored Division ( Hell on Wheels )

# 1997 REUNION

The "Last Hurra*h*" in Myrtle Beach South Carolina 1997. Only a few wonderful men left to attend. Most passed by 2014 -except Russ Allen who passed in 2022, J.E. and Russ spoke by phone weekly with a few others holding on to life. I could hear Dad's deepest voice holding back the tears, he would clear his throat to pat his fellow soldier one more time on the back and remind them of the days of all their great work on their half-track. It took a lot to make these calls, but Dad's I believe knew his calling. It was to comfort those falling. Sometimes he would just pick up the phone and call the wife, to cheer her up and tell a joke or two. Then on to memories of what their great husband in the war would do. I would stand in the doorway of Dad's WAR room; my heart would hurt and the strength it took. It was always a depth of deep emotion and pride with his heartfelt sigh, Dad would camouflage his cry. "There is no goodbye" Dad would reply, "I'll see you on the other side".

## Three Men at the Table
## The Ladies Auxiliary Room

FIGURE 136 J. E. 1997 Reunion

NORTH AFRICAN WAR - WITH MR. PEANUT & ME

After we the 2nd Armored Division landed at Casablanca and the ground fighting was over, we still had daylight strafing and nighttime bombing by German planes. After about 2 weeks we moved 20 miles North into a thick cork forest. The German U-Boats in the Atlantic were sinking most of our food supply so we were short on food.

So I wrote the story of MR. PEANUT & ME and sent it to Mr. Obesi the founder and owner of Planters Peanuts. He sent me 12 cans of Planters Peanuts. (During the war there was a limit of size and weight of packages.). I shared the peanuts with my halftrack crew.

Then I had another idea - write B&M Beans in Portland, Maine and ask for B&M Beans (we need food). Several of the women employees at B&M sent me 5lb boxes of B&M Beans with victory notes enclosed. The halftrack crew and I had a "Tooting Good Time".

52 years later before our 50th Annual Reunion of 125 members, family and friends, I again wrote the story of MR. PEANUT & ME to Planters Peanuts and they sent me 125 cans of Planters Peanuts to serve at each table for each person attending our banquet at the Sheridan Sand Key Reunion at Clearwater, Beach Florida.

Then I had another idea - Write the story of B&M Beans to Portland, Maine about the nice women employees of 1943. B&M Beans then sent me 2 cases of 48 cans each of B&M Beans for our 50th Reunion Celebration. "Another Tooting Good Time".

NOW YOU KNOW THE FULL STORY OF MR. PEANUT & ME
B&M BEANS AND - "ANOTHER TOOTING GOOD TIME"

Ed Sammons

North African war with Mr. Peanut

Peanuts were J.E.'s childhood that he truly enjoyed throughout his entire life. I remember Dad grabbling a handful, shaking around the salt in his hand then throwing them in his mouth with a perfect catch. Peanuts were everywhere. Large can by his TV stand. Upstairs in a candy dish. Always packets in his pockets and the gift from his family in Virginia.

Figure 137 Can of Planters – 50th Reunion

50th REUNION had a can of Planters Peanuts placed at each table setting.

August 2, 1995

Director of Marketing
Nabisco Foods
Planters Division
P.O. Box 41
Winston Salem, N.C. 27102

**PLANTERS PEANUTS WENT TO WAR - WWII**

In 1943 in North Africa while fighting the Germans, food was scarce thanks to the German U-Boats, so I wrote a V-Mail letter to Planters Peanuts at my home town of Suffolk, Va. and asked if they would send me some of my favorite food "NUTS", as we were very hungry.

Many thanks to Planters, I received in North Africa a carton of 12 - 8oz. cans of Planters Peanuts, which I shared with the crew on my Command Half-Track, that is - all but one can that I kept as emergency food in a safe compartment where we stored our extra ammo and land mines.

That can of Planters travelled from North Africa to England then on to "D" Day at Omaha Beach, France, Belgium, Holland, Battle of the Bulge to Berlin. In 1945 at Berlin, Germany, President Harry S. Truman personally decorated the men of Co."E" with the Presidential Citation for valor under extreme enemy fire and more than 1500 miles in combat from North Africa to Berlin.

I never used that emergency can of Planters Peanuts and found it recently in good sealed condition in my old army trunk in the attic along with several other items I saved from the war.

~~NOW - 100~~ of [A FEW OF] the remaining men & family of Co."E: 17th Armd. Engr. Bn., 2nd Armored Division from General Patton's Army will celebrate their 50th Golden Annual Reunion at the Sheraton Sand Key Hotel, Clearwater Beach, Florida, September 28, 29, 30, 1995.

NOW - We would like to tell the World - once again we have Planters Peanuts to enjoy while I tell this unusual story at the reunion. We would appreciate the appropriate number of Planters nuts so that one can be set at each place setting for the Saturday Night Banquet.

Thank you very much for your kind consideration.

Sincerely,

James E. Sammons, Chairman
2431 Grove Ridge Drive
Palm Harbor, Florida 34683-3220
Tel. 813 787 4147 (unlisted)

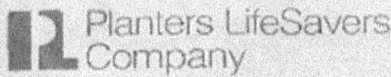

August 22, 1995

James E. Sammons
2431 Grove Ridge Drive
Palm Harbor, Florida 34683-3220

Dear Mr. Sammons:

We, at the Planters Company, were flattered to hear from you and your group and are pleased to contribute to your 50th Reunion Celebration.

Your team's brave campaigns during WWII were certainly worth a great deal more than peanuts. However, with Planters and Mr. Peanut there with you, we know that we helped to boost your endurance and your morale.

So, enjoy our fresh cans of Planters Peanuts and accept our praise for your victories.

And remember when you are food shopping, don't forget to grab a can of Planters Peanuts, and Eat Your Planters!

Congratulations,

Robert J. Gfeller, Jr.
Business Director - Planters Company

Letter from Planters Peanuts

Figure 138 1990 reunion (two pictures); above the "brave ladies", and below, their "brave heroes"

All these happy faces, I remember so dearly, and so clearly, as if it was yesterday....
Oh, then how the men and women were always separated. This was the way of life to keep the hardships and horrific memories of war from their wife…The "WAR ROOM" Dad always made sure it was set up at every hotel reunion for each soldier to share their stories, hold each other's arms, grab a tissue, and thank God and I heard several times "if it weren't for Patton we might not be here today.

Figure 139 Author portrait – Rita Sammons Harrell

After going through this whole experience of reading dad's writings and lots of research, I discovered a deep love for my father in a more honorable and heroic way. Always felt close and loved listening to all his stories, …. just wish I had known, when he was still alive, of all his most honorable glories…Everyone is a messenger of memories and moments.

```
            ALTAR OF BATTLES
         2nd ARMORED DIVISION WWII
      FREEDOMS FOUNDATION VALLEY FORGE, PA.
             DEDICATED JULY 1981
FOUGHT IN - FRENCH MOROCCO, SICILY, OMAHA BEACH NORMANDY,
      FRANCE, BELGIUM, NETHERLANDS AND GERMANY
   TRAVELED THRU - ALGERIA, TUNISIA AND ENGLAND
 INVASIONS - NORTH AFRICA, SICILY AND OMAHA BEACH, NORMANDY
 CAMPAIGNS - NORTH AFRICA, SICILY, NORMANDY, NORTHERN FRANCE,
      ARDENNES, RHINELAND AND CENTRAL EUROPE
```

```
THIS IS A BRIEF SUMMARY AND PICTURE OF THE ALTAR OF BATTLES AT VALLEY
FORGE. THE FLOOR IS MADE OF LARGE STONES FROM AND WITH NAMES OF EACH
STATE AND COUNTRY WE TRAVELED THRU FROM BENNING TO BERLIN. FROM THE
ALTAR THE LONG APPROACH WALKWAY HAS A BRASS PLAQUE ON EACH STEP NAMING
EACH BATTALION AND REGIMENT IN ORDER OF BATTLE CASUALTIES. THERE IS
A TREE PLANTED IN MEMORY OF EACH CONGRESSIONAL MEDAL OF HONOR RECEIPIENT.
THIS MEMORIAL IS A PERMANENT REMINDER TO FUTURE GENERATIONS AND A TRIBUTE
TO THOSE BRAVE MEN THAT GAVE THEIR ALL FOR FREEDOM. Co."E" REUNION CLUB
DONATED THE REMAINING REUNION FUND TO THIS HISTORIC MEMORIAL FOR PERPETUAL
CARE.   ED SAMMONS 1/98
```

Figure 140 Alter of Battles

Valley Forge altar of battles

Valley Forge where J.E. had the Reunion and was very much impressed with the Altar of Battles. Some of the engineering he thought might not withstand weather and time and wrote to the Freedoms Foundation and suggested to reinforce with metal some areas of the Altar.

Figure 141 J. E. with great grandson Brayden

Dad holding great grandson Brayden who got his great grandfather's blue eyes! How he loved his children and all his grandchildren. So humble, honest, and honorable. I remember the day before he passed 2 of his great grandchildren, Ryan and Addison made their love posters to send off with him in the parking lot from the hospital before his last journey home to heaven.

Figure 142 J. E.

J.E. taking it easy, and enjoying the Florida sun… an American hero deserves it!

# THE 1992 REUNION ROSTER

## 1992 Reunion Roster --- From: Russell G. and (Lillian) Allen To: Jo and (Pete) Zuko

Although many of them had passed, J.E. still continued to hold his most dearest event for 5 more years until his last hurrah in 1997.

```
1992 ROSTER                Co."E" Reunion Club 17th Armd. Engr. Bn.
                                   2nd Armored Division

Allen, Russell G. (Lillian)
Althouse, Charles E.
Barnes, Herbert J. (Lorraine)
Browne, Erwin P. (Zelda)
Campbell, Charles A. (Marge)
Cooper, Dwight A. (Marian)
Cortez, Adriano (Emelinda)
Correll, Lewis W. (Val) Bn.Comm.
Desiderio, Mario (Mary)
Diederickson, John J. (Anna)
Dudley, Edmond (Audrey)
Emig, Gerald M.
Erstein, Barnie (Rita)
Foy, Charles D. (Opal)
Gouge, Howard
Greene, Glen W. (Opal)
Griffin, Earl W. (Frances)
Griggers, Harold (Radio & Ruby)
Harmon, Frank Sr. (Norilynne)
Hedges, George K.
Illig, Herman H. (Lena)
Jackson, Charles C.
Kerr, William V. (Helen)
Leta, Joseph S. (Kay)
Marc, Arthur (Lois)
Masch, George A. (Angie)
Miller, George C. (Lillian)
Nissen, Herman (Margaret)
Powell, Charles W. (Dorothy)
Provenzano, Almond B. (Marian)
Rice, Jack (Bertha)
Sammons, James E. (Ed & Bea)
Scruggs, William R. (Margaret)
Seegmuller, Frank (Norma)
Sigrist, Arthur (Marian)
Sikora, Mathew (Esther)
Simpson, Orvell (Irmgard)
Sorensen, Melvin (Frieda)
Strickland, Edward L. (Shirley)
Sullivan, William J.
Sykes, Vernon F. (Myrtle)
Trail, Charles R. (Katherine)
Turner, James E. (Hennie)
Whisenant, George L. (Dottie)
Wiegman, Walter C. (Ella)
```

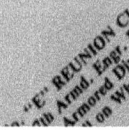

1992 ROSTER (continued)

Co."E" Reunion Club 17th Armd. Engr. Bn.
2nd Armored Division

Associates ;

Atkins, Keith (Donna Belle)
Bacon, Arthur (Rose)
Bechtel, Fritz (Arlene)
Dye, Clara (Leon Roberts)
French, Emily (Russ Sayce)
Gnau, Ruth (Charlie)
Jackson, Evelyn (Marshall)
Ketchpaw, Jean (Gordon)
Mecler, Ann (Leo)
Pfeifer, Martha (Joe)
Stewart, Doris (Walt)
Sutton, Bonnie (Al)
Veltman, Mary (Al)
Wright, Millie (Harry Young)
Zukow, Jo (Pete)

Figure 143 J.E. at the podium

At each Annual Reunion J.E. would give his Chairman of the Board speech. Many times, he would reflect on a war battle story and then when hankies came out of the purses-he would start with the war jokes and funny stories. It was a way they all got their support and relief from physical and mental battle wounds. I reflect on Robert Frost's "Mending Wall" poem- "Something there is that doesn't love a wall and wants it down."

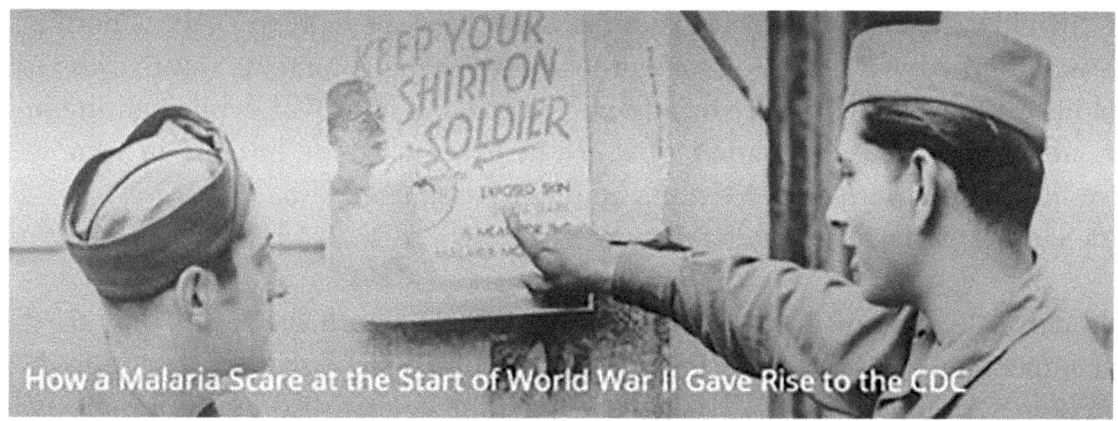

WWII and Malaria

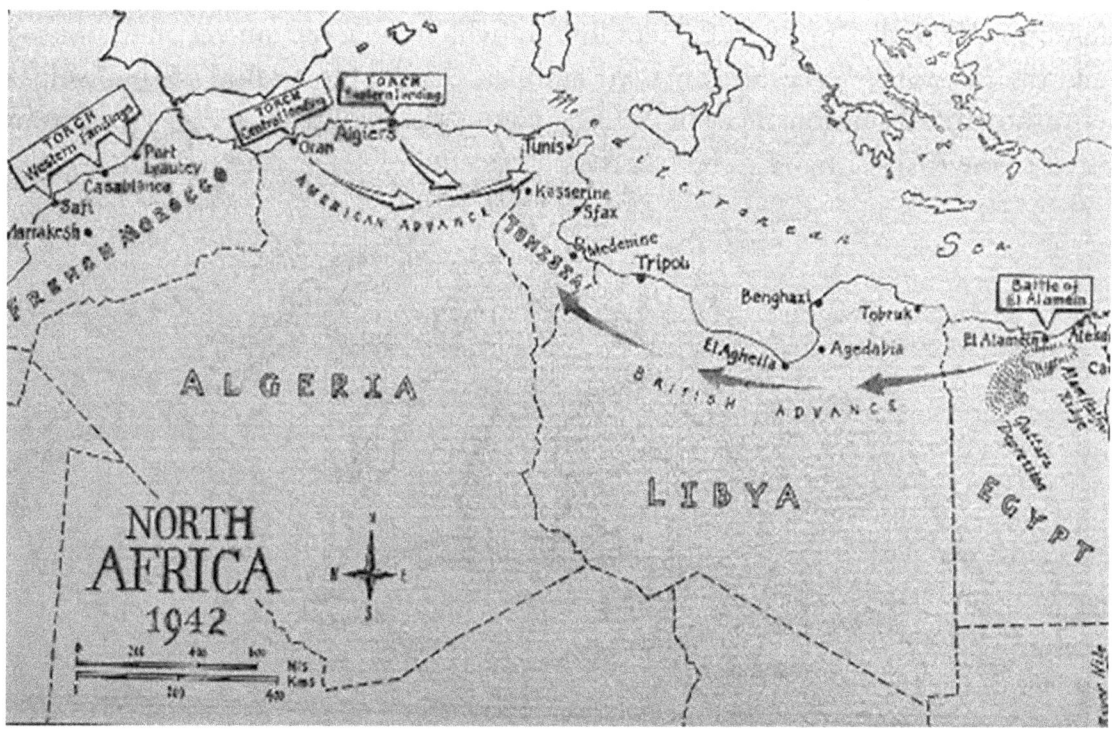

Figure 144., J.E., and the U.S. ARMY... Why???

Malaria and J.E. were not friends. My dad had the bitter fight of the Army's recognition until his end. Dad got malaria during the North African Theatre Battle Campaigns in 1943. I remember Dad with night sweats, and feverish chill-body aches. He wrote to the Army headquarters year after year in St. Louis. I still can hear his typewriter plugging away, with each of his index pointed finger so forcefully on his smith-corona. Then, asking for another stamp needed to mail yet another letter to the Army. Then like clockwork, every few months, came the same reply to Dad … "nothing on file… all records were burned in a fire". Even one of Dad's last dying comments was that the Army never recognized his lifelong torment of having contracted Malaria in WWII, while fighting in Northern Africa. J.E. never received compensation, of which he never asked for, but just an acknowledgement would have sufficed. I'm sure other Veteran Families have suffered also.

- **Rita Sammons Harrell**

I would dare say, that one of the first things we did to research the reason why the U.S. Army allowed a compensation or a simple "acknowledgement of the facts" that J.E. had indeed contracted a disease in North Africa during WWII, was to contact the Veteran's Administration in Washington, D.C., and especially one of Author Rita Sammons Harrell's childhood friends in Bethesda, former CDC Director Robert Redfield.

And we did get an answer, as to the reasons why, and the solution to this miscarriage of caring for our veterans, not only of the "Greatest Generation", of which there remain very few, but to ALL U.S. veterans, and their families. Yes, especially their families, that had to endure the hardships of watching, as the Author Rita Sammons Harrell did as a young girl, while her father typed away another letter directed to the Army…never to receive a reply, worthy of his sacrifices.

MEMORIES OF LONG AGO

Now that I'm 90 years young
My memory tells me many things I have done

I was drafted by President Roosevelt at age 21
Being a combat engineer in the Army was not fun

The famous Gen. Patton war speech we were told
At Fort Bragg in the sand and cold

I crossed the Atlantic Ocean twice
German U boats were not nice

I landed at Casablanca and covered French Morocco too
11 days fighting and then the Germans were few

It was on to Palermo Sicily to fight on the go
At Palermo General Patton was the big show

In England at Tidworth we did train
D Day at Omaha Beach Normandy was our aim

We fought the Germans from Casablanca to Berlin
Presidential Citation by Harry S. Truman for our win

Many hardships and casualties we did bare
You could only know if you were there

We were known as "Hell on Wheels" among the best
Hitler's soldiers know the rest

I have only 4 comrades that remain
We did our best for Freedom Reign


Ed Sammons   9/12/09

Memories of Long Ago

# J.E.'S SALUTE TO "HELL ON WHEELS"

## .... And let Freedom Reign!

A Casablanca and French Morocco poem Dad had composed, on his first fight to begin the war. It was a hot, dusty, and trying experience for J.E.'s first taste in real-time war. Many of his comrades would say later that they thought this time was the most trying of all, especially when many contracted Malaria and heat stroke. The "donkey story" Dad tells is quite compelling and you can visualize the ordeal of how they had to spy on the enemy. (Note: You'll find this story in "GRAMPA'S WAR")…Oh, the fun and heavy stories J.E. shared at all the reunions, of French Morocco. All of J.E.'s buddies would "donkey" into town to get in on all the info. On the next hit, as all the soldiers would gather round listening to the radio with a cigarette lit. J.E. with his sunburned face…sandy sweat drenched clothes and hot air you could practically slice through. But it wasn't just the enemy that was trying to stop the Allies…it was a disease. Some of the men including J.E. got Malaria. I remember Dad would be sick and with fever-he would say he got this from his time spent in Africa. For many years J.E. suffered with symptoms and wrote countless letters to the Army for compensation or just acknowledgement. Never a word back.

# EPILOGUE

Freedom's Sacrifices gave J.E.'s Family… a Future… This is not where this story ends…

My dad, J.E. wanted to leave these inspiring writings of these rare accounts of wartime for a soldier in WWII. A book for his grandchildren, their children, and generations to come to know the hardships and sacrifices that were made to keep the freedoms we hold so dear today.

Dad too was very successful in many endeavors while raising a family of six with mom. One important take-away bothering Dad was the story of needing a dime for a doughnut and cup of coffee with the Red Cross while in battle at the Rhine. J.E. had not a dime at the time. No dough and no doughnuts, but J.E. had plenty of cans of "Planters Peanuts." Dad thought it was a crime, not giving a soldier fighting four and half years of his lifetime! These feelings he could not get off his mind. Years after being a successful corporate controller for a major building company-he came home from work one day –laid several doughnut boxes on the table and asked which ones we liked best. Dad raised the dough as the story goes with the opening of our family's "Dixie Cream Donuts Shop" on busy Rockville Pike in Rockville, Maryland.

You might ask why the book is titled Patton's Hand of God… Many viewed Patton as too fierce and hard on the soldiers, but I do know that Patton's name was only mentioned in a remarkable sense with all of Company "E" at the Reunions. The power and relentless hand of Patton striking Dad's half-track with a "swaddle stick" yelling "Move It!" was a lasting imprint in the minds of these young soldiers of Company E who knew they could make it through the War following Patton's lead.

With the hand of my father, I have delivered to you his writings, poetry, and feelings of a humble and heroic soldier that gave four and half years of his life to "Pave the Way" for our troops to have the foundations to cross, ride, conquer and divide. This incredible unit of the 2nd Armored Division, 17th Battalion fought in deserts, mountainous terrain, winding hills, freezing cold battles with hungry bellies and hopeful hearts. Losing their commander, comrades, and officers in many battles by land mines, gunfire, and bombs. Just imagine being in a foxhole holding a tiny bible in the palm of your hand reading Psalm 23 *"even though I walk through the valley of the shadow of death, I fear no evil"*. I have Dad's little bible and it is kept in my palm now.

Every year starting in 1980 Dad would write his yearly poems. Many of these poems are an insight into what J.E. was really feeling during the wartime and later growing old with each passing birthday year. He cherished all his family and friends. The passing of many of his close war buddies were extremely hard and he would say "another day—and we lost another." Tears in his eyes he would continue to eat his favorite bread and butter.

Dad knew his years were few when he wrote his last poem at age 92. He was more than a soldier, father, and friend he was my hero until his end. Dad was an inspiration to all the fellow soldiers and would write and call them often. He would call and yell their sidekick name when they answered. Then they would talk and recall the wartime stories. He even would call the widowed wives and remind them of their husband's wartime glories.

Since I have a theatre background and have acted in many plays, Dad would always look at me and say; "Hey Reetz, you are like your cousin "Peggy Hopkins Joyce" who made her debut acting in the 1920's on the Hollywood stage!" I would laugh and never take it seriously, until one day when Dad approached me with his family roots writings where he was right! We are cousins to one of the first Hollywood's actresses who skyrocketed in the late 1920's. Peggy's grandmother is directly related to my grandmother and the Wilroy family. How incredible, that Dad had stored this information in the back of his mind, and I guess it is now my time to investigate and see what I can discover besides all her "lovers, Hollywood gossip, and crazy stories". Aside from the boarding school I attended in Chevy Chase, Maryland, I also attended a boarding school in Maple Mount, Kentucky, where I performed at "Jean Stapleton's Parkway Playhouse".

Peggy and I may have similar parallels, but I truly believe she has gotten a "bad rap" on who she really was. For this reason, I plan to finish another book project, "Cousin Peggy…the real One", and hope to show the warmer and more loving side of my former cousin. The 1920's were unforgivingly tough for women, in Hollywood, totally dominated by men, where women had to prove their worth, especially in a new industry called "motion pictures". My cousin Peggy was considered "too extreme" because she was way ahead of her time. I am hoping that I can also be ahead of our time, and provide women of today, that side of Peggy, as she was born and known as Marguerite Upton… a model of a "Modern Woman", for all times!

**Rita Sammons Harrell**

# TO MY DEAR DAD ...

Dear Dad,

I wish you were here to wipe away my tears. It has been a very difficult year.

Your book is going to be published just the way you wrote.

It reflects your love, courage, and so many wonderful quotes.

Finding all your stacked boxes filled with so much love. Your book is now complete with my hand and one above. Your hand always looked like mine.

I will now return a tribute to you of your heroic time.

Your soldier ghost haunted you in so many ways. Now its released into the world and no more replays.

The world will know you and forever cherish and discover. How you sacrificed and truly lived a life for others.

Yes Dad, you lived as you said-" A life not lived for others is not worth living" and coined the phrase:

Yesterday is gone Tomorrow may never come

So, I must enjoy the moment called today.

**Rita Sammons Harrell**

# ACKNOWLEDGEMENTS

I would like to acknowledge my husband, Blaine, who has always believed in me and encouraged me to get dad's book published. A contributor and counsel of book structure of words, gathering of material and keeping me motivated through my process of collecting heartfelt memories of dad. Hugs & kisses to my 3 beautiful daughters, Angie, Julie & Carrie for all their love and support.

Special thanks to a grade school classmate at St. Jane De Chantal School—Manuel Torres (M. Anton T.), a forever friend and publisher of *Patton's Hand of God*. I believe readers will agree, it is one of history's greatest books of untold stories of WWII. M.A.T.'s belief, knowledge, and expertise in publishing dad's true stories without transforming is monumental, and a legacy many generations will enjoy!

Special thanks to Melanie Sammons Garland and Richard Garland for their expertise and knowledge they shared to add to my memories.

Thank you Joan Sammons Tokarz, Merle Sammons Ivey, Sandy Sammons Cheatham and Vera Cutchins Hinnant-all who shared and gave information on dad and kept me going with inspiration.

Thank you Denise and Ramona Sammons—my sisters who helped tremendously, gathering, confirming and sharing information.

Great thanks to Joe St. Pierre for all your hard work with dad on assisting dad with his "Benning to Berlin" Video Taping and much more.

I feel the need to acknowledge the strength and faith that had influence on my writings: *Sister Mary Victoria Brohm* my mentor who taught me in my senior year at Mt. St. Joseph Academy, Maple Mount KY. Sister Victoria took me under her wing, and discovered the actor and storyteller in me. I loved drama and literature and she had me enter in the very competitive Kentucky State Original Oratory and Drama Competitions at Kentucky Wesleyan College. I won "first place" in my oratory on "Grandma's Crazy." I also won the "best actress" and was awarded an additional trophy for my part as "Myrtle Mae Simmons" in the play "HARVEY." I have had many future successful endeavors, which can all be attributed to Sister Victoria's inspiring belief in me, and her relentless drive, always pushing me to succeed. I kept in touch with Sister Victoria and she came to visit me once, before she passed. Even in her last letter, it was evident that she continued to push me. I strongly believe that I received her gift of faith, that I keep always, deep inside my heart and lean on it and turn it on when I feel lonely or have any doubts. I then auditioned for "the Boston Conservatory" Theatre Arts program with my, "Grandma's Crazy Dance", using my own inspirational and original oratory and was surprisingly accepted!

This led on to more theatrical endeavors and motivational projects. The helpful hand of God, that of my father, and of my own handful of persistence, I am now able to hand, *PATTON'S HAND OF GOD*, to future generations, and keep my dad's legacy alive.

- **Rita Sammons Harrell**

# ABOUT THE AUTHOR

## Rita Sammons Harrell

- Won "Best Actress" Award in State competition at Kentucky Wesleyan College.
- Auditioned with my interpretive dance called "Grandma's Crazy" at "the Boston Conservatory" and was accepted.
- Appeared in several stage productions at "Jean Stapleton's Parkway Playhouse in Burnsville, NC.
- An extra at Arena stage and performer with Washington Dance Company.

- Became the #1 salesperson selling "no run pantyhose."
- Was known in the community papers in Montgomery County as the "Coupon Queen."
- Coached and mentored—while at Montgomery County.
- Scholarship Director for the State of Maryland.
- Crowned Miss Bethesda, Miss Montgomery County and Miss PG County (4th runner up Camille Lewis). Sat at dinner tables with Kathleen Kennedy Townsend, Colin Powell, and many more.
- Director of Miss Preakness crowned Sonia Amir my Miss Montgomery County.
- Trained and motivated over 2,000 independent contractors for City Express Courier Service.
- Became Marketing Manager for Choice Hotels assisting with commercials and ad campaigns.
- 10 yrs. as basketball, and softball coach for the Boys and Girls Club in Laurel Maryland.
- Music Manager for Singer Songwriter "Bill Mott" "Dancing with Angels."
- Volunteer with the "Peace House" in Laurel Maryland—helping to coach troubled teenagers.
- Director of Sales & Marketing for Starwood Resorts—opening, training, and motivating.
- Sales Manager, CEM for the City of Myrtle Beach-booking citywide events to impact the city revenues.
- Married with 3 daughters, and 10 Grandchildren.
- Co-author of father's book "GRAMPA'S WAR".

# APPENDIX

## Special Contributors

The following is the list of *PATTON'S HAND OF GOD* "Special Contributors", which we welcome their personal comments of what J.E.'s book means to them, their families, and the legacy it preserves for their family member…who served.

In the future editions of "*PATTON'S HAND OF GOD*", all replies, by each family member, or friend will be added to printing and the publication of "Special Contributors. This list will grow, and soon to follow, with audibles for each family member to share and have forever inscribed in an audible format.

The Author, Rita Sammons Harrell will provide a personalized written "Thank You" to each family, when your ordered books are delivered.

### "Special Contributors List" "Special Comments"

Beatice Chaon Sammons Blaine Harrell
Melanie Sammons Garland and Richard Garland
Ramona Sammons
Merle Sammons Ivey and Dennis Ivey
Delane Cutchins Bailey
Bob Cutchins

Carrie Harrell Lansdale and Jeff Lansdale
Denise Sammons
Wilroy and Elizabeth Sammons
Joan Sammons Tokarz
Vera Cutchins Hinnant
William Wilroy Sammons

Sandy Sammons Cheatham
John Sammons
Darren Garland
Brayden Lansdale
Marshall Taylor
Addison Taylor
Alex and Dylan Nascimento
Jim Sanders Julie Harris
Larry and Julia Chaon
Paula and Bill Harris
Tim and Ann Lehan
Michelle and Dennis Freidel
Barbie DM Daisy
Elizabeth Lehan and Sarah Lehan
Bob and Judy Wolfe
Russell Allen
Pershing (MAC) Atkins
Herbert Barns
John Dierderickson
Charlie Gnau
Harry Kuppersmith
George Masch
Joe and Martha Pfeifer
Robert C Pryor
Frank Seegmuller
Bonnie Sutton
Thomas Walker

Hilda Wilroy Duke
Chaon Garland
Daisy Lansdale
Angela Harrell
Ryan Taylor
Julie Harrell Nascimento
Joe St Pierre
Jeanette and Merlin Newkirk
Don and Donna Dinges
Jim and Marge Lehan
Terri and Don Hettel
Maria and Ed Paine
Thomas and Brenda Lehan
Bill and Chris Cable
William and Pat Burk
Charles Althouse
Jim Barnhart
Dwight Cooper
Ray Ellis
William Karr
Mel LaScola
George Miller
Al Provenzano
William Scruggs
Jerome Strickland
Graham Walker
George Whisenant

# SPECIAL MENTION

## Michael O'Brien

Special thanks for his assistance, to my classmate Michael O'Brien of St. Jane De Chantal School in Bethesda, MD., and a Graduate of West Point, following his father, Col. James Kenneth O'Brien (pictured in a West Point cadet portrait; and as 2$^{nd}$ Lieutenant in combat calculating target settings for his field artillery platoon somewhere in Germany, after graduating with friend John Eisenhower (Ike's son) from West Point on D-Day, June 6, 1944.
**Rita Sammons Harrell**

Figure 145 James Kenneth O'Brien West Point cadet portrait

Figure 146 Col. James Kenneth O'Brien as 2nd Lieutenant in combat

# SPECIAL MENTION

Figure 147 Dean Michael Cheng

## Michael Cheng Ph.D. CHE
Dean at the Chaplin School of Hospitality & Tourism Management at Florida International University

I would like to extend a special mention to Dean Michael Cheng of the Chaplin School of Hospitality & Tourism Management. I want to personally thank Dean Cheng for providing a future forum at the Kovens Conference Center, so that F.I.U. students understand the "universality" of the word, HOSPITALITY by the hand of a solder and his mission to unite WWII Veterans and family.

Going the distance to cater beyond one's needs or what could be expected was the pleasure of J. E.
**-Rita Sammons Harrell**

A special mention page has been provided for the Dean of Chaplin's School of Hospitality & Tourism Management, Dr. Michael Cheng, for recognizing the work that J.E. Sammons demonstrated throughout his life, especially after WWII, proving that the word "hospitality" is not limited to the hotel restaurant sector, but rather can be implemented in our daily lives. J.E. did it during over half a century, after 1945, providing his "buddies", their wives, friends and families with the care and love that can only come, with a heart like J.E.'s… filled with "hospitality" to his fellow human beings.

# How *Hospitality* Kept a Unit Alive!!!

Let Hospitality be your guide It serves life from inside

This was J.E.'s lifelong pursuit A friendly handshake or salute Survival of the great depression

Provided strength over any oppression Hospitality is not taught it is lived

By the more you love and give No greater feeling

Than to serve those in needing Pleasure to deliver

A small price for a true giver

J.E. became a messenger of hope to soldiers and wives A caring letter, note to tell them of their heroic survive Just pass a note to a friend of soldier each day

It is just a little thing, J.E. would say Oh all the friends he had made

Over the years of as the soldier's band played A glimpse of hope kept him from astray

Being the hospitable home of the brave Let true hospitality thrive

It's the little things that keep it alive

Such a little thing, J.E. would say

To pass along and give a solider a smile today

J.E.'s life purpose to motivate the 17th unique engineers …All those fifty plus years!!!

## Special J.E. Things – All Starting with the Letter "F"

The following are things that meant most to J.E.… Starting with the letter "F"

**Family** and **Fatherhood**—loved his wife and children greatly and great provider—Up the ladder Dad would advance in his accounting career for his growing family –from Loves Park to Milwaukee to Maryland.

**Faith,** prayed daily—went to church every Sunday

**Friendships** (especially Army buds and wives) Dad loved to visit friends from all over, would drive the distance to see even a distant solider whom he never met—as long as he was in the 2nd Armored Division!

**Frankfurters**/Hot Dogs-J.E. loved his chili—dogs and would travel long distances to find the best chili—dogs

**Franchising** and opening a franchise Doughnut shop named "Dixie Cream Donuts"—a family business he embraced with challenges and loved teaching all his kids the art of doughnut making—His favorite saying: ***"Keep your eye upon the doughnut and not upon the hole"***

As a **Financial** Consultant, became a Chief Accountant for a large Montgomery County Maryland Builders of Gaithersburg Village known as the "Kettler Brothers". Building one of the largest developments in Montgomery County Maryland.

**Football**—loved to watch every Sunday—had several favorite teams: Redskins, Green Bay, and Bears

5/28/01

Dear Lou,

    Nice to talk with you today and to know you and Theda are O.K. Bea and I are doing good and try to enjoy each day.

    I keep busy writing stories I remember of our war years together. I have the first manuscript copy to the publishers its called -

GRAMPA"S WAR

BENNING TO BERLIN WITH HELL ON WHEELS

    Enclosed is one story from the book that is of great interest. When the book is published you are - copy # 1

    All the best to you and Theda. Keep in touch !

*Ed*

Ed & Bea Sammons

ENCL.
COL. & CORP.

June 5, 2001

Dear Mel,

Thanks for your letter in regard to my good friend Herbie. Having been in wartime service together for 4½ years, we were like brothers.

What a joy it was all those reunion years with your Dad and Mom and our frequent phone calls and Florida visits. After more than 50 years it was much easier to talk about the war.

I'm sure you have heard the story of how Herbie got the name - B.S. Barnes, if not, it will be in the book I'm writing for our children and grandchildren -

GRAMPA'S WAR
BENNING to BERLIN with HELL ON WHEELS

I know you miss your Dad, as every son would that had a Dad like Herbie. However, he provided many years of joy.

Your Dad and I were very lucky - of 12000 2nd Armored Division soldiers, 7089 were killed, wounded or captured. We were 2 of the 4911 that returned home. Rest assured your Dad did his duty as a soldier and helped us enjoy the freedom we have today.

God Bless - Take good care of Mom.

Herbie's Buddy,

Ed sammons

Note to Herbie's son (a "Salute to Herbie – The Herbie I Know" can in the Final Victory – Crossing the Rhine.)

# AND MORE SPECIAL "J.E. PHOTOS" ...

Figure 148 J. E. profile, waving

Dad was the essence of the most adventurous kid, motivational soldier, dedicated husband, comforting father, and truly a great friend to all his Co E until his end. What a man of courage and strength—he never gave up helping and reliving WWII every day. He was an inspiration and the meaning of hospitality thick and thin. He really cared about people. Dad started the Reunions right after WWII in 1946 and held it in Washington DC. He started with a handful of the 17th Battalion, Co. E veterans and spouses. This was the beginning of a great union of not just vets but families. J.E.'s hospitable charm was extraordinary to say the least. Always a hearty handshake, hold their arm to feel their pulse as J.E. would welcome his guests for a worthy cause.

Figure 149 Group photo of 1st Reunion - 1946

Registration card

One of J.E.'s last letters from Bob.

He passed shortly after. Dad was so sad sitting in his favorite chair, remembering all who had passed and he was one of the last.

## Reunion scheduled

World War II veterans of Company E, 17th Armored Engineers, 2nd Armored "Hell on Wheels" Division will hold their 41st annual reunion this weekend at the Reading Motor Inn.

The men of Company E saw action in North Africa, Sicily, Italy, and participated in the invasion of Normandy under Gen. George S. Patton.

"The men were together all but five years," said Ruth N. Gnau, Exeter Township, and widow of Charles S. Gnau, who helped organize reunion efforts 40 years ago.

"These men traveled together from Fort Benning, Ga., all the way to Africa," she explained. "For enough of them to travel together so long and for enough of them to come home after they were together, well, they became closer than brothers."

She said 87 people are registered for the annual banquet Saturday night. James M. Burt, a Colony Park resident, a former member of the 2nd Armored Division, and the only Congressional Medal of Honor winner in Berks County, is scheduled to speak at the banquet.

Reunion Scheduled (undisclosed newspaper)

Ruth Gnau, a great wife of Charlie who helped J.E. with several reunions. After Charlie passed, she kept coming to all the Reunions. A real trooper.

Figure 150. Graduation of Granddaughter Carrie, from US Air Force

Following the path of her grandfather in engineering and drove a half-track in the OPERATION FREEDOM IRAQ in Bala

Figure 152 Spencer, Nebraska for 1979 Reunion hosted by Joe and Martha Pfeifer

# LETTER TO THE EDITOR

Bethesda, Maryland September 25, 1979
An Open Letter to the American Legion World War II
Veterans, and the people of Spencer, Nebraska.

Dear friends and buddies,

For the past 34 years the members of Co. E of the 17th Arm'd. Engr. Bn. Of the Second Armored Division have been getting together for an annual reunion in which we re-live the experiences of our days in service and renew all the old friendships. This 1979 Labor Day weekend was no exception, as we came to Spencer! But that is where all similarity to previous gatherings ends--- for this year's affair hosted by Martha and Joe Pfeifer has topped them all! Joe and Martha were the perfect hosts with a beautifully planned get-together, but something more than that was experienced by all of us in Spencer.

We met you, the people, the World War II Veterans of the local American Legion Post, the neighbors, farmers, townspeople, family and relatives, and we were treated with a hospitality such as we had never known. We saw community spirit, love and friendship --- in action. You warmed our hearts, you wonderful people of Nebraska!

You showered us with love; you bestowed upon us flowers, food and home made crafts. Although many things in this life are fleeting, you can be sure that Co. E and its auxiliary will never, ever forget you, or the wonderful Labor Day weekend spent in your midst. We shall treasure our memories for years to come, and like another old soldier once said, "we shall return", if only to see if we dreamed all this.
God love and bless you all for bringing so much happiness to we visitors from the East.

Sincerely
Ed Sammons
(For all the members of the Co. E Reunion Club)

Figure 153 J. E. at podium, Bea laughing

J.E. as you can see loved talking and applying a theme to each year's reunion. Laughter became the sound at every reunion town. My mom Bea as you can see would laugh with tears. I remember Dad with his serious but funny speeches catching every ear.

Figure 154 This is a picture of us kids at the Reading PA reunion.

Where we all would look forward to seeing each other every year. My older sisters had some crushes. I did too. My youngest sister Ramona is sitting on the floor to the right. Left of her are twins Pam and Tam who we visited often in VA. Above Ramona is a blonde hair scratching her arm and unaware. Little did I know someday this bleached-blonde would be the messenger of the past to share?

Beside me to my left is Yvonne who was lots of fun. Beside me—right is my older sister Denise, who had all the boys at her feet, as Dad would always introduce me as REETZ!

Figure 155 Cousin Terri Lehan came to visit Uncle Ed!

Figure 156 Dylan and Great GRAMPA in Myrtle Beach, SC

Figure 157 1971 Reunion: Charlie Gnau, Mac Atkins, Ed Dunley, and J.E. Sammons

# FOR THE RECORD:

### In 1979...

J.E. pronounced touching words of praise for Major General Ernest Harmon, who passed on Tuesday, the 13th of November, 1979. In J.E.'s notes were the utmost of respect for the "old man" that led the 2nd Armored Division , "Hell On Wheels": *"We knew that we would be victorious with the general, and after breaking through the Siegfried Line, winning at Aachen, we were unstoppable at the Bulge… it was him that got us through the worst winter (Dec. '44 – Jan. '45) in our lives! Our prayers go to his family and we're extending an open invitation to any of our upcoming Co."E" Reunions to his son from Bethesda, Robert S."*

### In 1990...

General George S. Paton's "Hell on Wheels" was deactivated; formed in 1940, it is the longest active service armored division (5 years) in American history. Hell On Wheels participated in the *"first armored participation in an amphibious landing on a hostile shore"* with 10,000 GIs, 350 tanks, and made history when rolled onshore on November 2, 1942, in North Africa. It's "specialized engineering unit, called "WE Pave the WAY", was the first Allied unit to enter Belgium, and allow a record breaking 100 miles in one night charge, that helped win, the Battle of the Bulge in the winter of 1944-45; was the first American unit to enter Berlin on July 4, 1945.

*The passing of General Harmon and Hell On Wheels deactivation*

J.E. remembered Gen. Harmon and spoke highly of him. Many remembered war stories with the General and their "Hell on Wheels".

Figure 158. Seven battle campaigns....Banner used at Reunions.

## These SEVEN BATTLE CAMPAIGNS became J.E.'s words and language and of his life after WWII:

**Operation Overlord**—Coined by Winston Churchill for the Invasion of Europe.

**Dragon Wagon**-US Army truck trailer to carry the thirty-ton Sherman tanks to preserve for battles

**Four Freedoms**—President Franklin D Roosevelt to insure the US of the four main freedoms of the US and World in his radio speech in 1941: Freedom of Religion, Freedom from Want and Freedom from Fear

**Batter Up**—A code to indicate that the French were resisting the American troops landing in North Africa in 1942, followed by "Play Ball" order for the Allied troops to attack

**C-Ration**—Army's individual ration of food each day in the field that consists of 3 cans of meat, canned vegetables crackers, sugar, coffee and a confection. (Hersey candy bar) J.E. said he only got green beans!

**Bailey Bridge**—used by the 17th Engineers since it was light weight and easy to assemble, transport and repair

**Pontoon Bridge**—Used by the 17th at the Rhine River

**Desert Rats**—given to the British seventh Armored Division that fought in North Africa

**Falaise Gap**—Site of attempted Allied encirclement of German Forces in Western France. (Half of the Germans escaped and would not have if General Patton was not denied by Field Marshall Bernard Montgomery) This was a great rendition in J.E.'s Video

**Ardennes Offensive**—Advance of the German forces in Mountains of Belgium known as the "Battle of the Bulge"

**Bouncing Betty**—a nickname for German mines filled with steel pellets and set off by a tripped wire

**Fat Boy**—code for the atomic bomb

**Firefly**—A gadget placed in the enemy gas tanks setting the vehicle on fire

**D-Day June 6, 1944** the greatest invasion in history!

**Mickey Mouse**—Password used by US forces on D-Day

Figure 159. J. E. and Bea

Mom kept dad alive through the War dad would always say. Her daily letters during the war of love and faith encouraged J.E. to survive and live another day....

Figure 160 My wedding and Dad 1978

Figure 161 Mom and Dad after the War 1945

Figure 162. Group of soldiers, from above

If I could go back in time and have a doughnut for a dime
Savor the devotion of the cause, and applaud
To all those engineers who had no fears
Picked and labeled as those "Patton Boys"
They did not dance to the Germans with toys
They drove ahead in the mist of fire and bombs to "Pave the Way"
All for our Freedoms we hold dear today
Soldiers that had to demolish, rebuild roads and bridges with resilience in record time
Strength of a team of soldiers in unity under the influence of Patton's mind
These engineering soldiers had the belief would all survive
Holding on to each other's abilities to stay alive
I witnessed a unit with the strongest friendships I had ever seen
I felt the hearts of grown men you see
It had an extraordinary result on me
Time will tell so many WWII books will arrive
This one is for the generations to know the men who survive

Figure 163. The War Room, 1995

The "War Room" at every Reunion (this one was in 1995)
Many of tears were shed, the man looking at the camera is yes J. E. or known as ED.

Figure 164. 1958 reunion

This was the 1958 Reunion and my youngest sister Ramona with some of her dad's best buds: Curley, J.E., Stick, Charlie, Mac and Walker at the Reunion 1958.

How Ramona loved going to all the Reunions with Mom & Dad.
And I believe she attended them all!

Figure 165 Reunion in the 60's

I see so many familiar faces. And my grandmother Mable sitting with her white hair and glasses. See the reel of tape player we would see of last year's reunion.

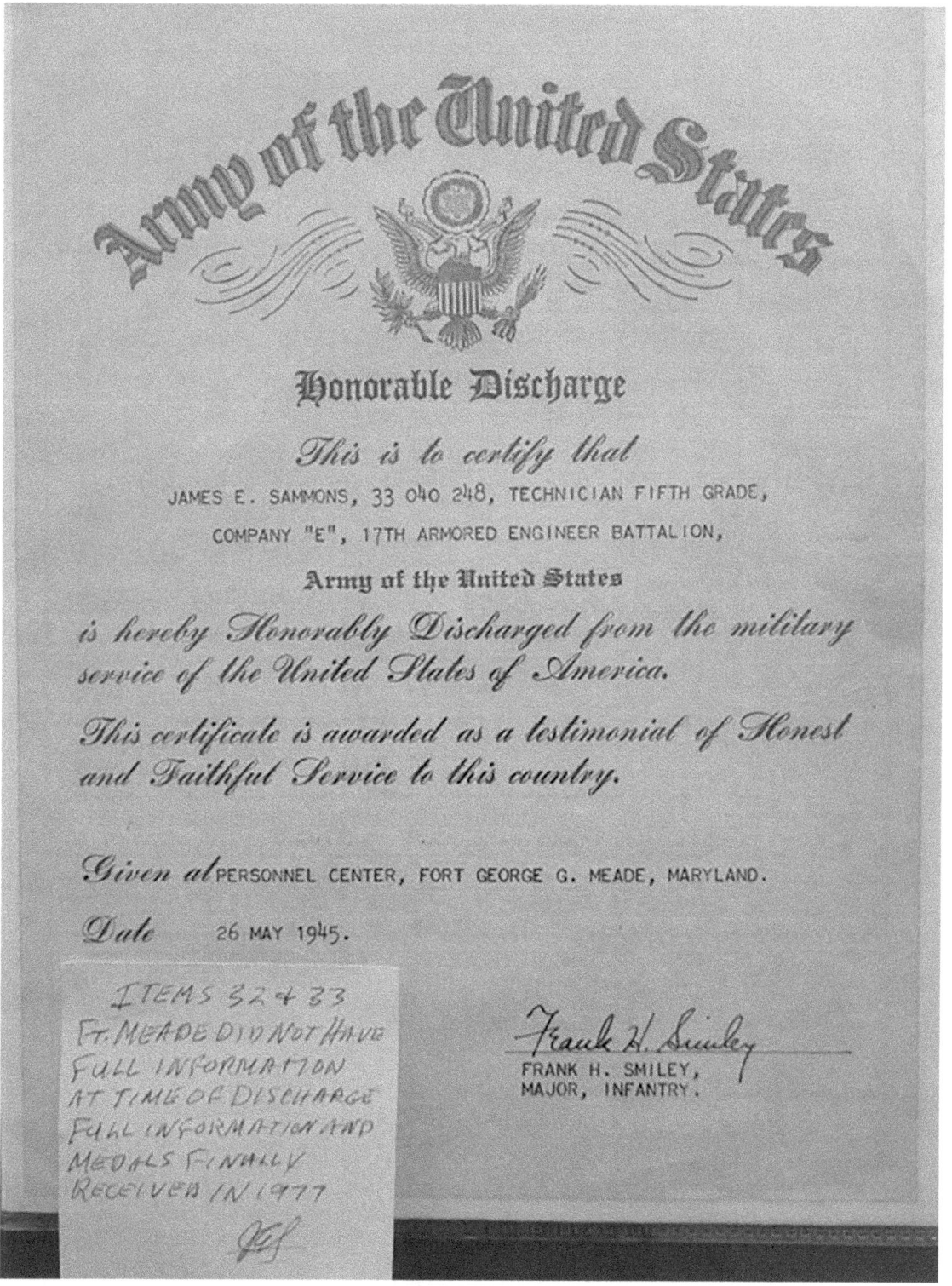

JE discharge papers

CERTIFICATE

APRIL 26, 1945.

"1. I certify that I have personally examined the items of captured enemy military equipment (~~~~~~~~) (in the possession of) James E. Sammons, that the trophy value of such items exceeds any training, service, or salvage value; that they do not include any explosives, and that the (~~~~~~) (possession) thereof is in conformity with the provisions of Sec III, Cir 353, WD, 21 Aug 1944, and the existing regulations of the Theater Commander.

"2. ~~I further certify that the items noted do not include any firearms capable of being concealed on the person, or any parts of firearms.~~

"3. The items referred to are:

1- CAL. 25 AUTOMATIC       1- CAMERA GERMAN
PISTOL SERIAL No.- 533768

\* Strike out one.
\*\* Not required for items being carried
Personally to the U. S.

_J.E. Michaud_
(Signature)

_Capt Inf_
(Rank and Branch)

Co "E" 17<sup>th</sup> Armd. Engr. Bn. A.P.O. 252
(Organization)

(Two copies of this certificate will be enclosed with each package containing captured enemy military equipment)

Figure 166 J.E. ready to serve as an Army Solider in 1941

His life and mission had just begun. Being the youngest son, J.E. was ready to enlist. And was heading back home from Basic Training for Christmas when the bombing of "Pearl Harbor" hit!... & everything in J.E.'s life changed!

The National WWII Museum, in memoriam

# APA PICTURE FILE LIST

The following *APA PICTURE FILE LIST* will have all of the photos within *PATTON'S HAND OF GOD* & *GRAMPA'S WAR* with as much reference information possible. Each picture will be numbered with a description.

Figure 1. J.E. and a young Rita Sammons Harrell/1950's/J. E. personal archives.

Figure 2. Picture of J.E. at Ft. Benning/1942/ location unknown/ J. E. personal archives.

Figure 3. Original crest insignia patch U.S. Army 2nd Armored Div./1940/ J. E. personal archives.

Figure 5 Mom and Dad 1930 J. E. Handwriting on 1930 picture/J. E. personal archives.

Figure 4 My Dog Snooks/ J. E. personal archives.

Figure 6. Family Photo /J.E. Handwriting on 1930 picture "Mom. Dad, Delane, Aunts Josephine and Paige, your Dad"/J. E. personal archives.

Figure 7. Sammons Family Picture J. E. Handwriting on 1930 picture "I'm eating cookies... Sammons Family"/J. E. personal archives.

Figure 8. Grampa Wilroy's Farm Home on the Nansemond River J. E.'s Handwriting /J. E. personal archive.

Figure 9. Family Photo J. E. Handwriting "Cousin Bill Faison...Your smiling happy Dad" on 1930 picture /J. E. personal archive.

Figure 10. Happy Days, 1927 - J. E. Handwriting/ J. E. personal archives.

Figure 11. J. E. portrait picture/J. E. personal archives.

Figure 15. Chow Time at the Mess Hall - March 1941, Ft. Benning, GA/ J. E. personal archives.

Figure 12. J. E. Latrine Duty/Ft. Benning, GA, 1942/J. E. personal archives.

Figure 16. Bridge Built on Louisiana Maneuvers – 1941, Ft. Knox, KY/J. E. personal archives.

Figure 13. J. E. on Basic Infantry Soldier Training with General Patton Jan. 1941/J. E. personal archives

Figure 17. J. E. Radio Command School – 1941 (Note Civilian Clothes)/ J. E. personal archives.

Figure 18. J. E. and soldiers - Nov. 9, 1942... Ed Sammons Ray Ellis Geo. Miller Herm Feldman...captured during Battle of the Bulge on picture/J. E. personal archives.

Figure 14. Patton picture from personal J.E. photo source "Col. George S. Patton addressing troops of the 67th Armored regiment..." /J. E. personal archives.

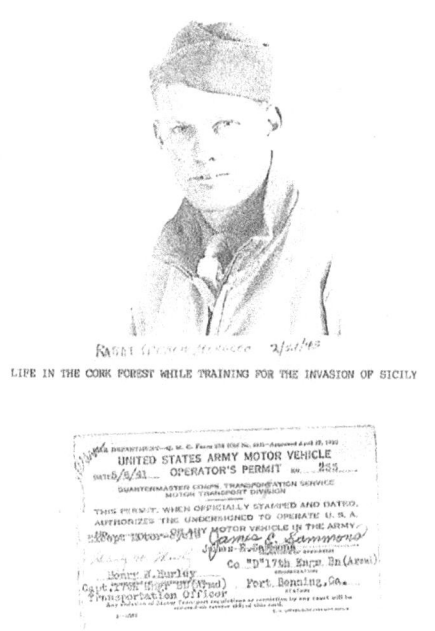

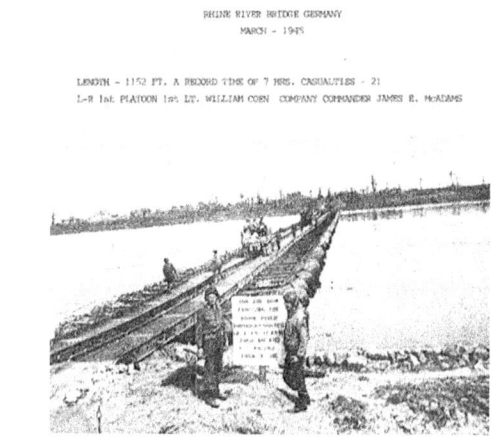

Figure 22. J. E. - Rhine River Bridge Germany March-1945... "The bridge constructed by the 17th Engineer Battalion (J.E.'s WE PAVE THE WAY) across the Rhine River in record time/J. E. personal archives.

Figure 19. J. E. Life in the Cork Forest while training for the invasion of Sicily/J. E. personal archives.

Figure 20. J. E. original army vehicle operator's license that travelled in his wallet from Benning to Berlin/J. E. personal archives.

Figure 23. J. E. – Hershey Chocolate Wrapper that survived/J. E. personal archives.

Figure 21. J. E. - Building a bridge across the Rhine, 1945/ J. E. personal archives.

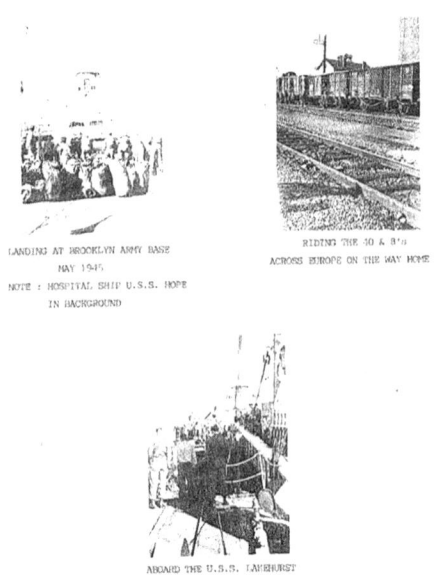

Figure 24. Brooklyn Army Base May 1945 Note: Hospital Ship U.S.S. Hope in the background/ J. E. personal archives.
Figure 25. J. E. Riding the 40 & 8s across Europe on the way home/ J. E. personal archives.
Figure 26. J. E. Aboard the U.S.S. Lakehurst coming home to America May/ J. E. personal archives.

Figure 28. Patton's son guest speaker - the 35th reunion Program/ J. E. personal archives

Figure 27. J. E. Family Photo - Handwriting "My Mom, Melanie, Eliz…Your beautiful Mom, pregnant with Vonnie…L to R - Bea Mom Melanie Ed Eliz – Joan & Wilroy – 1949/ J. E. personal archives.

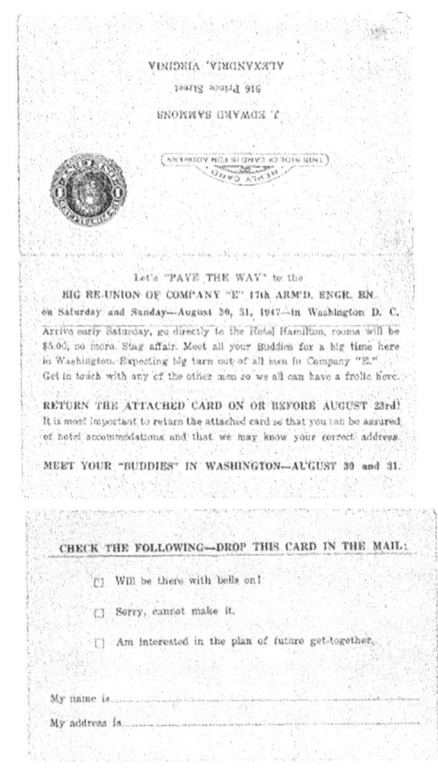

Figure 29. Original 1947 Reunion Reply Invitation Form/ J. E. personal archives

APA PICTURE FILE LIST | 381

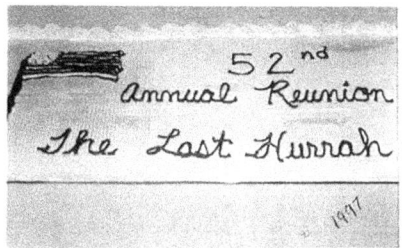

Figure 33. J.E. sitting on Army chest/ J. E. personal archives

Figure 30. Special Cake – Final Annual Reunion Myrtle Beach, S.C. Oct. 1997/ J. E personal archives
Figure 31. 1997 - The Last Hurrah! L/R Charlie Powell, Al Provenzano, Herbie Barnes, Ed Sammons, C harles Jackson, Russ Allen/ J. E. personal archives

Figure 34. J. E. Family photo/J. E. personal archives

Figure 32. Altar of Battles picture and typewritten notes/ J. E. personal archives.

Figure 35. Life As a Boy in Virginia/
J. E. personal archives

Figure 37. The Drugstore Cowboys/
J. E. personal archives

Figure 36. J.E. family photo – We picture/
J. E. personal archives

Figure 38. J. E. Boyhood wall hanging/
J. E. personal archives

APA PICTURE FILE LIST | 383

Figure 39. Samons Family/
J. E. personal archives

Figure 41. J.E. Leaving for Army Basic Training/
J. E. personal archives

Figure 40. J.E. on tank/
J. E. personal archives

Figure 42. J.E. at Ft. Benning, 1941/
J. E. personal archives

Figure 42. J. E. at Headquarters The Armored Force School/ J. E. personal archives

Figure 43 1941 Radio School Ft. Knox, KY/ J. E. personal archives

Figure 44. J. E. at Fort Knox/ J. E. personal archives

Figure 45. J. E with truck/J. E. personal archives

Figure 46. J. E. Driving a Jeep at Ft. Bening/ J. E. personal archives

APA PICTURE FILE LIST | 385

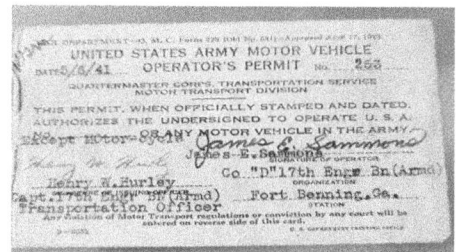

Figure 47. J.E. Arny motor vehicle license/
J. E. personal archives

Figure 48. We Pave the Way patch/
J. E. personal archives

Figure 49. Hell on Wheels patch/
J. E. personal archives

Figure 50. J.E. on his motorcycle at Ft. Benning/
J. E. personal archives

Figure 51. J.E. during maneuvers leaning on tractor tire/
J. E. personal archives

Figure 52. J. E. motorcycles with buddies
/J. E. personal archives

Figure 53. J. E. showing his skills as a driver
/J. E. personal archives

Figure 54. J.E. at Ft. Benning with his FORD GPW Jeep/
J. E. personal archives

Figure 55. J.E. in a half-track truck/
J. E. personal archives

Figure 56. The J. E. stance/
J. E. personal archives

Figure 57. Hitch a Ride/
J. E. personal archives

APA PICTURE FILE LIST | 387

Figure 58. J. E. on latrine duty/
J. E. personal archives

Figure 60. Two soldiers on a wall/
J. E. personal archives

Figure 61. Bridge Building, Ft. Benning, 1941/
J. E. personal archives

Figure 59. J. E. on Guard Duty/
J. E. personal archives

Figure 62. J. E. under combat conditions/
J. E. personal archives

Figure 63. Bridge across the Chat-a-hoo-chi River, 1942/ J. E. personal archives

Figure 66. North and South Carolina maneuvers/ J. E. personal archives

Figure 64. J. E. the Soldier on a bridge/ J. E. personal archives

Figure 67. J.E. at the Half-track gun/ J. E. personal archives

Figure 65. Building the bridges and roads Carolina and TX maneuvers/ J. E. personal archives

Figure 68. J. E. with a group on Patton's Tank/ J. E personal archives

APA PICTURE FILE LIST | 389

Figure 69. J.E. ready for action on one of Patton's tractor monsters/J. E. personal archives

Figure 71. General George S. Patton/ public domain photo

Figure 72. 2nd Armored Division Panoramic View/ J. E. personal archives

Figure 73. Chow Time/J. E. personal archives

Figure 70. Patton addressing soldiers at Ft. Benning, GA/ picture taken by J. E. Sammons/J. E. personal archives

Figure 74. The Engineers of the 17th/ J. E. personal archives

Figure 75. Company E 17th Engineers, J.E. circled/ J. E. personal archives

Figure 76. Riverside Bar and Grill, Madison Ave, NYC Nov 9th, 1942, and Paris R & R/J. E. personal archives

Figure 77. J. E. Rabat French Morocco, 1943/ J. E. personal archives

Figure 78. J. E. on a Camel in Rabat French Morocco/ J. E. personal archives

Figure 79. Morocco side street/J. E. personal archives

APA PICTURE FILE LIST | 391

Figure 80. Lt. Col Hurley/J. E. personal archives

Figure 82. Capt. Burt/photo in the public domain

Figure 83. President Truman and Capt. Burt/photo in the public domain

Figure 81. Uncle Welly/J. E. personal archives

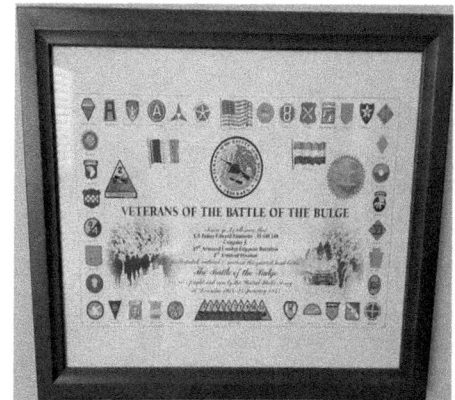

Figure 84. Battle of the Bulge veteran certificate/ J. E. personal archives

Figure 85. We Pave The Way original patch/
J. E. personal archives

Figure 86. Platoon Picture/J. E. personal archives

Figure 87. 1st Platoon Picture/J. E personal archives

Figure 88. 2nd Platoon Picture/J. E. personal archives

Figure 89. Engineering Platoo/J. E. personal archives

Figure 90. James Edward Sammons portrait picture 1945/
J. E. personal archives

Figure 91. James Edward Sammons' Medals, Citations,
Battle Theatre Ribbons/J. E. personal archives

APA PICTURE FILE LIST | 393

Figure 92. J. E.'s original dog tags/J. E. personal archives

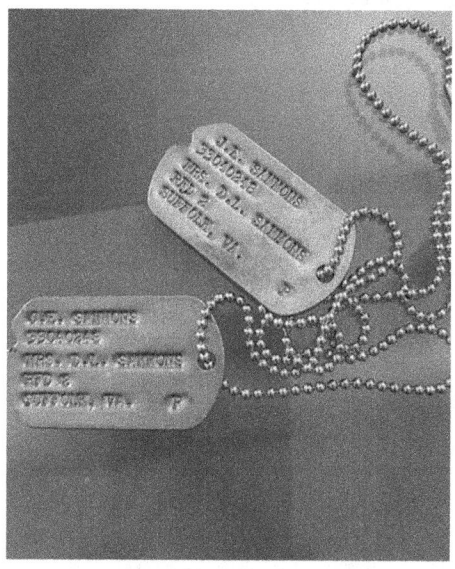

Figure 93. J. E. backup dog tags/J. E. personal archives

Figure 94. Tidworth England 1944/J. E. personal archives

Figure 95. J. E. in Tidworth, England, March, 1944/ J. E. personal archives

Figure 96. "Sidekicks" and long-lasting friendships/ J. E. personal archives

Figure 97. Full Field Inspection at Tidworth Barracks, West of London/J. E. personal archives

Figure 98. J.E. at the Rhine (collage)/
J. E. personal archives

Figure 99. J. E. standing in front of a truck on Hell Day/
J. E. personal archives

Figure 100. J. E sitting on a German Pillbox/
J. E. personal archives

Figure 101. Laundry service during Hell on Wheels...battle towards the River Rhine/J. E. personal archives

Figure 102. Crossing the Rhine Courtesy of E. Co. 17th armored Engr Bn/J. E. personal archives

APA PICTURE FILE LIST | 395

Figure 103. KRUP Iron Works, Germany, March 1945/
J. E. personal archives

Figure 104. Red Cross WW II patch/J. E. personal archives

Figure 105. J.E.'s personal European African Middle Eastern
Campaign medal/J. E. personal archives

Figure 106. Cpl. James Edward Sammons wearing his
stripes and the most important battle theatre ribbon...
Battle of the Bulge/J. E. personal archives

Figure 107. Rita and J. E./J. E. personal archives

Figure 108. J.E. and Bea/J. E. personal archives

Figure 110. J.E., Bea, and J.E.'s mom/ J. E. personal archives

Figure 109. J.E. and Bea in front of my Dad's new car after the war/J. E. personal archives

Figure 111. J.E. and his mom/ J. E. personal archives

APA PICTURE FILE LIST | 397

Figure 112. Hell on Wheels collage/
J. E. personal archives

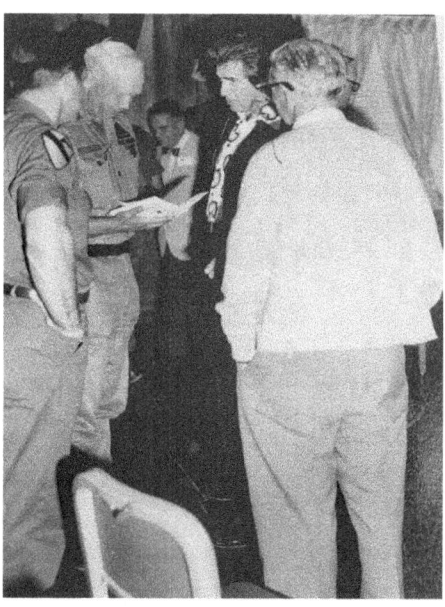

Figure 114. Robert Pryor interviews Patton photo courtesy
of Robert Pryor/J. E. personal archives

Figure 113. 35th Anniversary Reunion Program

Figure 115. J. E.'s Granddaughter, Carrie/
J. E. personal archives

Figure 116. J. E. and Bea at the head reunion table/
J. E. personal archives

Figure 117. 40th reunion cake, 1985/
J. E. personal archives

Figure 118. 1989 Reunión Gun Salute/
J. E. personal archives

Figure 119. Spencer, Nebraska J.E. on a float/
J. E. personal archives

Figure 120. Dad with Carrie at her wedding, 2006/
J. E. personal archives

Figure 121. Dad and Carrie dancing at her wedding/
J. E. personal archives

APA PICTURE FILE LIST | 399

Figure 122. Welcome to Canadaigua Reunion of 1992/
J. E. personal archive

Figure 123. Dad's 80th in Palm Harbor/
J. E. personal archives

Figure 124. My 3 beautiful daughters and cousin, Julie
Harris/Photo Rita Sammons Harrell

Figure 125. My husband, Blaine/
Photo Rita Sammons Harrell

Figure 126. J.E. and his blonde little girl, Rita/
J. E. personal archives

Figure 127. Our family in Milwaukee, WI/
J. E. personal archives

Figure 128. J.E. and Rita (Palm Harbor)/ photo Rita Sammons Harrell

Figure 129. Posted at every Reunion Registration table/ J. E. personal archives

Figure 130. Box of Cigars with note

Figure 131. 48th Reunion picture/J. E. personal archives

Figure 132. J. E/J. E. personal archives

Figure 133. Carrie/Photo compliments of Carrie

APA PICTURE FILE LIST | 401

Figure 134. Lucky Strike Cigarettes and note/
J. E. personal archives

"Patton was right" ...
said J.E.'s buddies in WWII,
Melchior Lascola and Al Provenzano

Figure 135 32nd Annual Reunion "Talks" /
J. E. personal archives

Figure 136. 1997 Reunion, three men at the table
(Ladies Auxiliary Room)J. E. personal archives

Figure 137. Photo of a Can of Peanuts at each table –
50th Reunion/J. E. personal archives

Figure 138. 1990 reunion photograph/
J. E. personal archives

Figure 139. Author portrait/photo by Rita Sammons Harrell

Figure 140. Altar of Battles picture and note /J. E. personal archives

Figure 141. J.E. with great grandson Brayden/ J. E. personal archives

Figure 142. J. E. in Florida/ J. E. personal archives

Figure 143. J.E. at the podium during an annual reunion/ J. E. personal archives

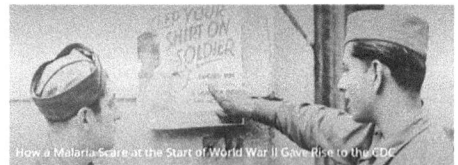

Figure 144. Malaria, J.E., and the U.S. Army/ J. E. personal archives

Figure 145. James Kenneth O'Brien West Pointe cade photograph/Compliments of Michael O'Brien

APA PICTURE FILE LIST | 403

Figure 146. James Kenneth O'Brien West Pointe cade photograph/Compliments of Michael O'Brien

Figure 147. Cheng, Michael, March 2022, Dr. Michael Cheng Global Hospitality Award Winner. Global Hospitality

Figure 148. J.E. profile, waving/J. E. personal archives

Figure 149. Group photo of 1st Reunion, 1946/ J. E. personal archives

Figure 150. Graduation of Granddaughter Carrie U. S. Air Force/compliments of Carrie/J. E. personal archives

Figure 152. Spencer, Nebraska, 1979 Reunion, hosted by Joe and Martha Pfeifer/J. E. personal archives

Figure 153. J. E. at the podium during an annual reunion/ J. E. personal archives

Figure 154. Photo of the kids at the Reading, PA. Reunion/ J. E. personal archives

Figure 155. Picture of Terri and J. E. /J. E. personal archives

Figure 156. Picture of Dylan and J. E. Myrtle Beach, SC/ J. E. personal archives

Figure 157. 1971 Reunion picture/J. E. personal archives

Figure 158. Seven Battle Campaign banner/ J. E. personal archives

Figure 159. J.E. and Bea/J. E. personal archives

Figure 160. Rita Sammons Harrell and J.E. on her Wedding day with her Dad, 1978/ J. E. personal archives

Figure 161. Author's Mom and Dad after the war, 1945

Figure 162. Group of Soldiers/J. E. personal archives

Figure 163. J. E. – The War Room at every reunion/ J. E. personal archives

Figure 164. 1958 Reunion picture/J. E. personal archives

Figure 165. Reunion in the 1960's. J. E. personal archives

Figure 166. J.E. ready to serve as an Army Soldier in 1941/ J. E. personal archives

# FINAL NARRATION AND FOLLOW UP

It is never "The End", when it comes to J.E. Sammons, who's proven that an ordinary individual, can beat hell, survive a general's push into one of history's bloodiest episodes, and come back home, forming a family, and finally, provide a wealth of friendships, that would help heal open wounds for thousands of veterans and their families, for over a half a century.

A young reader, someday, will go through this picture-text book, and relive some of the most desperate moments in American history, portrayed by our main character, and seconded by his closest listener of "J.E. stories" that finally compiled all the current original never-before-seen of "Grampa's War", and published into PATTON'S HAND OF GOD. Simply put, an American, that any young American girl or boy, can someday aspire to become.

--- **M. Anton T.**


And as my Dad would probably end his stories, to the many kids that would be listening at his Dixie Cream Donut Shop in Bethesda, …

"Keep your eye upon the donut…and not upon the hole…!!!!"

---- **Rita Sammons Harrel**

www.ingramcontent.com/pod-product-compliance
Lightning Source LLC
Chambersburg PA
CBHW080410170426
43194CB00015B/2763